Woolf Studies Annual

Volume 23, 2017

PACE UNIVERSITY PRESS • NEW YORK

Copyright © 2017 by
Pace University Press
41 Park Row, 15th Floor, Rm. 1510
New York, NY 10038

All rights reserved
Printed in the United States of America

ISSN: 1080-9317
ISBN: 978-1-935625-90-2

Member

Council of Editors of Learned Journals

∞ Paper used in this publication meets the minimum requirements of
American National Standard for Information
Sciences–Permanence of Paper for Printed Library Materials,
ANSI Z39.48–1984

Editor

Mark Hussey — Pace University

Associate Editor

Vara Neverow — Southern Connecticut State University

Book Review Editor

Amanda Golden — New York Institute of Technology

Editorial Advisory Board

Tuzyline Allan	Baruch College, CUNY
Judith Allen	Kelly Writers House, University of Pennsylvania
Morris Beja	Ohio State University (Emeritus)
Pamela L. Caughie	Loyola University Chicago
Kimberly Engdahl Coates	Bowling Green State University
Sarah Cole	Columbia University
Kristin Czarnecki	Georgetown College
Emily Dalgarno	Boston University (Emerita)
Beth Rigel Daugherty	Otterbein College
Claire Davison	Université Paris III–Sorbonne Nouvelle
Jane de Gay	Leeds Trinity University
Erica Gene Delsandro	Bucknell University
Madelyn Detloff	Miami University
Jeanne Dubino	Appalachian State University
Jane Goldman	University of Glasgow
Elizabeth Willson Gordon	King's University, Canada
Leslie Kathleen Hankins	Cornell College
Georgia Johnston	Saint Louis University
Alice Keane	Queens College, CUNY
Emily Kopley	McGill University
Karen V. Kukil	Special Collections, Smith College
Michael Lackey	Distinguished McKnight University Professor, University of Minnesota, Morris
Jane Lilienfeld	Curator's Distinguished Professor of English, Lincoln University of Missouri
Maren Linett	Purdue University
Gill Lowe	University Campus Suffolk
Celia Marshik	Stony Brook University
Ann Martin	University of Saskatchewan
Gabrielle McIntire	Queen's University, Canada
Toni A. H. McNaron	University of Minnesota (Emerita)
Eleanor McNees	University of Denver
Jeanette McVicker	SUNY Fredonia
Jean Mills	John Jay College, CUNY
Patricia Moran	London City University

Editorial Advisory Board (continued)

Steven Putzel	Penn State Wilkes-Barre
Beth C. Rosenberg	University of Nevada, Las Vegas
Victoria Rosner	Columbia University
Derek Ryan	University of Kent
Randi Saloman	Wake Forest University
Bonnie Kime Scott	University of San Diego (Emerita)
Urmila Seshagiri	University of Tennessee
Drew Shannon	Mount St. Joseph University
Kathryn Simpson	Cardiff Metropolitan University
Anna Snaith	King's College London
Helen Southworth	Clark Honors College, University of Oregon
Elisa Sparks	Clemson University (Emerita)
Peter Stansky	Stanford University
Alice Staveley	Stanford University
Diana L. Swanson	Northern Illinois University
Janine Utell	Widener University
Julie Vandivere	Bloomsburg University
Susan Wegener	Purdue University
Michael Whitworth	University of Oxford
Alice Wood	De Montfort University
John Young	Marshall University

The Editor welcomes the new members of the Editorial Board and profoundly thanks all those who served the Annual so well for so many years.

Many thanks to readers for volume 23: Michèle Barrett (Queen Mary U of London); Jennie-Rebecca Falcetta (Massachusetts C of Art & Design); Lise Jaillant (Loughborough U); Bryony Randall (U of Glasgow); Rachel Trousdale (Framingham SU); Adriana Varga (U of Nevada, Reno); Miriam Wallace (New College of Florida).

Woolf Studies Annual is indexed in *Humanities International Complete, ABELL,* and the *MLA Bibliography.*

Call For Papers

Volume #24/Spring 2018

Jane Marcus
(1938 – 2015)

Woolf Studies Annual invites articles responding to, in dialogue with, or related to the scholarship of the late Jane Marcus for a special section of the 2018 volume. Articles should be guided by the journal's usual submission policy (see http://www.pace.edu/press/journals/woolf-studies-annual), and should be submitted no later than June 15th, 2017, to woolfstudiesannual@gmail.com. Submission guidelines are listed on page 207.

Editors for this special section are listed below. Queries or proposals may be routed to them through our email address: woolfstudiesannual@gmail.com

Linda Camarasana, SUNY Old Westbury
J. Ashley Foster, Haverford College
Robin Hackett, University of New Hampshire
Clara Jones, King's College London
Jean Mills, John Jay College, CUNY

Contents

Woolf Studies Annual

Volume 23, 2017

	x	Abbreviations
		ARTICLES
Claire Davison	1	Hearing the World "in Full Orchestra": Voyaging Out with Woolf, Darwin, and Music
Patricia Novillo-Corvalán	33	Empire and Commerce in Latin America: Historicizing Woolf's *The Voyage Out*
Candis E. Bond	63	Remapping Female Subjectivity in *Mrs. Dalloway*: Scenic Memory and Woolf's "Bye-Street" Aesthetic
Amanda Golden	83	Textbook Greek: Thoby Stephen in *Jacob's Room*
Jacqueline Shin	109	It's You I Adore: On the Odes of Virginia Woolf
	141	**GUIDE** Guide to Library Special Collections
		REVIEWS
Jane Goldman	161	*Queer Bloomsbury* Brenda Helt and Madelyn Detloff, eds.
Benjamin D. Hagen	171	*The Value of Virginia Woolf* by Madelyn Detloff

Meghan C. Fox	175	*Virginia Woolf: Ambivalent Activist* by Clara Jones
Laura Doyle	179	*A Companion to Virginia Woolf* Jessica Berman, ed.
Ann Martin	183	*Woolf: A Guide for the Perplexed* by Kathryn Simpson
Patrick Collier	186	*Virginia Woolf and the Professions* by Evelyn Tsz Yan Chan
Angela Smith	191	*Natural Connections: Virginia Woolf and Katherine Mansfield* by Bonnie Kime Scott
		"Eternally in yr Debt": The Personal and Professional Relationship Between Virginia Woolf & Elizabeth Robins by Hilary Newman
		Saxon Sydney-Turner: The Ghost of Bloomsbury by Todd Avery
		Virginia Woolf as Memoirist: "I am made and remade continually" by Alice Lowe
		Mistress of the Brush and Madonna of Bloomsbury, The Art and Life of Vanessa Bell: A Biographical Sketch and Comprehensive Annotated Bibliography of Writings on Vanessa Bell by Suellen Cox
		Septimus Smith: Modernist and War Poet: A Closer Reading by Vara S. Neverow
Sunny Stalter-Pace	196	*Moving Modernisms: Motion, Technology, and Modernity* David Bradshaw, Laura Marcus, and Rebecca Roach, eds.
Benjamin Kohlmann	199	*Edward Upward: Art and Life* by Peter Stansky

203 International Notes

205 Notes on Contributors

207 Submission Guidelines

Abbreviations

AHH	*A Haunted House*
AROO	*A Room of One's Own*
BP	*Books and Portraits*
BTA	*Between the Acts*
CDB	*The Captain's Death Bed and Other Essays*
CE	*Collected Essays* (4 vols.)
CR1	*The Common Reader*
CR2	*The Common Reader, Second Series*
CSF	*The Complete Shorter Fiction*
D	*The Diary of Virginia Woolf* (5 vols.)
DM	*The Death of the Moth and Other Essays*
E	*The Essays of Virginia Woolf* (6 Vols.)
F	*Flush*
FR	*Freshwater*
GR	*Granite & Rainbow: Essays*
JR	*Jacob's Room*
L	*The Letters of Virginia Woolf* (6 Vols.)
M	*The Moment and Other Essays*
MEL	*Melymbrosia*
MOB	*Moments of Being*
MT	*Monday or Tuesday*
MD	*Mrs. Dalloway*
ND	*Night and Day*
O	*Orlando*
PA	*A Passionate Apprentice*
RF	*Roger Fry: A Biography*
TG	*Three Guineas*
TTL	*To the Lighthouse*
TW	*The Waves*
TY	*The Years*
VO	*The Voyage Out*

Hearing the World "in Full Orchestra": Voyaging Out with Woolf, Darwin, and Music
Claire Davison

Listening to music in King's College Chapel made Charles Darwin's "backbone shiver."[1] A romantic explanation for this sensual glow would have been spiritual transcendence, as the soul was elevated by the music; the down-to-earth naturalist sought more empirical causes, becoming intrigued by the physical, emotional, and biological materiality of musical affect. His curiosity for and love of music would last a lifetime, even if his confidence in his aesthetic sensibility declined over the years (F. Darwin 48-50).[2] Darwin took to listening daily to his wife, a highly talented pianist believed to have studied with Chopin, playing the prized family Broadwood, sometimes experimenting to see which animals responded likewise to the appeal of sweet sound. The earthworm, for example, remained apparently indifferent, but whether this meant it was deaf, nervously deficient, or emotionally unresponsive he never decided (Derry 37). However far-reaching on overtly unrelated scientific pursuits, all Darwin's writings reflect his fascination with the purpose and the appeal of music, and its signifying powers; to further his understanding and corroborate his own observations, he encouraged his correspondents to recount examples of musical ability and emotional reactivity in animals, findings which he duly reports in his own works. These include:

> a bullfinch which had been taught to pipe a German waltz (Darwin, *Descent* 417).

> the musical powers of an American species of mouse when the animal was kept in confinement (634).

> Crustaceans provided with auditory hairs of different lengths which have been seen to vibrate when the proper musical notes are struck ... and spiders attracted by thirds played on the piano, but repelled by sixths (635).

[1] Darwin evokes the phenomenon in a key passage of his autobiography describing the "musical set" he mixed with in Cambridge, and the choristers he would hire to sing in his rooms (F. Darwin 49); many early letters refer to his fascination with music, too. In the 1908-09 context that this article is exploring, it is worth noting that the passage was the focus of occasional unsigned notes and short retrospectives in a 1906 and 1908 issue of the *Musical Times* ("Occasional"; "Darwin and Lord Kelvin"). See Beer, "Backbone" for a broader study of Darwin's "backbone shiver."
[2] See Derry and Smocovitis 592-97 for excellent accounts of his lifelong musical awareness and interests.

Despite such meticulous groundwork, Darwin was still at a loss in his later years to explain music's complex physical, mental, and emotional effect, and its place in the rational, materialist plot of evolution. Rekindled by the Darwin-Spencer polemic in the latter half of the nineteenth century following Spencer's counter-Darwinian essay, "On the Origin of Music," the evolution and purpose of music was a field of enquiry Darwin would leave for later generations to explore:[3]

> Human song is generally admitted to be the basis or origin of instrumental music. As neither the enjoyment nor the capacity of producing musical notes are faculties of the least use to man in reference to his daily habits of life, they must be ranked amongst the most mysterious with which he is endowed (Darwin, *Descent* 733).

No less fascinated by musical expressivity, its intense communicative and aesthetic power as a non-verbal language, and what we would now refer to as its trans-species resonance, Darwin's near contemporary Richard Wagner was also attuned to the backbone shiver. The composer's interests, however, drew him to the tonal combinations and formal sequences most likely to defamiliarize listening habits and enthrall the listener; he then sought to yoke together "expansive" melodic forms, harmonic resonance, and rhythm on the one hand, and on the other the underlying pulse of narrative to bring new creative and organic intensity to music. The impact of his musical achievements and theoretical writings would change musical forms, patterns of composition, and the materiality of performance for generations to come. To this day, musicologists and music historians recurrently evoke the "Tristan chord" in the second bar of the Prelude to *Tristan and Isolde,* and the unresolved dominant-seventh chord to which it progresses, as that turning point in western music when high German romanticism first sounded the way from tonality to atonality.[4] This was no merely formal experiment; the lingering, unresolved, unfamiliar sequences literally play out Wagner's rejection of classical, predictable melodies and the conventional rules of harmonic resolution, in favor of

---

[3] The mystery of music has, of course, dogged philosophers and scientists from classical times to the present. A lifetime's experience as a music-lover and a neurologist, enabled by technology to "see the living brain as people listen to, imagine, and even compose music" led Oliver Sacks to conclude: "Our auditory systems, our nervous systems, are indeed exquisitely tuned for music. How much due to intrinsic characteristics of music itself —its complex sonic patterns woven in time, its logic ... the mysterious way in which it embodies emotion and "will"—and how much to special resonances in the immensely complex, multilevel neural circuitry that underlies musical perception and replay, we do not yet know" (Sacks xii-xiv). For the most up-to-date explorations of musical purpose, expression, and evolution from Darwin to neuroscience, see Altenmüller et al.

[4] For a full account of the Tristan chord and its historic and epistemological significance, see Magee.

organic musical forms. His essays defending such ground-breaking experiments in sound, which became familiar reading for so many of his musical contemporaries and musicologists, recurrently employ markedly evolutionist imagery, reflecting the extent to which Darwin's plot was shaping his own creative idiom (Grey 147-50).[5]

Tristan was completed in 1859, the same year that the fifty-year-old Darwin published *The Origin of Species*. Three landmarks for modernity therefore coincide in the year 1909: the coming-of-age of modern opera, the centenary of the naturalist's birth, and the fiftieth anniversary of *The Origin*. These were celebrated in style. Darwin commemorations occasioned "one of the most magnificent spectacles ever recorded in the annals of science … on a scale unsurpassed by other centennials of the time," receiving worldwide press coverage (Richmond 447-8).[6] The hub of these nationwide ceremonies was, of course, Cambridge; events included a formal reception on 23 June at Christ's College, the illustrious guest list for which included two children of one eminent Darwinian, Leslie Stephen.[7] New editions of all Darwin's works were commissioned for the occasion, numerous commemorative and biographical studies were published, and his enduring impact in biological and social theory was largely discussed in Cambridge, within Bloomsbury circles, and far beyond.

This culturally effervescent, commemorative context doubtless explains why Woolf, living in a milieu broadly steeped in Darwinian theory and with relations in the Darwin family, was reading or re-reading his major works at the time.[8] We can also surmise that some of the landmark publications of the day would have circulated in the Bloomsbury milieu: Cambridge University Press's centennial collection of essays *Darwin and Modern Science*, edited for the Cambridge Philosophical Society, for example. At least ten chapters out of a total of 29 would be likely to

---

[5] The influence of Darwin's theories and idiom on Wagner works was acknowledged by many of his own contemporaries (see for example Neumann), and has been the focus of critical attention, especially in the wake of Barzun's major work. See Østergaard and Grey for example.
[6] Various specialist reviews indicate that coverage began more than a year in advance. From mid-1908, articles in the *Musical Times*, *Mind,* the *Geographical Journal* and the *Journal of Philosophy*, for instance, reflect an interest not only in commemorating Darwin, but in re-reading Darwin's impact on contemporary arts and sciences, as will be seen in this article.
[7] See http://darwin-online.org.uk/1909.html (Accessed 13 July 2016). The seating plan for the formal dinner indicates the expected presence of a Mr and Miss Stephen. My thanks to Jane Goldman for providing this information.
[8] In the words of Elizabeth Lambert, "Throughout her youth [Woolf] read Darwin's works and was surrounded by luminaries of evolutionary thought, including her father, Leslie Stephen, and evolution's primary evangelist, T. H. Huxley" (Lambert 3). Lambert underlines the fact that Stephen himself had given his daughter a copy of Darwin's *Journal of Researches* (7), later known by the more appealing title, *The Voyage of the Beagle*. In 1906, Woolf had also inherited Thoby's personal copy of *The Origin of Species,* which he had been awarded as a school prize (Gillespie, in King and Miletic-Vejzovic xi).

have appealed to Bloomsbury's philosophical leanings, bearing on matters relating to language, mythology, and anthropology; these include key contributions by J. G. Frazer, Jane Harrison, and philologist Peter Gilles, which focus on dynamic, creative repercussions of Darwinian theory in the arts and ethnography—dance, ritual, primitive worlds, and animals' expressivity for instance.

While Darwin was being thus fêted, the intensely dynamic musical world of the new century looked back to the *Tristan* landmark to celebrate Wagner's lasting impact on modern music, which prompted new critical assessments, republications of his major essays, and specially commissioned biographies (including the first English translation of Nietzsche's *Richard Wagner in Bayreuth*).[9] This broader musical context of the times certainly enriches our appreciation of what were also Woolf's most intensely musical years, the highpoint of which was most certainly 1909. In this year alone, she attended performances of *Armide, Aida, Electra, Orpheus and Eurydice, Parsifal, Lohengrin, Lucia di Lammermoor, La Traviata*, and the English première of Ethel Smyth's *The Wreckers*—to mention only the principal operas. Diaries and letters confirm the impact of such musical hyperactivity, whether explicitly described or more subtly implied in entries with an intensified awareness of her acoustic environment. It was likewise in 1909 that Woolf contributed two major reviews to *The Times* on the Royal Opera Season at Covent Garden and the Wagner festival at Bayreuth (the hub of Wagner commemorative celebrations), both of which reflect not only her prolonged exposure to opera and musical performativity, but also a heightened awareness of the social, emotional, and communicative impact of music and its relation to linguistic expression—in resonance with ideas being propounded in Cambridge's philosophical circles, particularly within a Darwinist frame (*E*1 269-71; 288-92). The slippage from one expressive mode to another, and from one materialization to another, was indeed a characteristic feature of many of her early writings on music: in reference to *Parsifal,* Woolf explains that, "I expect it is the most remarkable of operas; it slides from music to words almost imperceptibly" (*L*1 406), a perception rich in Darwinian and Wagnerian echoes, as shall be explored below.[10]

---

[9]Although the notion of an "English Musical Renaissance" in the early 1900s has been contested, it is generally accepted that the years between the death of Queen Victoria and the outbreak of World War I were immensely, and jubilantly, musical in terms of concert programs, composition, the regularity and variety of musical events, and public and media response. *The Guardian*, to which Woolf contributed regularly, offered broad and detailed coverage of musical matters. It is furthermore worth noting that W. H. Hadow, the commissioning editor of the *Oxford History of Music*, and author of Volume Five, reviewed by Woolf in 1905 (E1 373-73), was renowned for his cultural liberalism and progressive championing of music's renewed dynamism. See Riley 16-20.

[10] As many critics have underlined since the 1990s, Woolf's musical life and awareness was far richer and of far greater consequence than had previously been acknowledged. See

There were not only centennial celebrations and musico-literary journalism at stake in 1909, however; it was an essential year in Woolf's creative and literary apprenticeship. In 1909, she undertook some of the most far-reaching, explicitly defined revisions of drafts for her first novel, the Darwinian underpinnings of which have been largely acknowledged, particularly in the wake of DeSalvo's first collation of early manuscripts to construct the finished novel's prototype, *Melymbrosia*.[11] It is this fascinating overlap of Darwinian models, musical expansiveness and voyages out that this essay seeks to clarify. I shall be linking the bolder Darwinian frame of the novel, its "zoological philosophy,"[12] and its gradual dissolution of individual character-drawing and plot to his own theories of musical purpose and the rich musical environment of the era. The expanded role given to music in later drafts leading to *The Voyage Out* becomes more striking and more significant when explored from an angle of cultural synchronism. Working from the premise that Woolf "worked all her life to give her fiction form and operatic structure" (Marcus, "Thinking" 22), I shall be foregrounding cultural, contextual connections that give a more substantiated, factually-grounded account of operatic and particularly Wagnerian influences, which "proved instrumental in helping her develop ideas about the connections between music and literature" (Kelley 420). These suggest why Rachel's musical life, for example, is given considerably more substance in *The Voyage Out* than in the novel's first drafts, and why there is a striking increase in musical events, musical references, and metaphorical allusions to music in the finished novel. In addition to explicit musical themes, there are also "fundamental parallels between operatic and novelistic narration" (Sutton, *Classical Music* 26) to be traced in the design of the final text. Foremost among these are a vivid Prologue or Overture scene on the London Embankment; a tripartite organization in three separate settings, like three acts: on board the *Euphrosyne*, at the South American hotel, and in the Amazonian forest. There is even a coda-like final storm—itself a dramatic, operatic convention, giving an agitated, virtuoso orchestral display while

---

Varga, Kelley, and Sutton "Space of Tears," "Fiction as Musical Critique," and *Classical Music* for rich accounts of Woolf's musical world, her musical reviews, and their potential interactions with *The Voyage Out*. As Sutton observes, referring to the years 1908-09, "at no other point in her life did [music] resurface so prominently in her non-fiction" ("Space of Tears" 52). For a splendid interlinking of literary modernism and Wagner's conception of "the unspeakably expressive speech beyond language that only the orchestra could provide," see Rasula 38-41

[11] The exact chronological sequence and dating of the extant manuscripts is as yet unclear, although the forthcoming Cambridge edition of the novel promises to provide the closest account of textual genesis to date. Meanwhile, see DeSalvo "Sorting, Sequencing," Froula, and Heine "Revisions of *The Voyage Out*," and "The Earlier Voyage" for essential contributions to this painstaking groundwork.

[12] I am deliberately echoing the title of Lamarck's *Philosophie zoologique* (1809), another landmark work whose centenary was marked and underlined the same year, especially in Franco-British scientific and philosophical reviews.

providing emotional relief and a background commentary on the workings of tragedy (Lindenberger 37-8). Auditory effect is likewise strikingly operatic, discernible in features such as contrasting voices, volume, timbre, the dramatic use of choric ensembles, and pacing. There are recitative-like dialogues, solo performances in the form of arias, strikingly choric scenes, and group exchanges explicitly orchestrated as musical events (for example, the first dinner party with the Dalloways [*VO* 40-5]), all of which will be evoked here within both a musical and a Darwinist frame.

Furthermore, it is a novel in which characters abandon ordinary speech and break into song at moments of extreme pain or pleasure, or to express excited feeling. This is, of course, the staple of operatic art, but it also gains from being set within the philosophical and scientific debates of the day, exploring the origins and function of music from an evolutionary perspective. The novel's soundscape, meanwhile, when read in counterpoint with that of Darwin's own "voyage out," is more resonant, both as a distant yet sonorous hum (at sea, in the hotel and during the jungle trip), and with remarkable outbursts of song from the human and the animal world—distinctions between which will prove decidedly tenuous, as Harrison and Giles, commemorating Darwin in 1909, had vividly underlined (Seward 506-08; 520-21). Exploring the literal appeal of the real world and how it sings (*D3* 260), I shall argue that "Musical Darwin" motifs (Smocovitis 592) in *The Voyage Out* can enhance the growing critical conviction that "Darwin's plot" was an essential feature of the "deeply embedded material [which] would have fed her imagination" (Ryan, *Materiality* 40), shaping the narrative and acoustic design of the text. The result is a first novel that theatricalizes Darwin's preoccupation with musical forms in the new world, "the real world," and the animal kingdom, and plays out Woolf's intuitive sense of emerging evolutionary repercussions for lives and literary patterns, the soundscapes of new worlds, and the musical imagination.

I. The Darwin Sound

The Sound is, of course, a waterway in South America rather than the naturalist's equivalent of Wagner's lingering chord sequence, but it provides a fitting metaphor when listening in parallel to Darwin's sense of a vaster, more unruly world, and to Woolf's urge to explore new fictional environments. As she explained in 1908 to Clive Bell, before explicitly setting out her creative ambitions in the new novel:[13]

> Ah, it is the sea that does it! perpetual movement, and a border of mystery, solving the limits of fields, and silencing their prose.... Nobody disturbs

[13] Woolf explains later in the same letter "how I shall re-form the novel and capture multitudes of things at present fugitive, enclose the whole, and shape infinite strange shapes," an ambition with strong echoes of the closing line of Darwin's *The Origin of Species*.

me, they light a lamp for me after dinner, and the only noises I can detect, with my window open, are distant sounds of cows, a bluebottle outside on the cistern and at the moment the flapping of a red admiral who has come in. (*L*1 356)

Woolf was seeking languages to transfigure modes of plot-composition and fictional expression as she listened thus to the world outside. Whether consciously listening with a naturalist's ear or not, these evocations of a resonant room where she sat writing, and the borders of mystery beyond, show a heightened sense of listenership as an allegorical mode—one where human agency could be decentered and human species' narcissism resisted—exactly those ambitions which made Darwin's evolutionary plot so revolutionary in its time (Beer, *Darwin's Plots* 29-35). It is this common attention to soundscape and allegories of listenership,[14] even when no human is there to listen, that I wish to start from.

The part played by Darwin's 1839 travelogue *The Voyage of the Beagle* in shaping Woolf's *The Voyage Out* has been insightfully explored by critics since Beer carefully mapped out the correlations.[15] Both works depict a naïve figure—the young naturalist aboard *The Beagle,* and Rachel, a young pianist aboard the *Euphrosyne*—who sets sail across the Atlantic and watches the contours of the familiar world dissolve. In both cases, the expanding horizon and the unexpected shapes and dimensions of uncharted lands prompt an awareness that conventional languages alone will not suffice to translate new territories into words. In the words of Darwin, "'When walking along the shady pathways, and admiring each successive view, I wished to find language to express my ideas. Epithet after epithet was found too weak ...'" (*Beagle* 507). His solution is not merely to observe and describe, but to record and represent sound—a fitting approach when we recall that "music filled Charles Darwin's life" (Smocovitis 592). He advises later generations of naturalists venturing thus into new worlds to adopt the method and acuity of the musician or of a musically alert listenership: "I am strongly induced to believe that, as in music, the person who understands every note will, if he possesses a proper taste, more thoroughly enjoy the whole, so he who examines each part of the fine view,

---

[14] I am deriving the concept from Stam's exploration of "allegories of spectatorship" at play in the reflexive mode of modernist film and literature (Stam 24-37).

[15] My reading of the novel's Darwinian heritage is indebted to Beer, but also to Elizabeth Lambert's essay on evolutionary discourse in *The Voyage Out.* Lambert's focus, however, is on the stylistic and thematic influence of Darwin's and later nineteenth-century evolutionary thinkers' writings in terms of the novel's representation of landscapes and vegetable / botanical references, rather than the novel's teeming animal imagery. Writing in 1991, however, Lambert's work predates contemporary animal and posthuman theory, and foregrounds Woolf's specifically feminist critique of evolutionary logic. For more recent explorations of the links between the Stephen family and Darwin, and between Darwinian thought and Woolf's perception of the natural world, see Alt, Czarnecki, and Ryan, "Spaniel to An*i*malous".

may also thoroughly comprehend the full and combined effect" (*Beagle* 513).[16] As a fine pianist, Rachel likewise thinks through musical sound sequences to make sense of new spaces, which are topographically undefined, or utopian spaces of an undefined future: "Now she stumbled; now she faltered and had to play the same bar twice over; but an invisible line seemed to string the notes together, from which rose a shape, a building (*VO* 58).[17]

In both works, the emerging perception of new territory, and an idiom and narrative to fit it, grows from a startling awareness of acoustic defamiliarization, which in turn is foregrounded and shaped into a "total" or inclusive "soundworld" (Halliday 12)—an auditory environment perceived and newly aggregated as "musical composition" or "precomposition" (Gandy 17). Background sound, from this perspective, is never a passive backcloth or a melodious, atmospheric accompaniment; it is powerfully performative and transformative. In their intuitive ways, both authors thus remind us that although the recent "acoustic" turn in cultural studies has vastly expanded our understanding of sonic modernity within an urban setting, a supposedly "natural" environment is just as "porous and disruptive a spatiality" as any early twentieth-century cosmopolis (Gandy 7).

Darwin defines his method as a "transposition" of flora, space, and sound (*Beagle* 310-11). The naturalist-as-listener makes a point of recording the landscape as a "great concert" of the world—an ambition that was soon to strike a chord with Wagner. The following telling example is but one of hundreds of sonic recordings in Darwin's travelogue, which capture the acoustic dynamics of the environment and rely on allegorical and metaphorical modes of listenership:

> Nature, in these climes, chooses her vocalists from more humble performers than in Europe. A small frog, of the genus Hyla, sits on a blade of grass about an inch above the surface of the water, and sends forth a pleasing chirp: when several are together they sing in harmony on different notes. I had some difficulty in catching a specimen of this frog ... Every evening after dusk this great concert commenced; and often have I sat listening to it, until my attention has been drawn away by some passing insect. (44)

---

[16] Darwin sums up his quest and achievements most explicitly in the final chapter; the "Retrospective" and peroration specifically define a comparative method and a blueprint for future researches. He draws recurrently on the techniques of the artist, composer, dramatist, and spectatorships—references most likely to have resonated with Woolf's "voyage out" (Beagle 494-517).

[17] This is one of three essential musical episodes in the novel in which Rachel's playing is truly performative, conjuring up uncharted, unspeakable spaces. I would link these musical events directly to the utopian imaginary of the novel, conjuring up worlds as yet unknown for the female musician. See also the end of the dance (87) and the last recorded "performance," interrupted by Terence (339-40). Darwin's utopian imaginary resounds in the closing lines of The Origin of Species, in which he looks ahead to "endless forms most beautiful and most wonderful that have been, and are being, evolved" (*Origin* 913).

Like Woolf writing to Clive Bell from the Pembrokeshire coast (where she was also "split[ting] her head" over *Principia Ethica*, which starts from a discussion of Darwinist and evolutionary ethics to expand out to aesthetic enjoyment), and like the awakening pianist Rachel, who would follow in his wake on the cliffs, along the coast and upriver in South America, the apprentice-naturalist is a listener in the world, for whom panoramic settings on land and at sea are an interwoven drama of natural and aesthetic sounds:

> At this elevation the landscape attains its most brilliant tint; and every form, every shade, so completely surpasses in magnificence all that the European has ever beheld in his own country, that he knows not how to express his feelings. The general effect frequently recalled to my mind the gayest scenery of the Opera-house or the great theatres. (Darwin, *Beagle* 47)

The same interrelated idiom of music's cultural setting and magnitude, woven into a naturalist's perception of the natural world, provides the keynote of "Impressions at Bayreuth," an essay revealing "Woolf's first recorded interest in the space 'between the acts' ... both inside, with the artificial performance space, and outside, within nature" (Kelley 420-21):

> In the next interval, between seven and eight, there is another act out here also ...These strange intervals in the open air, as though a curtain were regularly drawn and shut again, have no disturbing effect, upon *Parsifal* at least. A bat from the woods circled Kundry's head in the meadow and little white moths dance incessantly over the footlights. (*E1* 290)

Likewise, throughout *The Voyage Out*, Rachel's sense of being in an unfamiliar world relies on a comparable, specifically musical perception of the natural world: "her mind seemed to enter into communion, to be delightfully expanded and combined with the spirit of the whitish boards on deck, with the spirit of the sea, with the spirit of Beethoven Op. 111, even with the spirit of poor William Cowper there at Olney" (*VO* 35). Such passing, explicit interrelations, once appreciated as part of the novel's interlinked musical and natural backcloth, emerge as a more experimentally modernist idiom, one which "adumbrates a newer, more conjugated and convivial auditorium of the world" (Connor 22). If the novel is divided into the operatic movements suggested above, each setting has its own sonic background, as if recorded by a naturalist's sound-sensitive ear. The London embankment, for example, with its "shooting motor cars, more like spiders in the moon than terrestrial objects, the thundering drays, the jingling hansoms, and little black broughams" (*VO* 5); what we might call Act I, aboard the *Euphrosyne*, with its steadily beating heart (36) and "great bell;" Act II, in the hotel, where a resonant clock has a "silent hall to tick in," a wheezing chime and frenzied gong (129); and Act III in the forest:

> It echoed like a hall. There were sudden cries; and then long spaces of silence, such as there are in a cathedral when a boy's voice has ceased and the echo of it still seems to haunt about the remote places of the roof. (*VO* 312)

And finally, of course, the Coda or Epilogue, where the storm scene evoked above is explicitly dramatized as if it were being played out simultaneously in the closed setting of the hotel, beneath the lofty domes of the modern opera house, and upon the greater theatrical stage of the natural world:

> At a touch, all the electric lights were turned on, and revealed a crowd of people all standing, all looking with rather strained faces up at the skylight, but when they saw each other in the artificial light they turned at once and began to move away. For some minutes the rain continued to rattle upon the skylight, and the thunder gave another shake or two; but it was evident from the clearing of the darkness and the light drumming of the rain upon the roof, that the great confused ocean of air was travelling away from them, and passing high over head with its clouds and its rods of fire, out to sea. The building, which had seemed so small in the tumult of the storm, now became as square and spacious as usual. (*VO* 430-1)

As will be seen below, this pervasively sonorous world will prove decisive in Rachel's musical response to her environment, and in the novel's exploration of plot-resolution and musical conventions.

A fascinating cultural setting thus begins to take shape once the importance of the centennial celebrations are acknowledged. Darwin's accounts of new territories and narratives, comparing the naturalist's method to that of a composer and the great noise of the world to that of a symphony orchestra (*Beagle* 334), and his lifelong interest in the transformative energies of music, were being discussed and re-evaluated by Cambridge intellectuals (Harrison and Gilles in particular) and Woolf's immediate circles. This background chorus is in turn resounding in the musically vibrant, creative atmosphere of Woolf's evolving writing project. To return to her "Impressions of Bayreuth," we find the opera-goer who prefers "to step out of the opera house" in a decidedly naturalist mode, observing that "when the music is silent the mind inevitably slackens and expands, among happy surroundings: heat and the yellow light, and the intermittent but not unmusical noises of insects and leaves smooth out the folds" (*E*1 290). As the essayist concludes, in terms that recur in the closing words of Chapter Four of *The Voyage Out*, "we realise how thin are the walls between one emotion and another; and how fused our impressions are with elements which we may not attempt to separate" (292). It is exactly the effect that Halliday identifies in *Between the Acts*, "where the sonic and the non-sonic, and the musical and the non-musical, occupy a common space: a space, moreover, that is as much social as it is geophysical, as much conceptual as it is sensory, and as much imaginary, or subjective, as it is 'real.'"[18] The overall effect is one of the most striking examples in Woolf's work of the "uncanny prefiguring" (Hussey 131) of her mature writing in her earliest novel—listening to the real world in song in *The Voyage Out* anticipates by thirty years the pageant of prehistoric worlds, human-animal eclogues, and contemporary minstrelsy in "Anon" and *Between the Acts*.

II. A Carnival of the Animals

By the early years of the twentieth century, "Darwinism" was itself in the throes of extensive ramification and mutation, as is confirmed by a brief overview of the Cambridge Philosophical Society's imposing volume *Darwin and Modern Science: Essays in Commemoration of the Centenary of the Birth of Charles Darwin and the Fiftieth Anniversary of the publication of* The Origin of Species. Numerous contributors evoke the two essential offshoots for modern biology, on the one hand, and sociology, on the other, whether they problematize the relation between biological or organic evolution and social or selectionist evolution, or prefer quite simply to disregard one or the other. A third offshoot occupies an uneasy territory between the two: that of anthropology and primitive cultures, where essays by Frazer and Harrison in particular address questions of ritual, magic, and myth, describing examples of "a mystic bond" that unites "human kinsfolk to a species of animals or plants" (Frazer, in Seward 160) and thereby conjure up more complex, interrelated relationships between "Man," primitive peoples, and the lower creatures. Inevitably, these chapters draw at length on the five years of the *Beagle* voyage, and Darwin's later account of his observations of primitive worlds in unfamiliar settings. The focus of these contributions provides a fascinating access to Woolf's own "voyage out."[19]

---

[18] Halliday underlines Darwin's essential contribution to the theoretical groundings of sonic modernity by outlining its organic force in *The Descent of Man*, and its power to arouse "synoptic, if oblique impressions of this whole past in one fell swoop" (Halliday 24). Halliday equally explores the importance of Wagner as "an almost perfect guide" to modernism's literary "sound-worlds" (33), and compares Woolf's aesthetic strategies in creating a sound-world in *Between the Acts* to Wagner's vision of a "total" work of art (Halliday 11-3). I shall be returning to Darwinian and Wagnerian perspectives on sound in further detail below.

[19] From the perspectives of this essay, there are interesting but doubtless coincidental resonances between Woolf's novel and Frazer's account of his own experience of primitive narratives of origin which include a Melanesian legend from Santa Marina (the name Woolf gives to the fictional resort in South America), where man and woman are curiously intermingled, as are human and pig, and human and the tree (Seward 156).

As early works in each author's personal evolution, both texts invite phylogenetic and ontogenetic readings. Their protagonists' voyages are motivated by a desire to see the world and fathom their generic place in the patterns of life, from prehistory to the present, as an individual and as one of a species on a larger evolutionary scale. For Darwin, this was to be the entangled, intermingled mesh of the animal and human worlds, the processes of natural selection, and the potential for new species to evolve. For Rachel, the scale is more modest—she is to learn her place in the world as a woman, by observing the workings of upper-class English society, acquiring the etiquette required of a dinner party hostess, and improving her chances of marriage according to the exacting rules of domestic selection. The *bildungs* plot goes wrong, however; instead of rising to fulfill her destiny as a bride, Rachel proves "unfit" for survival: she falls sick with an unidentified tropical fever and dies.

The Darwinist underpinnings of this basic plot are surely anything but coincidental, and gain from being read within the context of organic versus sociological evolutionary schemes. Subtly Darwinian leitmotifs reflecting one or the other side of the debate play into the contrapuntal tensions of the novel, pulling against the smooth narrative surface. In either case, their comic, satirical, and ideological overtones confirm "Woolf's delight in Darwin's speculative imagination and her parody of science as a source of truth" (Lambert 1-2). They also suggest an underlying narrative project which, even while it critiqued evolutionary theory's imperialist goals and "the narrow empiricism of [its] sexual science" (Lambert 3), also explores the creative, transformative potential of Darwinist theory when it addresses mankind and animals as companion species, and as fellow performers of musicalized ritual. It is to these contending forces of early-twentieth-century evolutionism that I shall now turn.

Like the naturalist keen to abandon taxonomy to observe species interacting in their natural habitat, Rachel surveys "human beings" at one remove (*VO* 150). Woolf's external narrator proves a ruthless observer too, presenting the English travelers and the hotel guests as series of specimens, the comic incongruity of which creates a "Carnival of the Animals":[20]

> They saw Mr Pepper as though he had suddenly loosened his clothes, and had become a vivacious and malicious old ape. (VO 12)

> He's indescribably insignificant, and rather queer in his temper, poor dear. It's like sitting down to dinner with an ill-conditioned fox-terrier, only one can't comb him out, and sprinkle him with powder, as one would

---

[20] This is not to suggest any influence of Saint-Saëns' composition on Woolf's creative imagination at the time. Although performed in private in 1886, the work was kept hidden by the composer and not heard in public until 1922.

one's dog. It's a pity, sometimes, one can't treat people like dogs! (50)
Mr Pepper for all his learning had been mistaken for a cormorant, and then, as unjustly transformed into a cow. (94)

Whether figuring as conventional similes, startling metaphors, memories, real presences, or objects of trade, animals roam with often disarming ease throughout the pages of the novel, conjuring up a vision of the civilized world as a raucous menagerie.[21]

'My parrot can't bear dogs', said Mrs Paley, with the air of making a confidence. 'I always suspect that he (or she) was teased by a dog when I was abroad.' ... 'Animals do commit suicide' she sighed as if she asserted a painful fact. (132)

'What would you do if spiders came out of the tap when you turned on the hot water?' she demanded. (150)

Their silence, he said, reminded him of the silence in the lion-house when each beast holds a lump of raw meat in its paws. He went on, stimulated by this comparison, to liken some to hippopotamuses, some to canary birds, some to swine, some to parrots, and some to loathsome reptiles curled round the half-decayed bodies of sheep. (198)

These portraits far exceed witty characterizations. To the contrary, they have a firm place within Woolf's critique of "the cultural values that made evolutionary theory a compelling social force" (Lambert 19). They reverse Darwin's tendency, for example, to combine comic effect and exemplary strength by reading the animal world through the lens of the human.[22] In Woolf's text, it is the human who is "de-anthromorphized," losing the protective covering of culture and

---

[21] With over 600 animal references or metaphors, *The Voyage Out* may prove to be Woolf's most zoological text, although a much more thorough catalogue would be needed to affirm this. Despite a tremendous recent critical interest in the vital importance of animals in Woolf's creative imagination, little in-depth attention has so far been given to what Ryan terms the "animalous" of *The Voyage Out* (Ryan, "Spaniel to Animalous" 158-65, and Ryan *Materiality* 150-161). See for example the *Virginia Woolf Miscellany* vol. 84, "Virginia Woolf and Animals" (Czarnecki and Neverow).

[22] See for example Darwin's ants: "But having been attacked, the lion-hearted little warriors scorned the idea of yielding" (50), or his spiders "The little aëronaut as soon as it arrived on board was very active, running about, sometimes letting itself fall, and then reascending the same thread … On its first arrival it seemed very thirsty, and with exserted maxillae drank eagerly of drops of water" (*Beagle* 172-3).

refinement. The insistently intrusive, incongruous animal presences can be read as an all too discomfiting echo of the closing lines of *The Descent of Man,* which recall that benevolent human creatures, for all their noble qualities and god-like intellect, bear in their bodily frames the indelible stamp of their lowly origin.

On a more subversive, sociopolitical note, the cross-species parallels likening the human species to fossils and the lower animals bear comparison with Darwin's extensive discussion in *The Origin of Species* of variation under confinement and domestication. In the long term, he argues, this produces weaker specimens, less adapted to survive in the wild, making them more likely candidates for extinction or fossilization (although Darwin's 1859 masterpiece avoided alluding to the origins or possible extinction of the human animal). A Darwinian heritage can also be felt in the decentering of the dominant human gaze and the human organizer. These are not only animals looked at, but animals liable to assume their own subjectivity and look back:

> 'I don't know which alarms me the most—a cow or a tree. I once met a cow in a field by night. The creature looked at me. I assure you it turned my hair grey. It's a disgrace that animals should be allowed to go at large.'
>
> 'And what did the cow think of him?' Venning mumbled. (134)
>
> But Susan, who had been brought up to understand that the horse is the noblest of God's creatures, could not agree, and Venning thought Hirst an unspeakable ass, but was too polite not to continue the conversation.
>
> 'When they see us falling out of aeroplanes, they get some of their own back, I expect,' he remarked. (148)

As for the romantic liaisons that structure the central section of the text, these read as splendid variations of what Darwin in *The Descent of Man* refers to as "Love Antics and Dance." The most striking example is that of the dance party at the hotel (where the role of footman is played by a stuffed leopard [*VO* 167]), organized to consecrate the courtship rituals of two nondescript characters. From a supposedly genteel setting, despite being likened to "a farmyard scattered with grain on which bright pigeons were descending," the party changes drastically when Rachel takes over from the musicians and improvises dance music. The room is gradually transformed into a ludicrous carnival of interpretative dancing, in which the accoutrements of civilization are forgotten, and the blissfully lowly can reconnect with the elevated:

> St. John hopped with incredible swiftness first on his left leg, then on his right …Hewet, swaying his arms and holding out the tails of his coat,

swam down the room in imitation of the voluptuous dreamy dance of an Indian maiden dancing before her Rajah.... Miss Allen advanced with skirts extended and bowed profoundly to the engaged pair.... Mr Pepper executed an ingenious pointed step derived from figure-skating ... Mrs Thornbury tried to recall an old country dance ... As for Mr and Mrs Elliot, they galloped round and round the room with such impetuosity that the other dancers shivered at their approach. (*VO* 186-7)

The passage echoes disarmingly when read alongside the "ludicrous" courtship rites that Darwin records:

The gesticulations and parade of the males at the beginning of the love-season are extremely ludicrous.... our little white-throat often rises a few feet or yards in the air above some bush, and flutters with a fitful and fantastic motion, singing all the while, and then drops to his perch. The great English bustard throws himself into indescribably odd attitudes whilst courting the female ... An allied Indian bustard at such times rises perpendicularly into the air with a hurried flapping of his wings, and when they approach he trails his wings and spreads his tail like a turkey cock. (Darwin, *Descent* 430)

Another fine example of the constant shifts between animalesque farce, animalized satire, and reflexive cross-species exchange emerges in the latent rivalry between Hewet and Hirst when vying for Rachel's attentions. Both make rather ostentatious show of their learning and wit in public, and recommend suitable reading matter for Rachel; their choice is surely anything but fortuitous:

'What's that book?' 'It's Gibbon.' (*VO* 224)

'Would you happen to have a Gibbon, Uncle Ridley?' (*MEL* 117)

The book written by the man known to his friends as "The Gibbon" was of the course *The Decline and Fall of the Roman Empire*, a landmark proto-evolutionist narrative in which a great empire succumbs to degeneration, decline, and extinction.[23] Gibbon in Woolf's narrative, however, is an elusive, destabilizing factor, undermining stable hierarchizations and representations of species and class. Both suitors consider Gibbon-literacy to be an intellectual prerequisite and a reliable marker of human worth, and they incite Rachel to think likewise. When Terence reads pages aloud to convince Rachel of his rhetorical prowess, however, she fails

---

[23] By the early twentieth-century, the "decline and extinction" theme common to Gibbon and evolutionary theory was being propounded by imperialist Social Darwinists such as Cecil Rhodes. See Crook 162-3.

to admire his learning and eloquence as she is clearly intended to, her resistance being marked by her assuming a form of primeval, "pre-Gibbonesque" shell life:

> Hewet was still reading Gibbon aloud, and Rachel, for all the expression she had, might have been a shell, and his words water running against her ears, as water rubs a shell on the edge of a rock. (*VO* 229)[24]

In other words, well before succumbing to a mysterious fever, supposedly caught in the jungle, Rachel's body is resisting the call to rise to her destiny, and it does so by taking refuge in a less evolved form. It is a point I shall return to.

The passages evoking Rachel's Gibbon-related education provide comic and satirical relief (such as Hirst's fixed concentration as he peels a banana [VO 150]). More subtly, however, they suggest harsher, more "an*i*malous" Darwinian undercurrents (Ryan, "Spaniel to An*i*malous" 158). In both *The Descent* and *The Emotions*, the gibbon is singled out from other apes on account of his ability to "pour forth a whole octave of musical notes and may be said to sing" (Darwin, *Descent* 641). Darwin's detailed descriptions of the singing ape as part of his study of musical expressivity and its function within an evolutionary narrative gain from being read in parallel with Woolf's depictions of the eloquent suitors:

> The gibbon has an extremely loud but musical voice. In ascending and descending the scale, the intervals were always exactly half-tones; and I am sure that the highest note was the exact octave to the lowest. The quality of the notes is very musical; and I do not doubt that a good violinist would be able to give a correct idea of the gibbon's composition.... He [the gibbon] is much excited after his performance. (Darwin, *Descent* 633)

Suitors as singing apes would have been staple comic fair by the early 1900s. The classic example of Gilbert and Sullivan's "The Darwinian Man" from *Princess Ida* (1884) was only one of a kind:[25]

> The turn of the century witnessed an efflorescence of song and musical productions that evoked Darwin and his theory. The fact that they were no longer considered so new or shocking, but in fact daring and even risqué,

---

[24] The comment gains from being read in parallel with an earlier satirical note, when Rachel is observing a worshipper in church: "She was a limpet, with the sensitive side of her stuck to a rock, for ever dead to the rush of fresh and beautiful things past her" (*VO* 265).

[25] Gilbert and Sullivan's *Princess Ida* drew its comic satire from a blend of popular anti-Darwinism and hearty scorn for women's colleges; the parable of an ape enamored of an educated woman is told in its most famous song, "The Darwinian Man." *Princess Ida* is one of many examples of Darwin's musical posterity: popular Darwinism and anti-Darwinism, frequently targeting his theories of music, expressed in song, stage-plays, and operetta in the late nineteenth and early twentieth centuries (Smocovitis 592-600).

> fueled the appropriation of Darwinian themes for popular audiences who thrilled to scenes of monkeys, jungles, and humans in a more primitive, "natural" state. (Smocovitis 597)

Woolf's own figure of the performing gibbon, whether consciously inspired by popular, comic subversions of the era or not, is considerably more complex, however. It is to these singing animals and a broader operatic soundscape that we now turn, for these provide one of the most outstanding examples of how *The Voyage Out* interweaves themes of gender, sexuality, animality, and musical performance to sound the depths of courtship and mating in the hothouse world of the tropical hotel.

III. Here Comes the Bride? Opera, Music, and Matrimony

Extended studies of music making and musical perception in *The Descent of Man* enable Darwin to counter both the long-held belief that musical sensibility attested to the refinement and ascendancy of the human spirit, and the purely physiological explanations of music as an exaggeration of vocal utterance in primitive languages. In the Darwinian scheme of things, music is a startling reminder of man's lowly beginnings:

> The progenitors of man probably uttered musical tones before they had acquired the power of articulate speech; the males employ their voices to please the female. The impassioned orator, bard or musician, when with his varied tones and cadences he excites the strongest emotions in his hearers, little suspects that he uses the same means by which his half-human ancestors long ago aroused each other's ardent passions, during their courtship and rivalry. (*Descent* 639)

The link between song, primeval memory, and the propagation of the species provides a fascinating angle from which to observe "the impassioned orators and bards" of Woolf's novel, who break into song at moments of heightened emotion. Musically speaking, the novel's characters fall unequally into three categories: the male bipeds that sing or declaim, usually to a female listener; the female bipeds that listen and admire (Clarissa's recital of Shelley's *Adonais* being the one female "song" performed for Rachel); and Rachel, who prefers to observe, perform when alone, and remain mostly silent.

The male songsters include Ridley, who intones Pindar and other "songs" (*VO* 408) at every appropriate moment; Mr Pepper, who "strikes up" with Greek choruses from Sophocles (44); Mr Grice, who "recites in an emphatic nasal voice" (55), Richard Dalloway (whose predatory intrusions begin, revealingly, when he "sat upon Bach" [78]), who "soliloquizes" sententiously about icebergs and Burke before grasping Rachel in his arms (79-80), and rival suitors Hewet and Hirst, whose courtship rituals involve various poetry and song recitals—which in operatic terms would constitute the protagonists' solo arias: Hirst's extended Gibbon recitals and Sapphic odes in the place of the creed at Sunday service (267-8), and Hewet's effusive accounts of his own compositions, along with recitals of Whitman and Milton (380).[26] In all, there are fifteen separate performances of song or verse, each one clearly theatricalized with both a specific arena or stage and an appropriately designed listenership. Such breaks in the logic and efficiency of the spoken word, to transpose complex feeling into song, is the staple of the lyric arts from the masque to the musical, via opera. The result, whether on stage or in the novel, is to intensify or impede the linear, mimetic plot, and to introduce alternative aesthetics, rhythms, and mythic patterns into the formal and emotional architectonics of the work (Lindenberger 54-6).[27] At the same time, such interludes in song are consonant with Darwin's interest in ways in which song punctuates the natural rhythms of life, and with his wholly rational, evolutionary explanation of the origins and functionality of music. Darwin's earliest writings ascribe musical virtuosity to the male of the species; he later concedes that:

> Woman first acquired musical powers in order to attract the other sex. But if this is so this must have occurred long ago, before our ancestors had become sufficiently human to treat and value their women merely as useful slaves (*Descent* 639).

Approached from the angle of seemly courtship tricks, Rachel's preferred mode of music-making, in the intimacy of her room, is not merely solipsistic, as some critics have suggested. It marks a refusal to demean music and performance to the winsome graces of a female performer, and to the social spaces designed to stage seduction. Ostentatiously seeking solitude is a distinct model of resistance, and within the ideologically codified context of the conventional middle classes, it is political. Such political resistance can be passive, such as when she plays to herself in her own room, or sings when walking alone in the park; but it can also be pro-active. First voiced in passing when speaking to Helen in Chapter One (evoking Aunt Bessie's fear that a pianist's hypertrophied arm muscles might play against her marriageability [15]), her opposition becomes more forceful when she manifests her distinct distaste for the married woman's role that her social environment, and Terence in particular, plans for her; her rare outspokenness is prompted by his persistently talking aloud and interrupting her practice:

---

[26] We might note in passing the disastrous effects of Hewet's performances. His recital of Whitman elicits chuckles and laughter from the surrounding animals; his rendering of Milton will haunt Rachel until she dies. I shall be returning to this episode below.

[27] Lindenberger attributes specifically defamiliarizing techniques to operatic design in Wagnerian and post-Wagnerian opera, making a clear distinction with a more naturalist tendency sought by earlier schools of opera (218-227).

'Again, it's the fashion now to say that women are more practical and less idealistic than men, also that they have considerable organising ability but no sense of honour'—query, what is meant by masculine term, honour?—what corresponds to it in your sex? Eh?' ... Crashing down a final chord with her left hand, she exclaimed at last, swinging round upon him: 'No, Terence, it's no good; here am I, the best musician in South America, not to speak of Europe and Asia, and I can't play a note because of you in the room interrupting me every other second.' (340)

The presence of marked anti-Darwinist critique, countering the belief that a woman's musical skills serve to attract her mate, or that ungraceful animal noise is a sign of less evolved species, can be heard in the exchange that follows. Rachel is bound up in the musically demanding and emotionally rich textures of the last Beethoven sonata; Terence deflates her ambitions and expressivity with a peremptory and condescendingly animalesque metaphor:

'I've no objection to nice simple tunes—indeed, I find them very helpful to my literary composition, but that kind of thing is merely like an unfortunate old dog going round on its hind legs in the rain.' (336)

By adopting a Johnsonesque mode to ascribe musical virtuosity to men and "nice simple tunes" to women, and associating late Beethoven piano sonatas with dogs on hind legs in the rain, Terence is clearly making a tactical error. First, his condescending humor runs counter to the novel's decentering, "ani*m*alous" logic, which offers alternative worldviews to those of a self-centered, self-serving humanity, and lets animals speak back. Secondly, it runs up against the novel's networks of musical expressivity. Well before the 1910s, such wit would have been out of place in the advanced-thinking household Terence and Rachel supposedly aspire to, and more at home in the slapstick and comic patter of the music hall—Gilbert and Sullivan's comic operas, and their use of animal farce and blustering male chauvinism for example. In other words, Terence is revealing a mindset more suited to "singing apes" and patriarchy's operetta entertainments, where predictable plots, stable social hierarchies, and "happy endings" in marriage win the day—the dénouement that Rachel's family had been planning for her.

Rachel's plot, however, is going to evolve differently, thwarting the expectations of musical and social convention, but "recalling in a vague and distant manner" the rites and patterns from "long-past ages" (Darwin, *Emotions* 92). Such shifts of scale and plot are equally those that characterize Wagner's rejection of the conventional opera-dramas of the day in favor of differently designed, more complex compositions which reshaped long-forgotten myths. Explicitly defined in a Darwinist, evolutionary mode, his musical prose works define his quest for new melodic and harmonic patterns to be interwoven through movement, orchestral setting, song, and voice, thereby renewing the grandeur of opera for modern times.

Such musicalized worlds in Wagner's art-projects provide a fittingly evolutionist approach to Rachel's musical world.[28] What I am calling the operatic soundscape of the novel is not only provided by humans breaking into song. As we saw above, Woolf's novel is vividly depicted as a tapestry of sound, each of the novel's spatial settings being characterized as an acoustic sound-world, with a performative, transformative dimension. The most eloquent example within a Darwinist and musical frame is that of the forest, with its chorus of animal and vegetable inhabitants, where "the noises of the ordinary world were replaced by those creaking and sighing sounds which suggest to the traveller in a forest that he is walking at the bottom of the sea" (*VO* 315). The chorus of voices from humans, animals, and objects alike creates premonitory cross-species musical exchanges, harking back to more distant times. This too is what Darwin heard when he set out on a mule party to ascend the South American heights:

> When we reached the crest and looked backward, a glorious view was presented. The atmosphere resplendently clear; the sky an intense blue; the profound valleys; the wild broken forms; the heaps of ruins piled up during the lapse of ages ... all these produced a scene no one could have imagined.... I felt glad that I was alone: it was like watching a thunderstorm or hearing in full orchestra a chorus of the Messiah. (Darwin, *Beagle* 334)

This world "in full orchestra" resounds, for instance, throughout the excursion upriver, when Terence and Rachel first move from discreet courtship rituals to avowals of love. These will not be exalted, operatic love songs however, with a melodious accompaniment: Terence's efforts to recite Whitman[29] are met only by a bird's "wild laughter" and a monkey that "chuckl[ed] a malicious question" (312). The background chorus, meanwhile, grows equally cacophonous, creating a dissonant sonic backcloth for the blossoming love affair: "The sighing and creaking up above were broken every now and then by the jarring cry of some startled animal" (315). In this context, the first declarations of love are achingly hollow, the echoing words sounding like empty recitative:

---

[28] Wagnerian overtones, from *Lohengrin* to *The Ring* via *Tristan*, have been traced in a number of Woolf's works. See Kelley 420-3, DiGaetani 109-129, and Halliday 11-3 for example. For a masterly account of thematic interlinks between *Tristan und Isolde* and Rachel and Terence's romance, see Sutton, *Classical Music*.

[29] Terence's choice is indeed revealing, bearing in mind the huge influence of songs and opera in the poet's works; Whitman admitted to a follower that "But for the opera I could never have written *Leaves of Grass*" (Lindenberger 66).

> 'You like being with me?' Terence asked.
> 'Yes, with you,' she replied. …
> 'We are happy together.'…
> 'Very happy', she answered. …
> 'We love each other,' Terence repeated, searching into her face.
> 'We love each other,' she repeated. (316)

The haunting echo-effect is instantly followed by a powerfully-evocative silence, "broken by their voices which joined in tones of strange unfamiliar sound which formed no words. … They sat side by side. Sounds stood out from the background making a bridge across their silence; they heard the swish of the trees and some beast croaking in a remote world" (316). Once again, the intermingling of Darwinist, loosely operatic, and specifically Wagnerian motifs is striking here, all of which link back to Woolf's account of returning home from the opera house after hearing *Parsifal*. The "singing of the real world" resounding in the forest's medley of animal and vegetable voices recalls Wagner's belief that the antique Greek chorus should be "entirely transferred to the orchestra," so that an over-arching "melody-form" of the dramatic-musical whole can be heard throughout the opera house:

> But when, overwhelmed by this first general impression, the forest's visitor sits down to ponder; when, the last burden of the city's hubbub cast aside, he girds the forces of his soul to a new power of observing; when, as if hearing with new senses, he listens more and more intently—he perceives with ever greater plainness the infinite diversity of voices waking in the wood. Ever and ever a new, a different voice peers forth, a voice he thinks he has never heard as yet; as they wax in number, they grow in strange distinction; louder and louder rings the wood; and many though the voices be, the individual strain he hears, the glinting stream of sound seems again to him but just great forest melody. (Wagner, *CW* 3 339)

Like Wagner's orchestral chorus resonating from the depths of the concert hall,[30] itself a resurgent form of the Sophoclean choruses of Greek tragedy,[31] the "lower animals" in *The Voyage Out* are voicing the warning signals that Rachel is not quite ready to hear, their inarticulate cries opening up spaces for that which, if it cannot yet be said, can be heard.

---

[30] Wagner broke with operatic tradition by having the orchestra in a pit, hidden from the view of spectators, thereby creating a tighter interweaving of music, drama, and setting.

[31] In both "Music of the Future" and "Opera and Drama," Wagner presents the modern orchestra as "a bequest" from the chorus of Greek Tragedy in the ideal art-form to which he aspires (Wagner, *CW* 2 335-6; *CW* 5 338-9). In either case, the renewal of more primitive forms in modern music-drama is constantly apprehended in an explicitly evolutionary, Darwinist idiom.

IV. Preludes, Afternoons, Fauns

There is one last operatic performance to be fitted into the novel's musical and evolutionary counterpoint in which traditional plots—fictional and evolutionary—are diverted, where the natural world sings back, chorus-like to Rachel, and where "barbarous dissonance" takes over the soundscape. The return from the excursion upriver, with the marriage plot gaining momentum, finds Terence earnestly pursuing his endeavors to educate his future wife; he makes the most of an afternoon "so hot that the breaking of the waves on the shore sounded like the repeated sigh of some exhausted creature" (*VO* 380) to read aloud from Milton's *Comus*. Musical and intertextual resonances in this scene are powerful.[32] *Comus* is not merely poetry; it is a Baroque masque, conceived as a story in music, about music ("And listen why," the Prologue urges the spectator, "for I will tell you now / What never yet was heard in tale or song" [Milton, *Masque* 10]); it is set in a world where music can both beguile and protect, and where the woods themselves echo with luring melodies "that filled the air with barbarous dissonances' (Milton, Masque 21). The Red Riding Hood-type plot unfolds theatrically in song, recitative, dialogue, and musical interludes. A lady lost in the Wild Wood follows her "listening ear" (14) to the wicked sorcerer Comus's lair; here Comus will attempt to seduce her with song and sophistry—using the example of Nature's lush fertility to defend unbridled sexuality. After the Lady's brothers fail in their bid to save her, the Attendant Spirit sings to call up Sabrina, a river goddess who formerly relinquished human form to protect her own mind and body; Sabrina in turn sings to break Comus's spell, and return the Lady by magic to the safety of home.

As critics have underlined, the setting and climate of Milton's Wild Wood recall the tropical excursion and the garden where Terence reads to Rachel; likewise Milton's allegory of chastity, threatened by debauchery and magically preserved by song, resound in strange dissonance with Rachel's impending fate. It is just after struggling against the seeming inevitability of domesticity, suburbia, and child-raising that she hears Terence reciting the Attendant Spirit's song lines; at this point, her fever sets in. Lines from *Comus* continue to filter through her mind and her perception of the world (including the hirsute, faun-like doctor who doubles as an insidiously Comus-like figure) as the fever mounts, and she gradually fades from the narrative.

---

[32] Although possibly only part of the "traffic of ideas" (Hussey 61) by which Woolf in the late 1900s and early 1910s absorbed such French post-symbolist influences as "Matisse, Debussy, Scriabin, Mallarmé," there may also be intertextual, intermedial echoes of Mallarmé's eclogue "Après-Midi d'un Faune" in this episode, with Comus and the faun being fellow sexual predators, who are both traditionally represented as half human, half goat, sharing a carnal and profligate view of Nature's bounties provided for their pleasures. Debussy's symphonic poem inspired by the poem dates from 1894, and the Ballets-Russes performance from 1912.

In addition to verbal and thematic echoes, there are performance-related, intermedial resonances to be gleaned from this highly operatic intertext. When approached from the musical perspectives of masque, the death of Rachel gains in musical and narrative power.[33] It is important to note that the last glimpses the reader has of Rachel's consciousness present her not so much dying as receding from a world of trees and savages, dissolving in the heat, and, like Sabrina, quite literally becoming water:

> At last the faces went further away; she fell into a deep pool of sticky water, which eventually closed over her head. She saw nothing and heard nothing but a faint booming sound, which was the sound of the sea rolling over her head. While all her tormentors thought that she was dead, she was not dead, but curled up at the bottom of the sea. There she lay, sometimes seeing darkness, sometimes light, while every now and then some one turned her over at the bottom of the sea. (*VO* 397)

In fact, from the novel's outset, the lure of water as a site of otherness and freedom has been clearly part of Rachel's sketchily-evoked character:

> To be flung into the sea, to be washed hither and thither, and driven about the roots of the world—the idea was incoherently delightful. She sprang up, and began moving about the room, bending and thrusting aside the chairs and tables as if she were indeed striking through the waters. He watched her with pleasure; she seemed to be clearing a passage for herself, and dealing triumphantly with the obstacles which would hinder their passage through life. (*VO* 347)

Her withdrawing into a water world therefore pursues the logic of her previous moments of resistance to language and the ideologically-framed plots of patriarchy, when she pictured herself becoming a limpet, or shell, or "a fish at the bottom of the sea" (189). Furthermore, taking refuge in an aquatic element when threatened by logic, rationality, and predatory sexuality suggests she is also, quite literally, subverting Milton's plot, responding to Sabrina and the Attendant Spirit's songs, and fleeing to join them.[34] Recast in evolutionary terms, meanwhile, her escape

---

[33] An alternative, but not incompatible, reading of Rachel's death from a musical angle is suggested by Emma Sutton: "There are several reasons why Milton's words may be 'painful' (the drowning of the young virgin Sabrina, for instance, prefiguring the aquatic imagery of Rachel's own death), but the allusions to Rachel's 'pulse', and the repetitive echoing of 'listen', suggests that it is the regularity of this rhythm that is problematic. Milton's 'song' appears not only affective but also sinister" (Sutton, "Putting Words" 187).

[34] In Wollaeger's terms, "As water laps at the foot of Rachel's bed during her first day of fever, these lines haunt her, suggesting both the symbolic threat of Milton (author of the first domestic epic) and the more palpable threat of domestic life with Terence" (Wollaeger 66).

to the water means turning the evolutionary clock backwards, reverting to the element where life began.

There is one more link to be underlined to complete this reading of the masque's relevance in a musically-inclined Darwinian scheme of things. This relies on a contextual reading of the masque. First, as we know, Woolf, Vanessa, and Clive Bell, along with others from their play-reading society, performed *Comus* at home in autumn 1908, with Woolf playing the parts of the Lady and Sabrina (Lee 252). Absent from the earliest drafts of the text,[35] the embedded lines and Miltonic setting in *The Voyage Out* are thus no passing reference; Terence's recital voices and restages a familiar operatic and narrative text, the lull and rhythms of which Woolf had spoken and heard.

More important, however, are the links between Milton's work and Darwin's. In Gillian Beer's terms, Darwin "walks the tropical forests with Milton," his volume of "Paradise Lost" and "Comus" being "the one book he never left behind when he set out on his long isolated land-journey" (Beer, *Darwin's Plots* 30-2). She contends that the lewd villain Comus provided Darwin with a counter-model for his own definition of nature's plot. It was against Comus's carnal and profligate view of Nature's bounties provided for the gratification of man, Beer suggests, that Darwin began shaping a different narrative of the world, one in which man is displaced from his central position and subjected to the changing variables of time, space, and random interactions; and where nature was to be seen from the point of view of other species and orders of life.

Even had she been unaware of the Darwin-Milton connection, Woolf's expansive reading methods involved a keen perception of resonances between works and cosmologies. The cultural context during which the novel evolved, however, speaks in favor of her familiarity with this interconnection. The Christ's College Darwin commemorations of 1909 included an exhibition of Darwin's personal library and works, where his Milton volume, the *Beagle* library catalogue, and references from his *Autobiography* underlined his fascination with Milton. Furthermore, as the exhibition catalogue preface makes clear, there was also a commemorative link with Milton: the Milton tercentenary of 1908, just one year previously (Shipley and Simpson ii).[36] Not only had there been a library exhibition; there was also a

---

[35] It is worth noting that the entire episode (Chapter 25) diverges strikingly from the prompt onset of Rachel's illness in *Melymbrosia*. In Chapter 29, "a very strange thing had happened" (*MEL* 322): she wakes up with a fever. Terence doesn't recite, and there are no references to *Comus*.

[36] The catalogue begins: "Last year Christ's College celebrated the Tercentenary of our greatest Cambridge poet. This year the University is celebrating the Centenary of our greatest Cambridge Biologist, and the Jubilee of the publication of his most famous Work.

Twelve months ago a collection of portraits and of other memorials connected with John Milton was exhibited in the Old Library of Christ's College. This year the College has attempted to do the same in memory of Charles Darwin" (Shipley and Simpson. Accessed 12 July 2016).

production by the Marlowe Society of *Comus*, performed at Christ's College, in July 1908. Costume and scenery were designed by Frances and Gwen Darwin—occasional members of the Bells' Friday Club; and Jane Harrison attended the first night, her ambivalent response to its primitive beasts and dancing being recorded later in letters and also, in more indirect form, in various writings on ritual and sacred dance, from "On the Influence of Darwinism on the Study of Religions" to *Themis* (Robinson 200-02). The tricentenary prompted a new edition of *Comus*, featuring a detailed introduction, musical scores and programme notes. Textual layout favored performance rather than just reading. It may well have been the edition the Bells' play-reading society used, although no proof of this has yet come to light. Date, context, family ties, and the Cambridge environment, however, lend weight to an interlinked Darwin-Milton intertext working its way into Woolf's novel, not merely as theme or plot, but also as musical and theatrical resonance. These in turn reinforce alternative perspectives on the way the "comic operetta marriage plot" is diverted, in favor of more primeval, mythopoetic narratives.[37]

Rachel's resistance to the marriage model evoked by Terence and her withdrawal into a world of her own that is both musical and aquatic is clearly a prodrome of Woolf's formal resistance to the classic, linear marriage plot of conventional fiction.[38] In evolutionary terms, moreover, the two alternatives facing Rachel—reversion or nuptials—also reflect the opposing and contradictory ramifications of Darwinian theory that were identified earlier, weaving their way through Woolf's novel. On the one hand, by representing the world as an ever-changing environment of flux, where man and animal are ultimately intermingled species in varying degrees of evolution (linguistically, behaviourally, and physically), the novel adheres to the naturalist's ontological framework. On the other hand, however, Rachel's preference for music rather than marriage is in direct opposition with key components of Darwin's admittedly tentative conclusions about musical attributes and sexual reproduction. Is the finality of music really sexual showmanship and the propagation of the species? Is woman's "higher destiny" marriage and childbirth? Do the pillars of the British establishment as seen in the novel—the merchant, the colonialist, the parliamentarian, the academic—represent the highest degree of evolution so far reached by man, or are they reflections of an already degenerating,

---

[37] Although more likely that the play-reading society used the 1908 version, another older adaptation of *Comus* for theatrical production was also available: *Comus, Adapted from Milton, as it is now acted at the Theatres Royal*. This edition also invites rich parallels with Woolf's novel, including a long prologue developing a fable of human and animal metamorphosis, a speaking/singing role given to the muse Euphrosyne, and a recitative at the end sung by Sabrina and the Spirits before they return to the ocean. This replaces Milton's "happy ending" in which the Lady and her brothers return home safely.

[38] The animalous link continues here: the engagement announcements coincide with the hotel prostitute being "hoofed out" (*VO* 358).

overbred species caught willy-nilly in the inevitable processes of extinction? And what of the death of Rachel? Should we interpret it within an ontogenetic, individual scale, which implies that she is unfit to survive within the social and novelistic framework of an inherited order; or within an evolutionary, phylogenetic scale, in which case her singular existence dissolves into insignificance; she is but one tiny example of the slow processes of change—changes that will gradually favor new modes of existence, expression, and representation for female protagonists, women musicians, and the evolving forms of the novel?

By way of a conclusion, I would like to suggest an answer via Wagner and the opera. As musicologists and evolutionary scientists have pointed out, Darwin's epistemological quests and his recasting of ontological narratives provided Wagner with models and concepts that shaped his own theories of musical evolution, the cornerstone in either case being an unshakeable belief in streams of continuous change, or "whirlpools of becoming" as one biologist puts it (Østergaard 85). The opera, as Wagner began redefining it after the 1850s, had to break away from ready-made melodies, harmonic resolution, and familiar narrative schemes, in favor of "organic generation," "organic growth," and "endless melody," where recast myths from the long distant past would draw dynamically on "the natural thrust of life itself" in a "total artwork" (Wagner, *CW* 2 337; see also Rasula 27-8). Wagner's Gesamtkunstwerk was not a final goal towards which he aspired, but a model for transitions, transformative patterns, and organic changes to which he believed musical drama should continually aspire. His "Opera and Drama," for example, is a complex, ambitious definition of the poet and musician's joint pursuit of new musical, story-telling forms inspired by observing the evolutions of life itself rather than the will of the artist (Wagner, *CW* 2 356-7). The final peroration anticipates the artwork of the future as nothing less than a "voyage out" in melodic form where "the melody which appears at last upon the water-mirror of the harmonic ocean of the Future is the clear-seeing eye wherewith this Life gazes upwards from the depth of its sea-abyss to the radiant light of day" (366).

These were Messianic dreams, certainly, but they set out the principles for creative modernity in league with the scientific visions of the day, drawing the arts and the artist into evolutionary dynamics. They were cited copiously in all studies of Wagner's art, with choice extracts republished each year in the *Bayreuther Blätter,* and distributed, following Wagner's own designs, as program notes. They were thus widely available for new opera-going publics,[39] and were already familiar to seasoned music critics—like the classics scholar, "fervent Wagnerian" (Bell 149),

---

[39] As a later diary entry underlines, Woolf *read* program notes, feeling less confident in her specialized musical listening skills: "these musical people don't listen as I do but critically, superciliously, without programmes" (*D2* 239).

and occasional composer Saxon Sydney-Turner who accompanied Woolf and her brother to Bayreuth in summer 1909, and to numerous operas in London.[40] Virginia Woolf was thus being exposed to Wagner's aesthetic projects even while she attended operas, wrote about them, and pondered over the first drafts of her own text,[41] for which she too sought a less character- and plot-driven form, less reliant on readymade linear schemes and finalities, less causal and neatly tied up, and more random, tentative, and fragmentary—a form suited to showing that female protagonists too, as a species, were in the process of becoming other.

And so to return to Rachel. As she explains to Terence in *Melymbrosia*, "So I love the sea and music because they don't die" (*MEL* 224). Her alternative to death means opting for mutability, renewing the forms of life itself. From the point of view of poetics, she metamorphoses, like her mythical forebears Sabrina or Arethusa. In biological terms she reverts to an aboriginal state (as Darwin contends domesticated species may when returned to the wild), renewing her links with humanity's pelagic origin. She withdraws from the ontologically closed domains of rationality, consciousness, and knowledge, and reconnects with music and water—deterritorializing milieus where the human and the non-human, the prehistorical and the present, are mysteriously entangled and materialized, and where the self-posing subjectivity dissolves. There is thus a utopian otherness in her silent expressivity as a musical performer, as well as in the space of the future she consciously constructs:

> Rachel said nothing. Up and up the steep spiral of a very late Beethoven sonata she climbed, like a person ascending a ruined staircase, energetically at first, then more laboriously advancing her feet with effort until she could go no higher and returned with a run to begin at the very bottom again....Attacking her staircase once more, Rachel again neglected this opportunity of revealing the secrets of her sex. She had, indeed, advanced so far in the pursuit of wisdom that she allowed these secrets to rest undisturbed; it seemed to be reserved for a later generation to discuss them philosophically. (337)

[40] The *Bayreuther Blätter* from July-August 1909 reprints a shortened version of "Music of the Future," along with "On the Application of Music to the Drama." The program for *Parsifal* in 1909 includes Wagner's own program notes. I would like to thank Kristina Unger and the manuscript archive at the Richard Wagner Museum, Bayreuth, for providing information on these documents. See also Wagner, *CW* 6 302-11, and Grey 47-50.

[41] As veiled echoes from one to the other make clear, her novel was very much in her mind as she wrote about Wagner. In "The Opera," for example, giving a synoptic overview of Wagner's opera-going public, she remarks: "there is something primitive in the look of them, as though they did their best to live in forests, upon the elemental emotions, and were quick to suspect their fellows of a lack of 'reality', as they call it. They find a philosophy of life in the operas, hum 'motives' to symbolize stages in their thoughts, and walk off their fervor on the Embankment, wrapped in great black cloaks" (*E1* 271). The portrait strongly resembles Ambrose in the opening passage of the novel.

The same patterns of musically-shaped secrets and aquatic metamorphosis that "[g]ive the feel of running water, and not much else" (*L*1 383) shape the worlds as yet on the brink of discovery in the novel's wistful, but no less theatrical closing scene. Not only is the landscape of sea, land, and sky in a new configuration of intertwined transformations, but individual characters, lives, identities, and destinies have seemingly been dissolved by the storm, to be replaced by a fading chorus of voices, shapes, and textures of objects and shadowy figures perceived at the borders of consciousness, until, in a final *pianissimo*, they vacate the stage-space entirely:

> All these voices sounded gratefully in St John's ears as he lay half-asleep, and yet vividly conscious of everything around him. Across his eyes passed a procession of objects, black and indistinct, the figures of people picking up their books, their cards, their balls of wool, their work baskets, and passing him one after another on their way to bed. (*VO* 430)

Works Cited

Alt, Christina. *Virginia Woolf and the Study of Nature*. Cambridge UP, 2010.
Altenmüller, Eckart, Stanley Finger and François Bolter. *Music, Neurology and Neuroscience: Evolution, The Musical Brain, Medical Conditions and Therapies*. Elsevier, 2015.
Barzun, Jacques. *Darwin, Marx, Wagner: Critique of a Heritage*. Doubleday, 1941.
Bayreuther Blätter: Deutsche Zeiteschrift im Geiste Richard Wagner, Vol. 31: 1 – 12; Vol. 32: 1 – 12, 1908-1909.
Beer, Gillian. *Darwin's Plots: Evolutionary Narrative in Darwin, George Eliot and Nineteenth-Century Fiction*. 2nd ed., Cambridge UP, 2000.
———. "The Backbone Shiver: Darwin and the Arts." *After Darwin: Animals, Emotions and the Mind,* edited by Angelique Richardson, Rodopi, 2013.
Bell, Quentin. V*irginia Woolf: A Biography*, Vol. 1, Hogarth Press, 1972.
Connor, Steven. "Rustications: Animals in the Urban Mix." *The Acoustic City*, edited by Matthew Gandy, Berlin, Jovis, 2014, pp. 16-22.
Crook, David Paul. *Darwin's Coat-Tails: Essays on Social Darwinism*, Peter Lang, 2007.
Czarnecki, Kristin and Vara Neverow, editors. *Virginia Woolf and Animals*, special issue of *Virginia Woolf Miscellany,* no. 84, Fall 2013.
Darwin, Charles. *On the Origin of Species and the Voyage of the Beagle*, Vintage, 2009.
———. *The Descent of Man, and Selection in Relation to Sex*. 1871. Penguin, 2004.
———. *The Expression of the Emotions in Man and Animals*. 1872. Oxford UP, 2009.

———. *The Formation of Vegetable Mould Through the Action of Worms*. 1881. John Murray, 1883.
Darwin, Francis, editor. *The Life and Letters of Charles Darwin*, 3 vols., Murray, 1887. http://darwin-online.org.uk. Accessed 6 July 2016.
"Darwin and Lord Kelvin and Music." *Musical Times*, vol. 49, no.780 (1 February 1908), 97-99.
Derry, Julian. "Bravo Emma! Music in the Life and Work of Charles Darwin." *Endeavour*, vol. 33, no. 1, 2009, pp. 35-8.
DeSalvo, Louise. *Virginia Woolf's First Voyage: A Novel in the Making*. Rowman and Littlefield, 1980.
———. "Sorting, Sequencing, and Dating the Drafts of Virginia Woolf's *The Voyage Out*." *Bulletin of Research in the Humanities* no. 82, 1979, pp. 294-316.
DiGaetani, John Louis. *Richard Wagner and the Modern British Novel*. Associated UP, 1978.
Froula, Christina. "Out of the Chrysalis: Female Initiation and Female Authority in Virginia Woolf's *The Voyage Out*." *Tulsa Studies in Women's Literature* vol. 5, no. 1, 1986, pp. 63-90.
Gandy, Matthew. "Acoustic Terrains: An Introduction." *The Acoustic City*, edited by Matthew Gandy, Berlin, Jovis, 2014, pp. 7-15.
Gillespie, Diane F. Introduction. *The Library of Leonard and Virginia Woolf*, edited by Julia King and Laila Miletic-Vejzovic, Washington State UP, 2003.
Grey, Thomas S. *Wagner's Musical Prose – Texts and Contexts*. Cambridge UP, 2007.
———. *Richard Wagner and his World*. Princeton UP, 2009.
Hadow, W. H. *The Oxford History of Music*, Vol. 5, Clarendon Press, 1904.
Halliday, Sam. *Sonic Modernity. Representing Sound in Literature, Culture and the Arts*. Edinburgh UP, 2014.
Heine, Elizabeth. "The Earlier Voyage Out: Virginia Woolf's First Novel." *Bulletin of Research in the Humanities* no. 82, 1979, pp. 271-93.
———. "Virginia Woolf's Revisions of *The Voyage Out*." *The Voyage Out: the Definitive Edition*, edited by Elizabeth Heine, Vintage, 1992, pp. 399-452.
Hussey, Mark. *The Singing of the Real World: The Philosophy of Virginia Woolf's Fiction*. Ohio State UP, 1986.
Kelley, Joyce E. "Virginia Woolf and Music." *The Edinburgh Companion to Virginia Woolf and the Arts*, edited by Maggie Humm, Edinburgh UP, 2010, pp. 417-436.
Lambert, Elizabeth L. "'And Darwin Says They Are Nearer The Cow': Evolutionary Discourse in *Melymbrosia* and *The Voyage Out*." *Twentieth Century Literature*, vol. 37, no. 1, 1991, pp. 1-21.
Lee, Hermione. *Virginia Woolf*. 1986. Vintage, 1987.
Lindenberger, Herbert S. *Opera, The Extravagant Art*. Cornell UP, 1984.
Magee, Bryan. *The Tristan Chord: Wagner and Philosophy*. 2001. Picador, 2002.

Marcus, Jane. "Enchanted Organs, Magic Bells: *Night and Day* as Comic Opera." *Virginia Woolf: Revaluation and Continuity, A Collection of Essays*, edited by Ralph Freedman, University of California Press, 1980.

——. "Thinking Back Through Our Mothers." *New Feminist Essays on Virginia Woolf*, edited by Jane Marcus, Macmillan, 1981, pp. 1-30.

Milton, John. *Comus: A Masque*. 1634. *As it is now acted at the Theatres Royal, Altered from Milton,* London: Lister, 1787.

——. *The Masque of Comus, with the Original Music by Henry Lawes,* London: Novello & Co., 1908.

Neumann, Angelo. *Personal Recollections of Wagner.* Translated by E. Livermore, London, Holt, 1909.

Nietzsche, Friedrich. "Richard Wagner in Bayreuth." *Thoughts Out Of Season.* Translated by Anthony M. Ludovici, The Edinburgh Press, 1909.

"Occasional Notes." *Musical Times,* vol. 47, no. 762, (1 August 1906), 537-540.

Østergaard, Edvin. "Darwin and Wagner: Evolution and Aesthetic Appreciation." *The Journal of Aesthetic Education,* vol. 45, no. 2, 2011, pp. 83-108.

Rasula, Jed. "Endless Melody." *Texas Studies in Literature and Language*, vol. 55, no. 1, 2013, pp. 36-52.

Richmond, Marsha L. "The 1909 Darwin Celebration. Reexamining Evolution in the Light of Mendel, Mutation and Meosis." *Isis,* vol. 97, no. 3, 2006, pp. 447-484.

Riley, Matthew, editor. *British Music and Modernism* 1895-1960. Ashgate, 2010.

Ryan, Derek. "From Spaniel Club to Animalous Society: Virginia Woolf's *Flush*." *Contradictory Woolf*, edited by Derek Ryan and Stella Bolaki, Clemson U Digital P, 2012, pp. 158-65.

——. *Virginia Woolf and the Materiality of Theory: Sex, Animal, Life*. Edinburgh UP, 2013.

Sacks, Oliver. *Musicophilia*. 2007. Toronto: Vintage House, 2009.

Seward, A. C., editor. *Darwin and Modern Science: Essays in Commemoration of the Centenary of the Birth of Charles Darwin and of the Fiftieth Anniversary of the Publication of* The Origin of Species. Cambridge UP, 1909.

Shipley, A. E. and Simpson, J. C., editors. *The Darwin Centenary: The Portraits, Prints and Writings of Charles Robert Darwin Exhibited at Christ's College, Cambridge in 1909*, Cambridge UP, 1909. http://darwin-online.org.uk.

Smocovitis, Vassiliki Betty. "Darwin and his Theory in Song and Musical Production." *Isis*, vol. 100, no. 3, 2009, pp. 590-614.

Stam, Robert. *Reflexivity in Film and Literature. From Don Quixote to Jean-Luc Godard.* Columbia UP, 1992.

Sutton, Emma. "'Within a Space of Tears': Music, Writing, and the Modern in Virginia Woolf's *The Voyage Out.*" *Music and Literary Modernism: Critical Essays and Comparative Studies*, edited by Robert P. MacParland,

Cambridge Scholars Press, 2009, pp. 50-65.
———. "'Putting words onto the back of music'—Woolf, 'Street Music' and *The Voyage Out.*" *Paragraph*, vol. 33, no. 2, 2010, pp. 176-96.
———. "Music." *Virginia Woolf in Context*, edited by Bryony Randall and Jane Goldman, Cambridge UP, 2012, pp. 278-90.
———. "Fiction as Musical Critique: Virginia Woolf, The Voyage Out and the Case of Wagner." *Words and Notes in the Long Nineteenth Century*, edited by Phyllis Weliver and Katharine Ellis, Boydell P, 2013, pp. 145-64.
———. *Virginia Woolf and Classical Music*. Edinburgh UP, 2013.
———. "Silence and Cries: Soundscape of *The Voyage Out*." *A Companion to Virginia Woolf*, edited by Jessica Berman, Wiley & Sons, 2016, pp. 41-54.
Varga, Adriana, editor. *Virginia Woolf and Music*. Indiana UP, 2014.
Wagner, Richard. *Richard Wagner's Prose Works*. Edited and translated by William Ashton Ellis, London: K. Paul, Trench, Trübner and Co., 1892-7. 12 vols.
Wollaeger, Mark A. "Woolf, Postcards, and the Elision of Race: Colonizing Women in *The Voyage Out*." *Modernism/modernity*, vol. 8, no. 1, 2001, pp. 43-75.
Woolf, Virginia. *The Voyage Out*. 1915. Oxford World Classics, 2009.
———. *Melymbrosia*. 1982. Edited by Louise DeSalvo, San Francisco: Cleis, 2002.
———. *The Letters of Virginia Woolf*. Edited by Nigel Nicolson and Joanne Trautmann, Harcourt Brace Jovanovich, 1975-89. 6 vols.
———. *The Diary of Virginia Woolf*. Edited by Anne Olivier Bell, Harcourt Brace Jovanovich, 1977-1984. 5 vols.
———. *The Essays of Virginia Woolf*. Edited by Andrew McNeillie (1-4) and Stuart Clarke (5-6), Harcourt Brace Jovanovich, 1986-2009. 6 vols.

Selected List of Works Consulted

Bailey, Robert, editor. *Richard Wagner: Prelude and Transfiguration from 'Tristan und Isolde'*. Norton Critical Score, 1985.
Beckett, Lucy. *Richard Wagner's Parsifal*. 1981. Cambridge UP, 1995.
Beer, Gillian. *Arguing with the Past: Essays in Narrative from Woolf to Sidney*. Routledge, 1989.
Bernhart, Walter, Steven P. Scher and Werner Wolf, editors. *Word and Music Studies: Defining the Field*. Rodopi, 1999.
Bishop, E. L. "Toward the Far Side of Language: Virginia Woolf's *The Voyage Out*." *Twentieth Century Literature*, Vol. 27, no. 4, 1981, pp. 343-361.
Clausen, Christopher. "Charles Darwin on Music." *The Kenyon Review*, vol. 5, no. 4, 1983, pp. 72-3.

Froula, Christine. "Rachel's Great War: Civilisation, Sacrifice, and the Enlightenment of Women in *Melymbrosia* and *The Voyage Out*." *Virginia Woolf and the Bloomsbury Avant-Garde: War, Civilisation, Modernity,* Columbia UP, 2005, pp. 35-61.

Kivy, Peter. "Charles Darwin on Music." *Journal of the American Musicological Society,* vol. 12, no. 1, 1959, pp. 42-48.

Rodoway, Paul. *Sensuous Geographies.* Routledge, 1994.

Spotts, Frederic. *Bayreuth: A History of the Wagner Festival.* Yale UP, 1994.

Sutton, Emma. *Aubrey Beardsley and British Wagnerism in the 1890s.* Oxford UP, 2002.

Van Wyhe, John. *Charles Darwin in Cambridge: The Most Joyful Years.* Singapore, World Scientific Publications, 2014.

Wallaschek, Richard, James McKeen and James Cattell. "On the Origin of Music." *Mind,* vol. 16, no. 63, 1891, pp. 375-388.

Empire and Commerce in Latin America: Historicizing Woolf's *The Voyage Out*
Patricia Novillo-Corvalán

In this article, I seek to recuperate the overlooked Latin American contexts that inform Virginia Woolf's first novel, *The Voyage Out* (1915). Integrating archival research and a historicizing approach, I utilize documentary evidence drawn from the research notes that Virginia Woolf conducted for Leonard Woolf's study *Empire and Commerce in Africa* (1920), namely, empirical data relating to political-economic issues in Latin America and, more specifically, to countries such as Argentina and Brazil. In so doing, I demonstrate that Virginia Woolf puts the complex issue of Great Britain's neocolonial domination in Latin America squarely on the cultural agenda of *The Voyage Out*. In particular, I suggest that the archival documents (housed at the Leonard Woolf archive, University of Sussex) acutely illustrate the extent of Britain's disproportionate economic control of Argentina through the development of the meat industry that turned the Argentine Republic into the abattoir of the British Empire. I argue that this documentary evidence complements and complicates the overall political message of *The Voyage Out*, whereby Woolf mercilessly denounces Britain's attempt to gain economic control of the continent through the predatory figure of Willoughby Vinrace and his high stakes in the meat and rubber trade. His involvement in the latter, meanwhile, is discussed in the second part of the article, where I shift my attention to the rubber boom in early twentieth-century Amazonia. Specific references in *The Voyage Out* adumbrate Virginia Woolf's awareness of human rights abuses perpetrated in the upper Amazon basin, testifying to her engagement with the geopolitical issues of her time, especially the vexed relationship between empire, capitalism, and modernity.

Michèle Barrett has recently unearthed significant archival material preserved at the Leonard Woolf Archive, which has revealed Virginia Woolf's extraordinary contribution to her husband's book, *Empire and Commerce in Africa: A Study in Economic Imperialism* (1920) in her role as research assistant or, even more appropriately, collaborator. Leonard Woolf's book had been commissioned by the Fabian Society and was published under the imprint of the Labour Research Department and George Allen & Unwin in 1920. According to Barrett, the complex research and analysis of empirical data that Virginia Woolf conducted for the project in 1917 sheds new light on her "relationship with her husband, and the critical and intellectual and political ideas they shared about British imperialism" (83). She also observes that the research reveals an image of "Virginia Woolf as a meticulous, even slightly pedantic scholar [with a remarkable] facility with factual data" (83). Crucially, Virginia Woolf's research notes are not just confined to Africa but also cover extensive empirical data on Latin America, since Leonard Woolf had originally signed a contract for a more ambitious book on International Trade, yet gradually reduced its scope by specifically focusing on a single continent. Therefore, in the early stages of the research for the global version of the project, Virginia Woolf made copious and detailed notes of British Consular Reports concerning international trade relations with Latin America. The research notes are ordered alphabetically and begin with the Argentine Republic, a country to which she devotes 13 pages of notecards (most of them neatly written in longhand in her distinctive purple ink). The notes are itemized under the heading "Return of Foreign Trade of the Argentine Republic during the years 1893-1891."[1] Despite the fact that this research was undertaken two years after the publication of *The Voyage Out*, I suggest that Virginia Woolf's knowledge of political-economic issues related to the Latin American nations (her reports cover a wide range of countries, including Chile, Brazil, Mexico, Cuba, Costa Rica, Ecuador, Guatemala, and Argentina) can, potentially, seriously reconceive her depiction of the continent in the novel. In concert with Barrett and Anna Snaith, I recognize the significance of performing an "intertwined reading" of the Woolfs' engagement with imperialism (Snaith 20), particularly as this article seeks to provide a conceptual framework that strategically reads *The Voyage Out* alongside *Empire and Commerce*, while also paying rigorous attention to Virginia Woolf's research notes held at the Leonard Woolf Archive.[2]

In this way, I seek to explicate the way in which Virginia Woolf's research for the original International Trade project can retrospectively "legitimize" her aesthetic engagement with Latin America, in an attempt to challenge a critical paradigm that has anchored Woolf's knowledge of the continent in a rhetoric of exoticism and orientalizing images of butterflies linked to the Argentine writer, critic, and feminist, Victoria Ocampo. This implies that the "spatial" dimension of the novel, which E. M. Forster once dismissed as "a South America not found on any map and reached by a boat which would not float on any sea" (172), may be taken more seriously. Critics such as Fiona Parrot, Laura Lojo Rodríguez, and Giulia Negrello have shown that Woolf's imaginary excursions to South America anticipated her final and most significant encounter with the continent that was embodied in the larger-than-life figure of Ocampo. Parrot states that "Woolf enjoyed Ocampo's company but often imagined her as a fabulous character from a strange and distant land she knew little about" (1), while Lojo Rodríguez notes that "for Virginia Woolf, Victoria Ocampo was an example of remote and exotic exuberance" (219) and, in a similar vein, Giulia Negrello concludes that "Woolf projected onto Ocampo her

---

[1] Leonard Woolf Archive, University of Sussex Library Special Collections, Work Life section SxMS-13/I/L/6.

[2] Other crucial points of intersection in the Woolfs' shared concerns with Empire include their so-called "village in the jungle" novels. See Wollaeger, "The Woolfs in the Jungle."

idealised vision of South America" (122). Though it cannot be denied that in her correspondence with Victoria Ocampo Woolf narrowly defines a continent of the scale, diversity, and complexity of South America as "a land of great butterflies and vast fields" (*L5* 365), it must be borne in mind that such remarks were prompted by the lavish and stereotypical gifts that Ocampo bestowed upon Woolf:

> You are too generous. And I must compare you to a butterfly if you send me these gorgeous purple butterflies [orchids]. I opened the box and thought "this is what a garden in South America looks like!" I am sitting in their shade at the moment, and must thank you a thousand times *(L5* 348-9).

If Ocampo willingly encouraged Woolf's exotic fantasies through her extravagant gifts, it has to be said that she also patiently tolerated the latter's orientalizing responses. As Gayle Rogers points out, in her transmission of Woolf's works in her native Argentina, Ocampo tactfully revised "Woolf's Eurocentrism" (143) in order to convey her cultural politics as part of a liberating feminist agenda that the two women passionately shared through their aesthetic commitment to gender equality. The powerful confluence between two icons of twentieth-century feminism—one English, the other Argentine, one publisher of the Hogarth Press, the other of Editorial Sur—initiated an aesthetic fulcrum that played a decisive role in the formation and circulation of transatlantic modernist practices.

In the course of this article, though, I shall question some of the assumptions undergirding Woolf's relationship to Latin America in an endeavor to challenge the prevailing view that her knowledge of the continent was vague, deficient and, at its worst, non-existent. Rather, I seek to show that she was the possessor of a complex socio-economic knowledge of a country such as Argentina, a claim based not only on crucial documentation gathered from the research notes she undertook for *Empire and Commerce,* but also on textual evidence drawn from T*he Voyage Out* and *Melymbrosia*. By elucidating Woolf's complex awareness of pressing geopolitical issues in late nineteenth- and early twentieth-century Latin America, I seek to move beyond the romanticized rhetoric that constitutes an integral part of her epistolary relationship with Ocampo and that has so far framed the majority of scholarly work on this subject. Whereas my present intention is to historicize the contemporary political-economic contexts of *The Voyage Out* by recuperating Woolf's more sophisticated knowledge of crucial Latin American issues, this does not suggest that I am critically unaware of the novel's exoticizing proclivities nor, for the same matter, of its equally noticeable inattention to regional details. A number of scholars have drawn attention to the contradictory ideology underpinning the novel, a political tension marked by Woolf's strong anti-imperialist and feminist agenda, on one level, and by a tendency to orientalize and stereotype colonized nations, on another. Critics such as Mark Wollaeger,

Steven Putzel, Alissa Karl, Carey Snyder, and Andrea Lewis are among those who claim that Woolf's resistance to British imperialism and patriarchal institutions has been partially undermined by her dehumanizing depiction of the native women in *The Voyage Out*. For example, Wollaeger states that whereas Woolf "clearly indicates that the gender politics informing Rachel's life also govern the native village," her colonial critique is further complicated by the fact that she is transforming "the native women into a mere backdrop for Rachel's inner drama," which "partially reproduces the imperial hierarchy the novel otherwise attacks" ("Postcards" 66). Meanwhile, Jane Marcus's oft-quoted observation that in *A Room of One's Own* Woolf was not immune to racial prejudice despite her best intentions to "dissociate herself from the racism of her family and class by announcing that she could pass even a 'very fine Negress' without wanting to 'make an Englishwoman of her,'" further exposes her complicity with orientalism (149). At the same time, John Batchelor has devoted some thought to Woolf's deeply problematic representation of the tropical setting in South America, a continent she had never visited. He claims that Woolf "makes elementary mistakes: forgetting that the seasons are reversed in the Southern Hemisphere, she has the climate in this imaginary country advancing from mild early spring to intolerably hot summer between the months of March and May" (13). Batchelor is referring here to the way Woolf's Georgian personages often make embarrassing geographical slips, such as forgetting that in South America the month of March should announce the arrival of autumn, not spring:

> The three months which had passed had brought them to the beginning of March. The climate had kept its promise, and the change of season from winter to spring had made very little difference, so that Helen, who was sitting in the drawing-room with a pen in her hand, could keep the windows open though a great fire of logs burnt on one side of her (*VO* 103).

At the other end of the spectrum, however, Woolf is not unaware of the politics of representing imperial locations, an aspect that is constantly interrogated in the novel and that is indissolubly linked to the phenomenon of economic imperialism. As Kathy Phillips points out, "despite Virginia Woolf's residual insensitivity to colonized people and her lack of first-hand knowledge of the colonies, she felt strongly that the English civilization which the British imposed on their subjects was not worth exporting" (xxxv). Her rejection of colonialism, Julia Kuehn explains, "sprang from her great-grandfather's, grandfather's and father's nationalist fervour and critique of Empire respectively [as well as] her relationship with Leonard Woolf" (168). Therefore, it is hardly surprising that the British imperial mindset, together with its ingrained sense of racial, moral, and cultural superiority is constantly questioned, mocked, and satirized in the novel. Notice, for example, the discussion that takes place at the beginning of Chapter XI:

> One of these parties was dominated by Hughling Elliot and Mrs Thornbury, who, having both read the same books and considered the same questions, were now anxious to name the places beneath them and to hang upon them stores of information about navies and armies, political parties, natives and mineral products – all of which combined, they said, to prove that *South America was the country of the future* (*VO* 151, my emphasis).

While the above extract appears to end in a note of optimism, the assertion is ironic since to succinctly claim that "South America was the country of the future" in a politically-loaded debate about empire, cartography, militarization, and the acquisition of raw materials, implies a tacit endorsement of British imperialism, not least since the "future" of the *continent* of South America has been irreversibly blighted by the atrocities committed (or about to be committed) by the dominant European powers. Manifestly, the pompous Hughling Elliot and Mrs. Thornbury arrogantly uphold South America as the "future" of Europe, namely, as the world's richest source of raw materials to be liberally plundered by the European colonizer. Furthermore, Mrs. Thornbury glorifies the colonial exploits of the British Empire by boasting that she has sons "in the navy [...] and in the army too; and one son who makes speeches at the Union – my baby!" (*VO* 125). Later on, moreover, another character raises the inevitable set of questions: "Conquer a territory? They're all conquered already, aren't they?" (*VO* 152), echoing the Conradian realization that "the blank spaces on the earth" have been conquered by Western imperialism and have inevitably "become a place of darkness" (Conrad 8-9). Such exchanges show that Woolf responded critically to questions of Empire at a time when "European imperial rule over the non-European world extended to nearly two-thirds of the Earth's land surface, and Britain's Empire accounted for much of those holdings," as Andrea White points out (180).

To be sure, the ideological discourses of taxonomy and cartography remain one of the main preoccupations of Woolf's characters; their relationship with the South American landscape is always evocative of Empire, as the Amazon is constantly refashioned into a *terra incognita* awaiting colonization (and reinvention) by the "imperial eyes" of the European explorer, in Pratt's well-known phrase. Even Woolf's young and naïve heroine, Rachel Vinrace, is depicted in the imperial act of scrutinizing "the soil of South America so minutely that she noticed every grain of earth and made it into a world where she was endowed with the supreme power" (*VO* 157). "Imperialism after all is an act of geographical violence," writes Edward Said, "through which virtually every space in the world is explored, charted, and finally brought under control" (*Nationalism* 77). And yet here, by provisionally endowing a female character with imaginative power, Woolf astutely finds a new way of critiquing the intimately intertwined discourses of imperialism and patriarchy by denouncing, as Kathy Phillips points out, a masculine tradition that associates conquest and adventure as roles "traditionally reserved for men" (70).

The transnational epistemology complexly operating in *The Voyage Out* may be further contextualized within a wider Anglophone tradition that similarly embarked on the immensely challenging task of representing Latin America, a continent that was still regarded (in the Humboldian paradigm) as a New World awaiting reinvention by the European observer. "South America was very much on the minds of novelists at the time," writes Linda Dryden, and "was becoming fertile ground for the literary imagination at the turn of the century" (71). In a dialectical mixture of romance, ethnography, and travel writing, a cluster of imperial adventure novels set in South America including, Conrad's *Nostromo* (1904), W. H. Hudson's *Green Mansions* (1904), Arthur Conan Doyle's *The Lost World* (1912) and Woolf's *The Voyage Out*, as well as (more belatedly) Evelyn Waugh's *A Handful of Dust* (1934), give renewed and urgent meaning to the question of whether, from the point of view of Western imperialism, South America was the continent of the future. Moreover, it is possible to locate James Joyce's short story "Eveline," first published in the *Irish Homestead* in 1904 and subsequently reprinted in *Dubliners* in 1914 (just one year before *The Voyage Out*), as part of this tradition of narratives of "voyaging out," even though Joyce ironically suggested the reverse, a story of paralysis and thwarted emigration in which its eponymous heroine, Eveline Hill, refuses to elope to Buenos Ayres (spelled in the story in the Edwardian fashion). Katherine Mullin has historically positioned "Eveline" within the cultural contexts of the white-slave trade in late nineteenth-century Argentina, noting that the port city of Buenos Aires rapidly earned itself an international reputation as the "the worst of all centres of immoral commerce in women" and that the semantically-loaded phrase "going to Buenos Ayres" was interpreted as "taking up a life of prostitution, especially by way of a procurer's offices" (70-1). *The Voyage Out* similarly emerged within a European climate of anxiety about white slavery propaganda (Bradshaw) though, as Celia Marshik notes, Woolf "mocked the myth of 'white slavery' and encouraged her readers to confront their hypocrisy in moral matters" (Marshik 103).

Peter Childs perceives an epistemological shift in the genre of imperial adventure fiction, a marked movement from pro-imperial British authors such as John Buchan and Henry Rider Haggard—whose fictions celebrate the thin veneer of Western civilisation—to a sense of crisis exemplified by the skeptical and deeply ambivalent attitude towards Empire displayed by writers such as Conrad, Joyce, Woolf and, to a lesser extent, Kipling: "In the modernist period the gradual change from confidence to doubt comes to fruition as a literary ambivalence evidences a shift towards imperial disquiet" (17). Such sense of disquiet for the colonial enterprise is evident in Woolf's deeply ambiguous and satirical use of the clichéd tropes of the quest romance, which are reflected in her repeated attempt to interrogate the genre by subverting it for her own aesthetic purposes and by using her European "explorers" as a foil to launch a trenchant critique of British imperialism and gender politics. This is nowhere more evident than in her ironic construction of *The Voyage Out* as the failed *bildungsroman* of her young heroine, Rachel Vinrace. Woolf paints a largely unflattering portrait of the artist as a young woman *manqué*, whose aborted marriage, failed conquest, and untimely death seriously expose the cracks of the colonial enterprise, while foreshadowing the end of the British Empire. For Jed Esty, modernist authors such as Joyce, Conrad, and Woolf consciously destabilize the framework of the bildungsroman by blatantly showing that their youthful protagonists refuse to "*grow up*": "From Conrad's Asian straits to Woolf's South American riverway to Joyce's Irish backwater, colonialism disrupts the bildungsroman and its humanist ideals, producing jagged effects on both the politics and poetics of subject formation" (73). Woolf's uneasiness towards Empire is also conspicuous in her problematic representation of Rachel's fragmented consciousness, who remains inscrutable and tongue-tied throughout most of the novel, prompting her fiancé, the Cambridge intellectual and aspiring writer, Terence Hewet, to bitterly remark: "'I don't satisfy you in the way you satisfy me,' he continued. 'There's something I can't get hold of in you'" (*VO* 352). And, earlier in the novel, Terence is similarly baffled, yet transfixed, by Rachel's mysterious, sphinx-like face: "But what I like about your face is that it makes one wonder what the devil you're thinking about" (*VO* 347). As Julia Kuehn points out, Woolf's modernist innovation in this novel is manifested in her movement "from moral certainty to moral ambiguity" (185) in an aesthetic project in which "silences and ambiguities speak louder than words and deeds" (180).

"The country of the future": Argentina, Modernity, and the Meat Trade

In *The Voyage Out* Woolf provides vital links with New World historiography, its discovery, exploration, and conquest, having as its main satirical target Western notions of "progress," European racial superiority, and the economic exploitation of the New World's natural resources and their local inhabitants. Set in the fictitious British colony of Santa Marina, Woolf provides an imaginary "history" of the South American settlement by deploying an unmistakable parody of European travel writing and mythologized accounts of the conquest. At the heart of Woolf's fabricated "history" of Santa Marina is the deployment of a critique of British imperialism and an unmistakable parody of early modern travel writing in the mode of Sir Walter Raleigh, intertwined with mythologized accounts of the conquest and Renaissance anti-Spanish propaganda:

> Three hundred years ago five Elizabethan barques had anchored where the Euphrosyne now floated. Half-drawn up upon the beach lay an equal number of Spanish galleons, unmanned, for the country was still a virgin land behind a veil.... When the Spaniards came down from their drinking,

a fight ensued, the two parties churning up the sand, and driving each other into the surf. The Spaniards, bloated with fine living upon the fruits of the miraculous land, fell in heaps; but the hardy Englishmen ... despatched the wounded, drove the dying into the sea, and soon reduced the natives to a state of superstitious wonderment (*VO* 96).

Note, for example, Woolf's deliberate use of the trope of the gendered "virgin land" commonly employed by early European explorers, whose accounts portrayed the New World as an uninhabited paradise, a new Eden waiting to be ravished by the European colonizer. Woolf emphasizes how Santa Marina was fought over by Spanish, Portuguese, and British powers, describing their warring over the colony in a satirical manner reflected in her use of the mocking epithets, "the hardy Englishmen," the "vengeful Spaniards," and "the rapacious Portuguese" (*VO* 96) that turn the three leading imperial nations into recognizable caricatures symbolizing the reckless arrogance of European expansion and their failure to occupy the area and establish a settlement. Meanwhile, after three centuries of Spanish rule, the peripheral Santa Marina has been finally reclaimed by the British and is now a far-flung neocolonial destination for British tourists seeking an exotic getaway in the exuberant tropics of South America. Crucial to this transatlantic Empire is the figure of Willoughby Vinrace, proud owner of the *Euphrosyne*, the cargo ship that transports the British tourists to Santa Marina. The name of the colony, meanwhile, is not bereft of symbolic connotations, absorbing a semantically-loaded imperialist signification. The word "Marina" literally signifies "born in the sea" ("nacida en el mar"), and it is obviously linked to the activities of shipping and maritime affairs, creating, by extension, associations with Christopher Columbus's largest ship, *La Santa María,* a near-namesake of Santa Marina. Additionally, the name of the colony may open further associations with Doña Marina, Hernán Cortés's interpreter and alleged concubine, known as La Malinche. According to Susan Bassnett and Harish Trivedi, the figure of La Malinche "serves as an icon to remind us that a dominant metaphor of colonialism was that of rape, of husbanding 'virgin lands', tilling them and fertilizing them and hence 'civilizing' them" (4).

As far as spatial economics is concerned, the reader learns in Chapter One of *The Voyage Out* that the transatlantic route of Willoughby Vinrace's commercial enterprises ambitiously extends between "London and Buenos Aires" (*VO* 18), therefore specifically situating the Argentine capital as the final, strategic destination in a long chain of global networks. Willoughby's capital investment in southern South America is centered on the agrarian market and it is based on the commerce of "poor little goats" (*VO* 18), as his daughter Rachel laments, which has apparently generated enough wealth to pay for her music education, among other things, as well as advancing the expansion of his "empire" in the Southern Hemisphere. "Willoughby, as usual, loved his business and built his Empire," muses his sister-in-law, Helen Ambrose, neither approving nor condemning the imperialist ideology of her brother-in-law (*VO* 19). When the crusty Cambridge scholar and fellow traveler Mr. Pepper brusquely asks the pragmatic Willoughby to deploy one of his cargo ships to "investigate the great white monsters of the lower waters," the latter amusingly replies:

> "No, no," laughed Willoughby, "the monsters of the earth are too many for me!" Rachel was heard to sigh, "Poor little goats!" "If it weren't for the goats there'd be no music, my dear; music depends upon goats," said her father rather sharply, and Mr. Pepper went on to describe the white, hairless, blind monsters lying curled on the ridges of sand at the bottom of the sea, which would explode if you brought them to the surface... (*VO* 18-9)

Woolf uses this seemingly causal exchange to articulate the two men's opposing conceptions of imperialism. While the eccentric Mr. Pepper casts himself as an Elizabethan explorer and harks back to a bygone era of Renaissance voyages of discovery and travelers' tales populated with images of oceanic monsters (illustrating Stephen Greenblatt's notion of "the production of a sense of the marvellous in the New World" [73]), Willoughby, by contrast, exemplifies a late nineteenth-century model of capitalism in South America as he "sharply" reminds his daughter that "music depends upon goats."[3] Here, Woolf seeks to emphasize the uncomfortable truth that the genteel lifestyle, privilege, and education of a British lady such as Rachel Vinrace is intricately connected to Britain's imperial history and to Willoughby's concentration of capital in South America. Alissa Karl rightly situates *The Voyage Out* within the context of the publication of Vladimir Lenin's pamphlet *Imperialism: The Highest Stage of Capitalism* (1917) in order to argue that Woolf participates in "a rendering of imperialism as function of capitalism's development that was undertaken not only by Lenin, but by theorists like J. A. Hobson" (Karl 45). In effect, the laborious composition of *The Voyage Out* (written between 1907-1915) emerged in the wake of Hobson's devastating critique of British imperialism in his groundbreaking work, *Imperialism: A Study* (1902) while, within the space of two decades, Leonard Woolf would emerge as the foremost critic of imperialism with the publication of *International Government* (1916) and the aforementioned *Empire and Commerce in Africa* (1920). In the latter, Leonard Woolf defines economic imperialism as:

> The international economic policy of the European States, of the U.S.A., and latterly of Japan, in the unexploited and non-Europeanized territories

---

[3] Note, too, the symbolically-loaded name "Pepper" that is evocative of the spice trade, especially since Christopher Columbus had originally sailed to India in search of lucrative spices, leading to his inadvertent "discovery" of a new continent.

> of the world.... I call it imperialism because the policy always implies either the extension of the State's territory by conquest or occupation, or the application of its dominion or some form of political control to peoples who are not its citizens. I qualify it with the word economic because the motives of this imperialism are not defence nor prestige nor conquest nor the "spread of civilization" but the profit of the citizens, or of some of the citizens, of the European State (*Empire and Commerce* 19).

Dominic Davies points out that the anti-imperialist tradition of thought developed by Leonard Woolf, Hobson, and Lenin precisely interrogated "the interrelation between capitalism and imperialism as two separate, but mutually sustaining, modes of exploitative practice" (47). Whereas Leonard Woolf's study primarily focuses on the economic exploitation of Africa by Western imperial nations, his exposé of the rampant inequalities created by a profit-driven capitalist system is also applicable to Latin America. Europe's desperate need for raw materials and natural resources led to aggressive competition for the acquisition of new colonies in the "underdeveloped" world, whether in Africa, Asia, or Latin America. Virginia Woolf, who deemed *Empire and Commerce* "masterly and brilliant" (*L2* 416), attentively utilizes the epistemology of a global economic system regulated by the leading European nations as the cornerstone of *The Voyage Out*, a rapacious capitalist system that she mercilessly critiques via the figure of Willoughby Vinrace.

After most Spanish colonies gained independence in the first decades of the nineteenth century, ending three grievous centuries of Spanish rule, the Northern European powerhouses (especially Britain) responded swiftly to this geopolitical change by forging trade relations with the young republics as part of a concerted plan of global economic expansion. Mary Louise Pratt has shown how the nineteenth-century European "scramble for Latin America" was complexly tied up in a neocolonial capitalist project that went hand-in-hand with travel writing, particularly the ambitious task of reinventing America through totalizing methods of classification and geographical rediscovery. According to Pratt, the towering figure of Alexander von Humboldt remains the single most influential author in the conception of Latin America as a "virtual *carte blanche*" in need of reinvention: a virgin land ready to be exploited by enlightened Europeans (115). Building on Pratt's work, postcolonial critic Jennifer L. French claims that Britain's aggressive policies of economic "development" in the young republics rapidly supplanted imperial Spain as the foremost exploiter of Latin America's natural resources. As political and military intervention in postcolonial Latin America were quickly replaced by the economic system and ideology of capitalism, Britain pursued what French calls an "invisible" Empire there: "A hegemonic formation that was effective enough to dominate economic (and consequently, social and cultural) life in Latin America, and yet almost imperceptible" (7). This is precisely what the British historian Eric Hobsbawm implies when he refers to countries such as Argentina and Chile as Britain's "honorary dominions" in what was largely conceived as Britain's "informal" Empire (125).

Therefore, Willoughby's emphatic retort, "No, no," to Mr. Pepper's outmoded rhetoric of "white monsters," and his repeated insistence on the trading value of domestic goats that have enabled Rachel's education, exposes the wide-reaching impact of the "invisible Empire" in the exploitation of southern South America's natural wealth. A shrewd British financier such as Willoughby would have bred goats for their valuable skin and for their meat. This offers a more complex image of Willoughby as a daring British entrepreneur willing to take risks in a constantly shifting and volatile world market, yet deriving handsome profits as a result. If anything at all, the "white monster" metaphor that looms large throughout the novel is none other than the exploitative forces of economic imperialism represented by Britain's aggressive capitalist penetration in South America and what Christine Froula interprets as the "living allegory of realities drowned by the exigencies of empire" (40). Consequently, Woolf's strategic choice of Buenos Aires as the final commercial hub in Willoughby's lucrative empire should not be underestimated, not least since the Argentine capital remains the only "real" Latin American location in the novel, particularly if compared with the "unreal" Santa Marina. As the "rising star in an internationalized economy" (Rocchi 1), Argentina is, indeed, a case in point and it is undeniable that in identifying Buenos Aires as one of the commercial arteries of Willoughby's South Atlantic route, Woolf would have been cognizant of the close links that developed between British capitalists and Argentine producers. Winthrop Wright notes that during the second half of the nineteenth century Argentina became an important agricultural producer and exporter and that the railway network built there by the British with the backing of President Domingo Faustino Sarmiento (a supporter of economic liberalism, in office between 1868-1874), helped to transform "Argentina from a backward rural country into a modern food producer" (Wright 4-5; see also Lewis 5).

The so-called Argentine economic "miracle" was owed both to the export of meat and raw materials such as wool, gaining the country, as Argentine historian Hilda Sábato remarks, "a significant place in the world market, thus developing its internal productive capacity and promoting a rapid process of capital accumulation centred in Buenos Aires" (23).[4] During his visit to Argentina in 1929, the Spanish philosopher José Ortega y Gasset summed up the vastness and richness of the fertile pampa with an essay appropriately entitled: "La Pampa … promesas" ("The Pampa … promises").[5] One major technological factor responsible for Argentina's colossal

---

[4] Moreover, Stephen Bell pertinently notes that "by the 1860s, wool had become Argentina's most valuable export and was already offering serious competition to the American producers" (306).
[5] All Spanish translations are mine, unless otherwise stated.

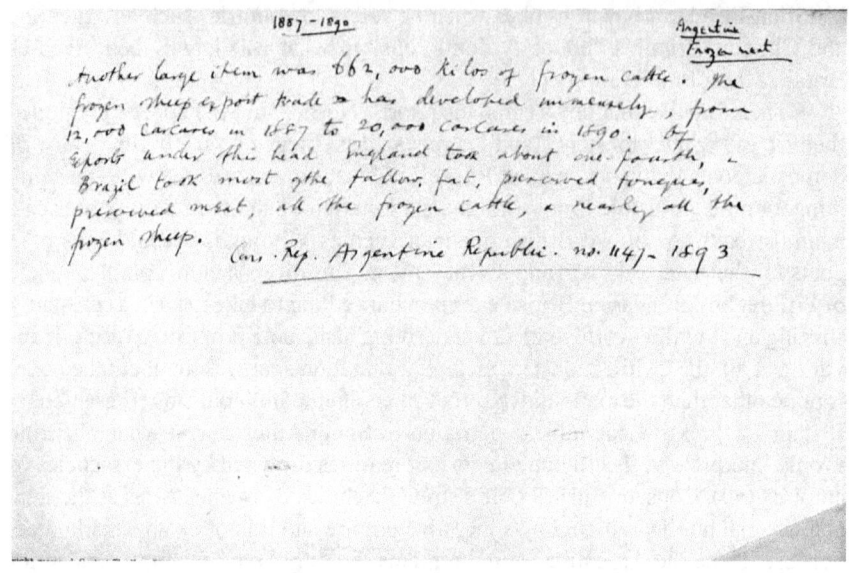

Figure 1: Virginia Woolf: Notecard from British Consular Reports, Argentine Republic, 1893. With the permission of the Society of Authors as the Literary Representative of the Estate of Leonard Woolf.

economic growth was the modern development of industrial refrigeration units that permitted the transportation of large quantities of meat across the Atlantic (Cardoso and Helwege 43). It is therefore hardly surprising that Argentina's beef-export boom made repeated appearances in the handwritten notecards Virginia Woolf copied out for *Empire and Commerce*. Consider, for example, the following stomach-turning account she extracted from the British Consular Reports:

> Another large item was 662,000 Kilos of frozen cattle. The frozen sheep export trade has developed immensely, from 12,000 carcasses in 1887 to 20,000 carcasses in 1890. Of exports under this head England took about one-fourth & Brazil took most of the fallow, fat, preserved tongues, preserved meat, all the frozen cattle & nearly all the frozen sheep.

What was Virginia Woolf thinking as she methodically copied out this gargantuan catalogue of frozen animal parts in her trademark purple ink? This report, evidently, emphasizes the impact of modern technological advances (in this case artificial refrigeration) that turned the Argentine Republic into the abattoir of the British Empire. Leonard Woolf later added the underlined heading "Argentine Frozen meat" on the right-hand side of the notecard: the capitalized adjective

EMPIRE AND COMMERCE   Novillo-Corvalán   45

	1901 Argentine Rep.	
Value of exports and imports to and from Argentine Rep., 1901	Imports	Exports
United Kingdom	7,292,160	5,984,150
Germany	3,344,908	4,295,976
United States	3,106,726	1,859,290
Italy	2,947,220	863,790
France	1,991,908	5,727,424
Belgium	1,757,730	2,691,546
Brazil	877,208	1,940,496
Spain	782,506	426,342
Paraguay	353,528	43,210
Uruguay	135,846	742,132
Netherlands	114,682	350,786
Bolivia	27,786	108,208
West Indies	8,734	73,236
Africa		578,250
Other Countries	49,858	7,144,750
	22,791,949	33,543,220

C.R. No. 2867 Buenos Ayres. 1902

Figure 2: Notecard from British Consular Reports, number 2867, Buenos Ayres, 1902. With the permission of the Society of Authors as the Literary Representative of the Estate of Leonard Woolf.

"Frozen," again, accentuates the tremendous economic impact of the new technology that significantly increased the consumption of meat worldwide. At the same time, Anglo-Argentine trade relations are indicated in the numerous economy tables reproduced by Virginia Woolf. As the table in Figure 2 indicates, Britain enjoyed the lion's share of the value of exports and imports to and from the Argentine Republic: in the year 1901 alone imports reached £7,292,160, and exports came to £5,984,150. Britain's overwhelming monopoly is further accentuated when compared with Argentina's economic activity with other Western nations (Germany ranks second).

In the context of Argentina's spectacular agro-export "boom," Rachel Vinrace's pointed exclamation "poor little goats" acquires an even more sinister political-economic signification. The Consular Reports clearly show the extent of Britain's economic colonization of the country through the development of the meat industry (especially meat-packing plants), whereby Britain not only consolidates its hegemony in the Argentine market but also becomes the foremost consumer of the country's natural resources. In this way, the Consular Reports reflect the overall political message of *The Voyage Out*, in which Woolf denounces Britain's attempt to gain economic control of the continent through the predatory figure of Willoughby and his high stakes in the meat trade. Considering that Woolf compiled these reports only two years after the publication of *The Voyage Out*, she would have been in a privileged conceptual position to understand the empirical data she was gathering, essentially associating issues pertaining to empire, commerce, and food markets with the economic maneuvers of Willoughby Vinrace and his aggressive capitalist infiltration in the Latin American market.

The importance of raw materials and the discourse of food is widely acknowledged in the novel. In Chapter XIV, Hewet brings to the fore the interplay between Empire and excessive meat consumption. Utilizing predatory imagery such as, "the animals had been fed" (*VO* 198), to evoke the stifling after-dinner atmosphere of the Santa Marina resort, each British resident is reimagined as an extreme example of a rapacious form of capitalism, "each beast holds a lump of raw meat in its paws" (*VO* 198). The degrading imagery continues, as Hewet compares the residents with, among others, "the half-decayed bodies of sheep" (*VO* 198), evoking both the "hunger" of the colonizer for foods and essential commodities and the industrial machinery of the slaughterhouse driven by the voracious consumption of food in the imperial metropolis. The ethical, political, and economic issues I have outlined so far would have led to Virginia Woolf's decision to set her colonial novel in South America, a continent that had become utterly subservient to Britain's capitalist maneuvers. As Said points out, "at the end of the nineteenth century, scarcely a corner of life was untouched by the facts of Empire; the economies were hungry for overseas markets, raw materials, cheap labour, and hugely profitable land" (*Culture and Imperialism* 6-7). Furthermore, the interplay between Empire, food, and commodification reappear in Woolf's political essay "Thunder at Wembley" (1924) that undermines the imperial project by ridiculing Britain's excessive consumption of foreign foods: "They say, indeed, that there is a restaurant where each diner is forced to spend a guinea upon his dinner. What vistas of cold ham that statement calls forth! What pyramids of rolls! What gallons of tea and coffee!" (*E3* 411).

Whereas the arrival of industrial refrigeration methods proved highly advantageous for the British investors involved (and the ruling Argentine oligarchy), its overall effect manifested itself in an ever-increasing demand for more arable land. This rocketing demand detonated Argentina's genocidal military campaign against its indigenous population, known as the "Campaña del Desierto" (1878-79; "Conquest of the Desert"). Led by future President General Julio Argentino Roca (a supporter of liberal economics; in office between 1880-86 and 1898-1904), and undertaken by the Argentine armed forces, Roca's brutal extermination of the Amerindian communities was intended to send a clear message to European investors that the Argentine Republic was open for business and had finally cleaned up its "uncivilized" backyard. For Roca, therefore, the indigenous peoples, "who were believed to embody racial inferiority, stood in the way of civilization and modernity" (Nouzeilles and Montaldo 104). Carlos F. Díaz Alejandro notes that at the time "public lands were quickly turned over to private owners in large chunks, mainly as a result of pressing government financial needs" (38). It is significant, in this respect, that in *Melymbrosia* Woolf satirizes Britain's insatiable "hunger" for land and raw materials by showing a picture of a megalomaniac Willoughby Vinrace obsessively building his mercantile empire and shipping "thousands of tawny little goats" for the future prosperity of the Vinrace family and, by extension, for the glory of the British Empire:

> Ships went out at his command and lured thousands upon thousands of tawny little goats from the uplands of South America into their holds. To have established one's family, so that they need only draw dividends as long as the world lasts, and to be able to do something for one's country by the time one is forty is a great achievement; it was probable that Willoughby Vinrace would be one of the exceptional people who make an accurate image of themselves in some kind of substance before they die, and render it back to the world. (*Melymbrosia* 19)

The historical, political, and economic significance of European capital investment in late nineteenth-century Argentina is also the subject matter of several of Virginia Woolf's notecards for the International Trade project. Woolf astutely perceived the complex relationship between capitalism, Empire, and modernity, especially within the context of British neocolonialism in Latin America. Therefore, she revisits these problematic issues in one of the handwritten cards from the British Consular Reports. Here, British economic interests in Argentina are clearly indicated through the imminent arrival of electricity and tramways to the city of Buenos Aires (note, though, how she transcribes the old British spelling of "Buenos Ayres" in contrast with her use of the modern spelling in *The Voyage Out*):

> Also two new electric light companies will shortly be in a position to give current in the City of Buenos Ayres, & a third is likely to be established; of these one is worked by English & the other two by German capital. An English tramway company has also been acquired by German capitalists, & an Argentine company has been taken up by capitalists of German nationality. In fact, German capital is flowing into the River Plate & is commencing to take up public works, wh. until quite recently were almost exclusively capitalised by British financiers.

It is clear that Woolf is witnessing here the sudden irruption of Western modernity in the sprawling Argentine metropolis, as part of a historical process which, in this case, serves as further proof that for imperial Europe, Argentina was "the country of the future." Above all, the notecard reinforces the notion that the process of

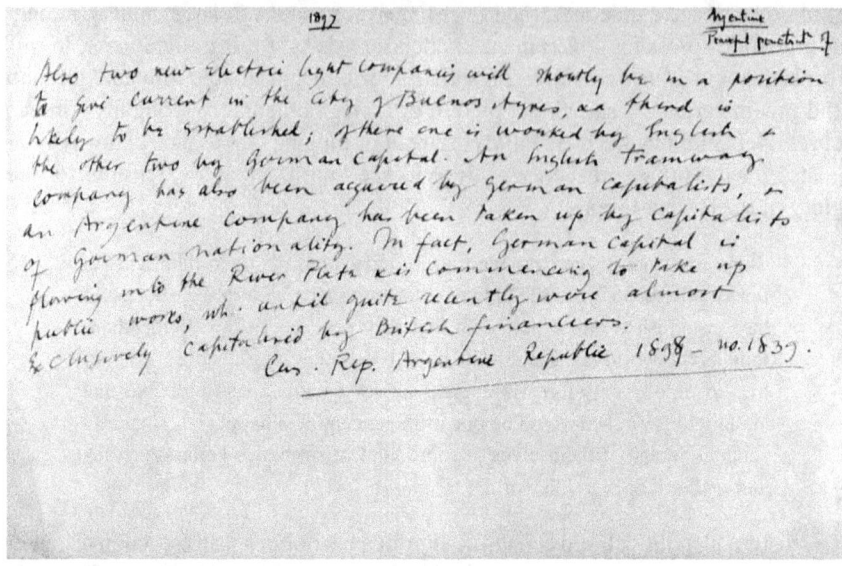

Figure 3: Notecard from British Consular Reports, Argentine Republic, 1898, number 1839. With the permission of the Society of Authors as the Literary Representative of the Estate of Virginia Woolf.

modernity is inextricably bound up with the ideologies of empire and capitalism. Consequently, the accelerated urbanization and Europeanization of the port city of Buenos Aires (soon to be reinvented as the "Paris of South America") went hand-in-hand with British and German economic penetration during a historical period in which the country experienced the unprecedented phenomenon of mass European immigration, aptly captured in the famous slogan pronounced by the political theorist, Juan Bautista Alberdi, "governar es poblar" ("to govern is to populate" [219]). More specifically, the card highlights the economic "scramble" for the Argentine Republic between British and German financiers fiercely competing for the monopoly of the country's economic resources (i.e. the banking, transportation, and public utilities sectors). The last sentence unequivocally states that the vast riches of the River Plate had so far been "almost exclusively capitalised by British financiers" and that such monopolization had, of late, been challenged by German investors. The fierce economic competition between Great Britain and Germany for the control of Argentina's wealth recalls Lenin's definition of capitalist imperialism as "a world system of colonial oppression and of financial strangulation of the overwhelming majority of the population of the world by a handful of 'advanced' countries" (28).

In the cultural sphere, moreover, the rapid growth of Buenos Aires into a gigantic urban conglomeration brought about "social dislocations that heightened the sense of crisis among its writers" (17), as Cathy Jrade points out. Latin American writers and intellectuals reacted ambivalently to the conditions of modernity. The negative after-effects of Britain's economic penetration in Argentina can be best explicated by examining the revisionary historicism put forth by prominent left-wing Argentine intellectuals such as Raúl Scalabrini Ortiz (1898-1959), who was writing in the wake of the Wall Street Crash and the political crisis brought about by the so-called "década infame" of the 1930s. In the case of Scalabrini, his idiosyncratic, anti-imperialist approach to the national dilemma was framed, according to Mark Falcoff, "in terms of an unholy alliance between 'country-selling' (vendepatria) oligarchs and foreign imperialists" (78). Attacking the positivist Roca administration that had "sold out" the nation to British financiers, for Scalabrini, Argentina rid itself of one imperial power (Spain) in order to be subjected to a new one (Great Britain). In *Política británica en el Río de la Plata* (1940; *British Politics in the River Plate*) and *Historia de los ferrocarriles argentinos* (1940; *History of the Argentine Railways*), Scalabrini adopts a Marxist approach to denounce Argentina's subservient role as Britain's economic "colony," in order to push an image of the country as a "sort of gigantic estancia whose agricultural and stock-raising capacities were being mercilessly exploited by Great Britain through a pliant Argentine elite" (Falcoff 78). In *Ferrocarriles*, he laments that "the fruits of the pampas are for others ... Argentina is a representative example of America: its problems are the problems of a martyrized [martirizado] continent" (Scalabrini 11). The Christian imagery denounces an agro-export economy that plunders the natural wealth of the ravaged nation for the principal benefit of the European consumer (although by "America" Scalabrini refers exclusively to the Spanish-speaking countries in the full knowledge that British neo-colonialism was being quickly replaced by the new giant of US domination).

Scalabrini's contemporary, the Argentine writer and critic Ezequiel Martínez Estrada (1895-1964), is also representative of this anti-imperialist, anti-modernity trend. In his highly polemical treatise *Radiografía de la Pampa* (1933; *X-Ray of the Pampa*), he pessimistically utilizes a medical register to diagnose the disease afflicting the ailing *patria*, a malaise inflicted by centuries of imperialism and, more recently, by the dehumanizing advances of the industrial world. Unsurprisingly, Martínez Estrada profoundly admired the Anglo-Argentine writer and naturalist, W. H. Hudson who, as Peter Earle notes, "[was] a nostalgic defender of a pastoral and mythical golden-age Argentina of the 1850s and 1860s" (9), a rural idyll populated by heroic gauchos whose equestrian lifestyle and trademark freedom had been radically displaced by the arrival of Western modernity. Born in 1841 in Quilmes (a province of Buenos Aires) to New Englanders and later naturalized as a British subject, William Henry Hudson (otherwise known in Argentina as "Guillermo Enrique") earned himself a dual identity as both reserved English gentleman and semi-barbarous gaucho, his reputation fluctuating between two names, languages, and nations.

On the other side of the Atlantic, meanwhile, Hudson was the subject of intense admiration from the literary coterie associated with Joseph Conrad, Edward Garnett, John Galsworthy, and R. B. Cunninghame Graham, who gathered at the Mont Blanc restaurant in London's Soho. Hailed by this circle as "a master of English prose" and praised by Conrad as the possessor of a unique, effortless style—"You may try for ever to learn how Hudson got his effects and you will never know. He writes down his words as the good God makes the green grass grow" (Conrad in Ford 72-73)—by the time *Far Away and Long Ago: A Childhood in Argentina* (1918) was released, the elderly Hudson was at the peak of his fame. This explains why, when *The Times Literary Supplement* asked Virginia Woolf to review Hudson's memoir, she accepted at once. "I feel pressed & important & even excited a little," she writes in her diary, "for a wonder, the book, Hudson, was worth reading" (D1197). Christina Alt has recently tracked the presence of Hudson in Woolf's work, revealing a voluminous number of references in her letters, diary, and essays, including a positive nod in her 1925 essay "Modern Fiction" (Alt 152-4). Alt also describes the important link between Woolf, the study of nature, and contemporary developments in the "new biology" (2-3). She examines Woolf's engagement with the study of nature in her fiction and non-fiction writings, particularly focusing on the late nineteenth-century shift from "the museum-based taxonomic tradition" to the "new biology of the laboratory," an important development running broadly in parallel to evolutionary theory (2). Alt also focuses on Woolf's subsequent interest in the theories and methods of the rising fields of ethology (the study of animal behavior) and ecology (the study of the relationship between organisms and their environment), both of which were directly associated with Hudson's pioneering study of living birds in their natural environment. For example, in her review of Hudson's *Far Away and Long Ago* in the TLS entitled "Mr Hudson's Childhood" and published in September 1918, Woolf is full of praise for Hudson's ability to conjure up "the bird flying, settling, feeding, soaring through every page of the book" (*E*2 301).

Considering that Virginia Woolf conducted her empirical research for the International Trade project in 1917 and, within roughly a year, published her review of Hudson's memoir, this trajectory implies that she essentially understood the two faces of Argentina, a duality framed, on the one hand, by the vanished rural idyll depicted in *Far Away and Long Ago*—"And when I recall these vanished scenes ... I am glad to think I shall never revisit them, that I shall finish my life thousands of miles removed from them, cherishing to the end in my heart the image of a beauty which has vanished from earth" (191)—and by the emergence of what Paula Young Lee defines as the nineteenth-century institution *par excellence*, the slaughterhouse, which radically transformed traditional agricultural methods, on the other (1, 12). Moreover, the image of the Argentine Republic as the abattoir of the British Empire later reappears in Virginia Woolf's only poem, the lavishly-titled "Ode Written Partly in Prose on Seeing the Name of Cutbush Above a Butcher's Shop in Pentonville" (1934).[6] A mock, albeit compassionately told, "ode" that chronicles the harsh working life of London butcher John Cutbush, the poem contains a crucial line about the Argentine agro-export industry:

> And he hires a barrow and goes to Smithfield
> at dawn; at chill dawn sees the cold meat,
> shrouded in white nets borne on men's shoulders;
> meat from the Argentines; from haired and red pelted
> hogs and bullocks (*CSF* 232).

The stanza signals Woolf's continued awareness of the global meat industry and the prominent role played by Argentina's meat packing plants in supplying vast quantities of frozen meat to Great Britain, as carcasses and animal parts are shipped from the industrial slaughterhouses of Buenos Aires to Smithfield meat market in Farringdon (London), to be finally handled, chopped, and sold by a local, hard-working butcher such as "little John" (*CSF* 231).

Britain, Empire, and the Rubber Trade

By also situating the novel within the historical context of the rubber boom in Amazonia, Woolf is addressing another vital aspect of capitalist imperialism in Latin America which, once again, is embodied in the predatory figure of Willoughby Vinrace and his ballooning transatlantic Empire:

> They heard of the *Euphrosyne*, but heard also that she was primarily a cargo boat, and only took passengers by special arrangement, *her business being to carry dry goods to the Amazons, and rubber home again* (*VO* 38, my italics).

Notice, for instance, how the sentence ends with a description of the alleged shipping affairs of the *Euphrosyne*, to clarify that one of *her* chief purposes as a "cargo boat" is the transportation of imported European goods to South America and, later, lucrative Amazonian rubber back to Europe. Therefore, the ship's sole purpose is trade, rather than to give a free ticket to the pompous Conservative politician

---

[6] I am most grateful to Derek Ryan for astutely drawing my attention to this key text.

Richard Dalloway and his arrogant wife Clarissa (both featured as minor characters), to whom the plural pronoun "they" is alluding to here. In this way, an explicit link between the Dalloways (who represent the British upper-middle classes) and imperialist politics is foregrounded, "for they came of a class where almost everything was specially arranged, or could be if necessary" (*VO* 38). Aboard the *Euphrosyne*, Clarissa Dalloway forcefully asserts her Englishness by uttering a patriotic speech strewn with imperialistic clichés:

> "D'you know, Dick, I can't help thinking of England," said his wife meditatively, leaning her head against his chest. "Being on this ship seems to make it so much more vivid – what it really means to be English. One thinks of all we've done, and our navies, and the people in India and Africa, and how we've gone on century after century, sending out boys from little country villages – and of men like you, Dick, and it makes one feel as if one couldn't bear *not* to be English!" (*VO* 51).

At the same time, the crucial use of the semantically loaded word "rubber" situates the novel within a recognizable colonial discourse of slavery and exploitation, while establishing vital links with the "scramble for Africa" depicted in Conrad's *Heart of Darkness*. Nonetheless, by strategically setting *The Voyage Out* in South America (rather than Africa), Woolf is drawing attention to the troubled history of the rubber trade in the Amazon region and, more specifically, to the so-called "Putumayo scandal" that made startling newspaper headlines in London in 1909 and that run in parallel with Roger Casement's denunciation of human rights abuses in South America (1910/1911) in his capacity as British consul-general in Rio de Janeiro, having previously exposed the atrocities committed in the Congo (1903).

The principal detonator of the highly inflammatory revelations of human rights abuses committed in Amazonia was the American engineer and explorer, Walter E. Hardenburg, who strategically decided to publish his highly sensitive material in the British periodical *Truth*. Founded in 1877 by the Liberal politician Henry Labouchère, *Truth* operated as a whistle-blower publication widely known for its ruthless "exposé of financial swindlers and [for its role as] public watch-dog" (Weber 38, 41). Hardenburg originally travelled to the Amazon basin motivated by greed as he was lured by the promise of fabulous riches in the lucrative rubber trade. However, in an ironic twist of fate, the self-styled conquistador suffered innumerable hardships, including unfair imprisonment at the hands of corrupt Peruvian rubber traders, an experience that exposed him to the systematic abuse and exploitation of the Amazonian Indians. Upon his release, however, the one-time conquistador astutely reinvented himself as a great humanitarian resolutely determined to air the atrocities in the British press. Michael Stanfield notes that

Hardenburg's sensationalist allegations, first published in *Truth* under the explosive headline, "The Devil's Paradise: A British-owned Congo" (Hardenburg 663-6), "were reported in the same sober voice used by Bartolomé de las Casas some 370 years earlier when he decried the excesses of Spanish colonialism in the Americas" (Stanfield xv). But, crucially, Hardenburg pointed the finger of blame at the British government. Westminster, he argued, was at the heart of the exploitative rubber industry in the Amazon (*The Putumayo* 21; 29; 31; 33-4). The unscrupulous Arana rubber company that enslaved the natives and used them as sources of cheap labor was in fact owned by British investors, hence denouncing Great Britain as the chief culprit in this tale of horror.

The so-called "rubber fever" that held sway at the end of the nineteenth century was the culmination of a long series of scientific discoveries that had revealed to the modern world the remarkable versatility of natural rubber and its potential manufacturing uses. Prominent among these pioneers is the Scottish chemist, Charles Macintosh (1766-1843), celebrated for the invention of waterproof garments by ingeniously creating a rubber-coated fabric that was extremely versatile and impermeable (the "mac" or "mackintosh" with an added "k," takes its name after him). Another seminal figure is the American chemist Charles Goodyear (1800-1860)—nowadays a name associated with a global brand of tires—who has been credited with discovering the vulcanization of rubber in 1839, a discovery that, in turn, proved crucial to the development of the first pneumatic tire by another Scotsman, Robert William Thomson (1822-1873) in 1867. The latter invention, not least, would trigger the archetypal emblem of modernity: the motorist revolution. Even Leonard Woolf, the arch-anti-imperialist, would later admit in his autobiography: "Nothing ever changed so profoundly my material existence, the mechanism and range of every-day life, as the possession of the motor-car" (*Downhill* 78).

These scientific breakthroughs notwithstanding, the fact remains that "Indians had been making expert use of rubber from time immemorial," writes Alain Gheerbrant, and it was the Indians who first showed the Portuguese "how latex could be moulded into boots and containers, or used as a waterproof coating for canvas" (79). World demand for rubber, by implication, brought into existence a plethora of industrial and domestic products, ranging from telephone cables to new "rubber" domestic products such as boots, bands, toys, erasers, gloves, and a long et cetera. The mythical legend of "El Dorado" fantasized by greedy conquistadors in search of precious metals during the Spanish conquest of America rapidly mutated into the ultimate capitalist dream symbolically described as "white gold," denoting the milky color of the liquid latex extracted from the rubber trees autochthonous to the Amazon region. The great rubber "boom" led to the destruction of the Amazonian ecosystem and to the slavery, murder, and forced prostitution of the native indigenous population, most of whom were forcibly "recruited" to work in the rainforests under threat of death, as Casement reports in the *Amazon Journal* that contains his harrowing reports of the official investigation:

> [The Indians] are not only murdered, flogged, chained up like wild beasts, hunted far and wide and their dwellings burnt, their wives raped their children dragged away to slavery and outrage, but are shamelessly swindled into the bargain. These are strong words, but not adequately strong.... It far exceeds in depravity and demoralisation the Congo regime at its worst (294-5).

Casement soon realized, as Helen Carr points out, that "much of colonialism was about capitalistic profit, not about improving the conditions of the indigenous people; the colonialists, he began to realise, were in fact only too ready to use these so-called primitive races as subhuman instruments for the accumulation of European wealth" (177). Predictably, implicit parallels were quickly drawn between the Congolese and Putumayo atrocities, although Casement went so far as to contentiously claim that the latter even exceeded the former. For Casement, if the genocidal acts in the Putumayo held a mirror to the unspeakable atrocities committed in the Congo, there was a crucial difference underlying both forms of human exploitation: Rule of Law. Whereas King Leopold II's ironically-named "Congo Free State" represented a form of "legalised tyranny," Casement asserts, the disputed territory of the Putumayo remained a "lawless tyranny," implying that "slavery under law" is better than "slavery without law" (295). This alarming "lawlessness" made the region an easy target for unscrupulous exploitation, opening a backdoor to corrupt rubber enterprises such as the infamous Casa Arana (later renamed the Peruvian Amazon Company). Founded by the Peruvian entrepreneur Julio César Arana, the company rapidly grew into a multimillion-pound empire financed by British foreign capital (with London, the imperial capital, as its headquarters) and enabled by the ideology of economic imperialism. Angus Mitchell underscores Britain's economic interest in the area through the backing of the first steamboat company in the upper Amazon basin and by forging British-South American banking alliances (50). The latter, precisely, are the types of trade networks that Virginia Woolf had painstakingly copied out from the British Consular Reports. For example, one notecard from the British Consular Report, Brazil, 1890, states that two central banking institutions in Brazil are owned and controlled by British financial establishments, thus exposing, once again, the profound economic penetration of the invisible empire:

> Other native banks are spoken of, but I am assured, on the best authority, that neither these nor those already in existence can in any way interfere with the two English financial establishments here i.e., the London & Brazilian Bank Ltd, & the English Bank of Rio de Janeiro, which continue their operations steadily & creditably.

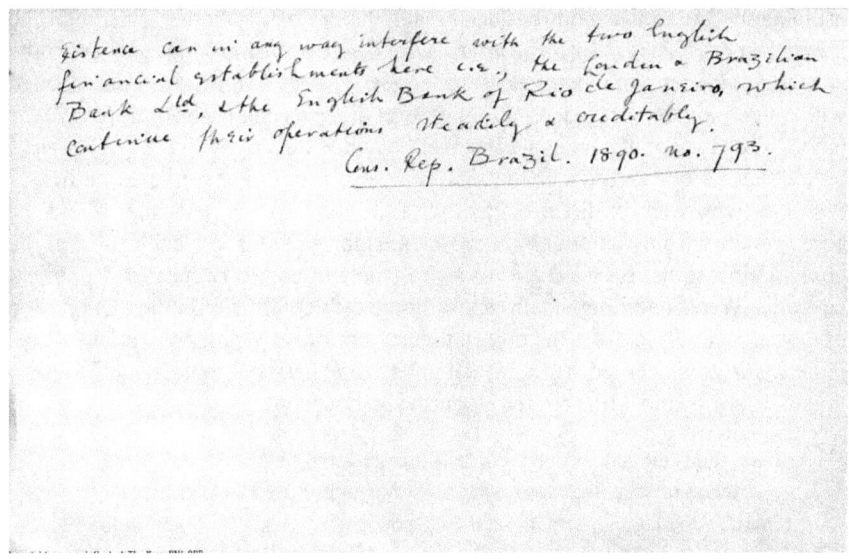

Figure 4: Notecard from British Consular Report, Brazil, 1890, number 793. With the permission of the Society of Authors as the Literary Representative of the Estate of Virginia Woolf.

No wonder, then, that Julio César Arana knocked on the doors of British financiers to secure the multimillion-pound loan for his rubber empire. In effect, British capital flowed freely to fund the Casa Arana, a company that operated a labor system based on slavery conditions thinly disguised as debt-peonage. In the aftermath of the abolition of slavery in Latin America and the Caribbean in the nineteenth century, debt-peonage rapidly became the successor to formal slavery. In his *Amazon Journal*, Casement exposes the harsh reality behind modern-day slavery practices operated by *aviadores* (middlemen), with whom the *seringueiros* (rubber tappers) exchanged their rubber for imported goods (tinned meats, sugar, beans, and candles). Casement makes overwhelmingly clear that these basic goods were only worth a miniscule fraction of the real market value of the latex (see, for example, 294-5).

If read within the context of *The Voyage Out*, such historical evidence raises renewed questions about the exact provenance of Willoughby's income. Where, once again, does the money that pays for Rachel's music education come from? Clearly, the source of his wealth originates from two separate transatlantic enterprises: the commerce of goats and the rubber trade, although Willoughby refrains from acknowledging the latter in his conversation with Mr. Pepper and Rachel, presumably due to the morally questionable nature of this "other" income. The import/export business of the *Euphrosyne*, the "cargo ship" that arrives to the Amazon crammed with European "dry goods" and later sails back home loaded with rubber, indubitably places Willoughby at the epicenter of the corrupt *aviador* hierarchical system of exchange, whether he traded directly with the *seringueiros* or whether he operated under the assistance of further intermediaries known as *patrones*, who were in direct contact with the workers. Of particular relevance here is a letter from Willoughby that Helen Ambrose reads in Chapter XV of the novel. Utilizing the epistolary form as a vehicle to address ethical and political concerns, Woolf unfailingly satirizes Willoughby's complicity in the exploitation of the natives. While, from the outset, the letter portrays Willoughby in his role as *pater familias* concerned with "his daughter's manners and morals" (*VO* 220), it gradually shifts into a less courteous and vulgar account:

> And then [the letter contained] half a page about his own triumphs over wretched little natives who went on strike and refused to load his ships, until he roared English oaths at them, "popping my head out of the window just as I was, in my shirt sleeves. The beggars had the sense to scatter" (*VO* 221).

In casting the otherwise "honourable" Willoughby into an immoral rubber baron who subjects his laborers to the type of bullying, ill-treatment, and forced labor that Casement had documented in his Amazon diary, Woolf is subversively emphasizing here that Britain—the archetypal progressive and humanitarian nation that had proudly abolished slavery in 1807—is in fact the main economic engine driving the genocidal acts committed in the Amazon. What Woolf makes overwhelmingly clear in the above extract is that the rubber industry was operated by an army of unscrupulous British investors eager to cash in during a period of record demand for latex, while blatantly turning a blind eye to the genocide of the native population, whether such capitalists operated remotely from London (a global financial center) or, in the case of Willoughby, were directly involved in the abuse of the workers. In many ways (again), the Putumayo recalled the horrors of the Congo, which means that Leonard Woolf's critique of the European mentality that sees the natives as disposable sources of cheap labor can be equally applied to the Amazonian system: "But ivory and rubber were of no value to Leopold unless he had the labour to collect them and to bring them to the coast for transport and sale in Europe" (*Empire and Commerce* 311).

At the same time, Virginia Woolf's satirical purpose is to attack the jingoistic patriotism of the British imperial colonist/adventurer who is ridiculed through Willoughby's grotesque account of his "triumphs" against defenseless indigenes. His callous behavior can be associated with Hobson's definition of jingoism as a form of "inverted patriotism whereby the love of one's nation is transformed into the hatred of another nation, and the fierce craving to destroy the individual members of that other nation" (1). Furthermore, Woolf's anti-imperialist condemnation (albeit couched in the guise of social satire) is intricately connected with the militaristic fervor of Richard and Clarissa Dalloway (cited earlier). In keeping with the pervasive anti-imperial tone of the novel, Woolf sets in motion a wider cast of nationalistic characters, disreputable minor figures who either flirt with extreme forms of patriotism (the Dalloways) or are abiding symbols of the ensnaring forces of capitalism (the Flushings). The latter are depicted in the novel as eccentric art-collectors eager to capitalize on the cheap labor generated by the Amazonian natives. Scholars such as Alissa Karl, Andrea Lewis, and Anna Snaith have persuasively shown the link between capital and empire in *The Voyage Out*, particularly the role played by the Flushings in reinforcing the "uneven relationship between native producer and imperialist consumer" (Karl 51) that is justified by the assumption that the colonized people occupy a "zero-degree of existence" (Lewis 116) and that is further propelled by "a metropolitan fetishization of the 'primitive' as the sign of the modern" (Snaith 31). Thus, cheap labor and colonial exploitation emerge as the chief concerns of the novel, whether the white colonizers are business magnates such as Willoughby Vinrace who have robbed "a whole continent of mystery" (*VO* 220) or, as exemplified in the extract below, small-scale opportunists such as Mr. and Mrs. Flushing:

> Mrs. Flushing came up once more, and dropped a quantity of beads, brooches, earrings, bracelets, tassels, and combs among the draperies.... "My husband rides about and finds 'em; they don't know what they're worth, so we get 'em cheap. And we shall sell 'em to smart women in London" (*VO* 272).

Woolf strategically uses this unscrupulous English pair as the embodiment of a deeply corrupt and unregulated system that shamelessly exploits the local indigenous communities, especially the labor produced by its women. Ultimately, their function in the novel is to illustrate the deeply intertwined relationship between imperialism with a "small i" (the Flushings) and a "big I" (Willoughby Vinrace). In the case of the former, the exotic jewelry and accessories crafted by the natives will be sold at inflated prices to wealthy women in the imperial metropolis, eager to purchase the types of tribal artifacts they would have seen exhibited in British Imperial Exhibitions, such as the 1924 Wembley Stadium Exhibition that Woolf described in apocalyptic undertones in "Thunder at Wembley." Part of what *The Voyage Out* sharply critiques, therefore, are the inner workings of imperial commerce in South America, particularly Britain's increasing reliance on both cheap labor and raw materials from its "honorary" dominions, exemplified in

Willoughby's commercial ventures. Consequently, Woolf presents a complex picture of Britain as one of the leading capitalist economies that has become overwhelmingly dependent on what Fredric Jameson defines as an economic system "located elsewhere, beyond the metropolis, outside of the daily life and existential experience of the home country, in colonies over the water whose own life experience and life world—very different from that of the imperial power—remain unknown and unimaginable for the subjects of the imperial power" (50-51). Informal colonies in the Tropical and South Atlantic rapidly emerged as the Empire's workshops, abattoirs, and suppliers of essential commodities such as rubber, wool, and beef.

By critically positioning *The Voyage Out* within the political-economic history of early twentieth-century Latin America, it is possible to reconceive the novel as an aesthetic platform for a scathing critique of an emergent global capitalist modernity, particularly the economic impetus behind Britain's disproportionate presence in Buenos Aires and Amazonia. The archival evidence in the form of Virginia Woolf's notes for the early International Trade project preserved at the Leonard Woolf Archive in Sussex has enabled the recuperation of the largely overlooked Latin American historical contexts embedded in the novel. At the same time, the notes seriously revise and rectify our understanding of Woolf's awareness of geopolitical issues pertaining to Latin America, enabling us to firmly situate *The Voyage Out* within a transnational economic network that serves as further proof of Woolf's concern with both "political space" and "global space" (Snaith and Whitworth 2), even if she was writing from the center of Empire and had never visited Latin America. Above all, her merciless critique of British imperialism opens up new routes of enquiry that delineate an economically-focused trajectory involving, in this case, Britain's overseas honorary dominions, which were crucial in supplying the privileged European consumer with essential raw materials. Highly attuned to the geopolitical changes of her time, Virginia Woolf, as Barrett has demonstrated, may now be firmly positioned as a political commentator (113-5), advancing, in the case of *The Voyage Out*, an unflinching denunciation of British economic imperialism in post-independence Latin America. This also means, as I suggested earlier, that the longstanding critical assumption that Woolf's knowledge of the continent was hopelessly vague and deficient can be conclusively put to rest.

Works Cited

Alberdi, Juan Bautista. *Bases y puntos de partida para la organización política de la República Argentina*. Buenos Aires, La Cultura Argentina, 1915.

Alt, Christina. *Virginia Woolf and the Study of Nature*. Cambridge UP, 2010.

Barrett, Michèle. "Virginia Woolf's Research for Empire and Commerce in Africa (Leonard Woolf, 1920)." *Woolf Studies Annual*, 19, 2013, pp. 83-122.

Bassnett, Susan and Harish Trivedi. "Introduction: Of Colonies, Cannibals, and Vernaculars." *Post-colonial Translation: Theory and Practice,* edited by Susan Bassnett and Harish Trivedi, Routledge, 1999, pp. 1-18.

Batchelor, John. *Virginia Woolf: The Major Novels.* Cambridge UP, 1991.

Bell, Stephen. "Aimé Bonpland and Merinomania in Southern South America." *The Americas,* vol. 51, no. 3, 1995, pp. 301-23.

Bradshaw, David. "'Tut, Tut': Censorship, Propriety and Obscenity in *The Voyage Out.*" *The Voyage Out: Centenary Perspectives,* edited by Sarah M. Hall, Mary Ellen Foley, Lindsay Martin and Claire Nicholson, Virginia Woolf Society of Great Britain, 2015, pp. 57-75.

Cardoso, Eliana A. and Ann Helwege. *Latin America's Economy: Diversity, Trends and Conflicts.* MIT Press, 1995.

Carr, Helen. "Roger Casement in the Amazon, The Congo, and Ireland." *Writing, Travel, and Empire,* edited by Peter Hulme, Tauris, 2007, pp. 169-94.

Casement, Roger. *The Amazon Journal of Roger Casement,* edited by Angus Mitchell, Lilliput Press, 1997.

Childs, Peter. *Modernism and the Post-Colonial: Literature and Empire 1885-1930.* Continuum, 2007.

Conrad, Joseph. *Heart of Darkness and The Congo Diary.* Edited by Owen and Robert Hampson, Penguin, 2007.

———. *The Collected Letters of Joseph Conrad: 1923-1924.* Edited by Laurence Davies and Gene M. Moore, Cambridge UP, 2008.

Davies, Dominic. "Critiquing Global Capital and Colonial (in)justice: Structural Violence in Leonard Woolf's *The Village in the Jungle* (1913) and *Economic Imperialism* (1920)." *Commonwealth Literature,* vol. 50, no.1, 2015, pp. 45-58.

Díaz Alejandro, Carlos F. *Essays on the Economic History of the Argentine Republic.* Yale UP, 1970.

Dryden, Linda. *Joseph Conrad and H. G. Wells: The Fin-de-Siècle Literary Scene.* Macmillan, 2015.

Earle, Peter G. *The Works of Ezequiel Martínez Estrada.* UP of Texas, 1971.

Esty, Jed. "Virginia Woolf's Colony and the Adolescence of Modernist Fiction." *Modernism and Colonialism: British and Irish Literature, 1899-1939,* edited by Richard Begam and Michael Valdez Moses. Durham UP, 2007, pp. 70-90.

Falcoff, Mark. "Raúl Scalabrini Ortiz: The Making of an Argentine Nationalist." *The Hispanic American Historical Review,* vol. 52, no. 1, 1972, pp. 74-101.

Ford, Ford Madox. *Mightier than the Sword: Memories and Criticisms.* Allen & Unwin, 1930.

Forster, E. M. "The Novels of Virginia Woolf." *Virginia Woolf: The Critical Heritage,* edited by Robin Majumdar and Allen McLaurin, Routledge, 1975, pp. 171-8.

French, Jennifer L. Nature, *Neo-Colonialism and the Spanish American Regional Writers*. UP of New England, 2005.

Froula, Christine. *Virginia Woolf and the Bloomsbury Avant-garde: War, Civilization, Modernity.* Columbia UP, 2005.

Gheerbrant, Alain. *The Amazon: Past, Present, and Future.* Harry N. Abrams, 1992.

Greenblatt, Stephen. *Marvellous Possessions: The Wonder of the New World.* Oxford UP, 2003.

Hardenburg, W. E. "The Devil's Paradise: A British-owned Congo." *Truth,* vol. 22, 1909, pp. 663-6.

——. *The Putumayo: The Devil's Paradise: Travels in the Peruvian Amazon Region and an Account of the Atrocities Committed Upon the Indians Therein.* T. Fisher Unwin, 1913.

Hobsbawm, Eric. *Industry and Empire: From 1750 to the Present Day,* rev. by Chris Wrigley, New Press, 1999.

Hobson, J. A. *The Psychology of Jingoism.* Grant Richards, 1901.

Hudson, William Henry. *Far Away and Long Ago: A Childhood in Argentina.* Eland, 2005.

Jameson, Fredric. "Modernism and Imperialism." *Nationalism, Colonialism, and Literature,* edited by Seamus Deane, U of Minnesota P, 1990, pp. 43-68.

Jrade, Cathy L. *Modernismo, Modernity and the Development of Spanish American Literature.* U of Texas P, 1998.

Karl, Alissa G. *Modernism and the Marketplace: Literary Culture and Consumer Capitalism in Rhys, Woolf, Stein, and Nella Larsen.* Routledge, 2009.

Kuehn, Julia. *A Female Poetics of Empire: From Eliot to Woolf.* Routledge, 2014.

Lee, Paula Young. "Introduction." *Meat, Modernity and the Rise of the Slaughterhouse,* edited by Paula Young Lee, U of Hampshire P, 2008.

Lenin, Vladimir. *Imperialism: The Highest Stage of Capitalism,* introduction by Doug Lorimer, Resistance Books, 1999.

Lewis, Andrea. "The Visual Politics of Empire and Gender in Virginia Woolf's *The Voyage Out.*" *Woolf Studies Annual* vol.1, 1995, pp. 106-19.

Lewis, Colin M. *British Railways in Argentina 1857-1914: A Study of Foreign Investment.* Athlone, 1983.

Lojo Rodríguez, Laura María. "'A gaping mouth, but no words': Virginia Woolf Enters the Land of Butterflies." *The Reception of Virginia Woolf in Europe,* edited by Mary Ann Caws and Nicola Luckhurst, Continuum, 2002, pp. 218-46.

Marcus, Jane. "Britannia Rules The Waves." *Decolonizing Tradition: New Views of Twentieth-Century "British" Literary Canons,* edited by Karen R. Lawrence, U of Illinois P, 1992, pp. 136-62.

Marshik, Celia. *British Modernism and Censorship.* Cambridge UP, 2006.
Martínez Estrada, Ezequiel. *Radiografía de la Pampa.* Losada, 1953.
Mitchell, Angus. "The Diaries Controversy." *The Amazon Journal of Roger Casement,* edited by Angus Mitchell, Lilliput, 1997.
Mullin, Katherine. *James Joyce, Sexuality and Social Purity.* Cambridge UP, 2003.
Negrello, Giulia. "Wild Nature, Afternoon Teas and Butterflies: Virginia Woolf, Victoria Ocampo and the South-American Dream." *The Voyage Out: Centenary Perspectives,* edited by Sarah M. Hall, Mary Ellen Foley, Lindsay Martin and Claire Nicholson, Virginia Woolf Society of Great Britain, 2015, pp. 120-8.
Nouzeilles, Gabriela and Montaldo, Graciela. "Frontiers." *The Argentine Reader,* edited by Gabriela Nouzeilles and Graciela Montaldo, Duke UP, 2002.
Ortega y Gasset, José. *Obras completas,* volume 2, Revista de Occidente, 1957.
Parrott, Fiona G. "Friendship, Letters and Butterflies: Victoria Ocampo and Virginia Woolf." *Scotland's Transatlantic Relations Project Archive,* 2004, pp. 1-7.
Phillips, Kathy J. *Virginia Woolf Against Empire.* U of Tennessee P, 1994.
Pratt, Mary Louise. Imperial Eyes: *Travel Writing and Transculturation.* Routledge, 2008.
Putzel, Steven. "Virginia Woolf and British 'Orientalism.'" *Virginia Woolf Out of Bounds: Selected Papers from the Tenth Annual Conference on Virginia Woolf,* edited by Jessica Berman and Jane Goldman, Pace UP, 2001, pp. 105-112.
Rocchi, Fernando. *Chimneys in the Desert: Industrialization in Argentina during the Export Boom Years,* 1870-1930. Stanford University Press, 2006.
Rogers, Gayle. *Modernism and the New Spain: Britain, Cosmopolitan Europe, and Literary History.* Oxford UP, 2012.
Sábato, Hilda. *Agrarian Capitalism and the World Market: Buenos Aires in the Pastoral Age,* 1840-1890. U of New Mexico P, 1990.
Said, Edward. "Yeats and Decolonization." *Nationalism, Colonialism, and Literature,* edited by Seamus Deane, U of Minnesota P, 1990, pp. 69-98.
——. *Culture and Imperialism.* Chatto and Windus, 1993.
Scalabrini Ortiz, Raúl. *Historia de los ferrocarriles argentinos.* Plus Ultra, 1974.
Snaith, Anna. "Leonard and Virginia Woolf: Writing Against Empire." *Journal of Commonwealth Literature* vol. 50, no.1, 2015, pp. 19-32.
—— and Michael H. Whitworth. "Introduction: Approaches to Space and Place in Woolf." *Locating Woolf: The Politics of Space and Place,* edited by Anna Snaith and Michael H. Whitworth, Palgrave, 2007, pp. 1-28.

Snyder, Carey. "Woolf's Ethnographic Modernism: Self-Nativizing in *The Voyage Out* and Beyond." *Woolf Studies Annual,* vol.10, 2004, pp. 81- 108.

Stanfield, Michael Edward. *Red Rubber, Bleeding Trees: Violence, Slavery, and Empire in Northwest Amazonia: 1850-133.* U of New Mexico P, 1998.

Weber, Gary. "Henry Labouchere, 'Truth' and the New Journalism of Late Victorian Britain." *Victorian Periodicals Review,* vol. 26, no.1, 1993, pp. 36-43.

White, Andrea. "Conrad and Imperialism." *The Cambridge Companion to Joseph Conrad,* edited by J. H. Stape, Cambridge UP, 1996.

Wollaeger, Mark. "The Woolfs in the Jungle: Intertextuality, Sexuality, and the Emergence of Female Modernism in *The Voyage Out, The Village in the Jungle,* and *Heart of Darkness.*" *MLQ* vol. 64, no.1, 2003, pp. 33-69.

——. "Woolf, Postcards, and the Elision of Race: Colonizing Women in The Voyage Out." *Modernism/modernity,* vol. 8, no.1, 2001, pp. 43-75.

Woolf, Leonard. *Empire and Commerce in Africa: A Study in Economic Imperialism.* George Allen and Unwin, 1920.

——. *Downhill all the Way: An Autobiography of the Years 1911-1918.* Hogarth Press, 1967.

Woolf, Virginia. *The Voyage Out.* Edited by Lorna Sage, Oxford UP, 1992.

——. *Melymbrosia.* Edited by Louise DeSalvo, Cleis Press, 2002.

——. *The Diary of Virginia Woolf.* Edited by Anne Olivier Bell, 5 vols. Hogarth Press, 1977-84.

——. *The Complete Shorter Fiction.* Edited by Susan Dick, Hogarth Press, 1989.

——. *Essays of Virginia Woolf.* Edited by Andrew McNeillie, 4 vols. Hogarth Press, 1986-94.

——. *The Letters of Virginia Woolf,* edited by Nigel Nicolson and J. Trautmann Banks, 6 vols. Hogarth Press, 1975-80.

Wright, Winthrop R. *British-Owned Railways in Argentina: Their Effect on Economic Nationalism,* 1854-1948. U of Texas P, 1974.

Remapping Female Subjectivity in *Mrs. Dalloway*: Scenic Memory and Woolf's "Bye-Street" Aesthetic
Candis E. Bond

In *Mrs. Dalloway* (1925), Clarissa Dalloway's daughter, Elizabeth, takes a solitary omnibus ride through a range of traditionally masculine spaces: the monumental space of Whitehall, filled with its memorials to war, the professional spaces of the Strand, including Somerset House and the Temple, and the religious spaces of Fleet Street, most notably St. Paul's Cathedral (*MD* 132-6). On this ride, Elizabeth is described as a "pioneer," and the physical streets are connected to Elizabeth's longing for "a profession" as she muses: "She would become a doctor, a farmer, possibly go into Parliament ... all because of the Strand" (*MD* 133). Elizabeth experiences the patriarchal streets and buildings—particularly those around St. Paul's—as intimidating; she moves through the area "shyly, like someone penetrating on tiptoe" (*MD* 134). But she is also intrigued by the urban space, particularly the "queer alleys" off Fleet Street, which she also refers to as "tempting bye-streets" (*MD* 134). The image of the bye-street suggests a detour, an alternative way of being in the urban space that is marginal yet somehow still central to its operation. But Elizabeth hesitates to enter the alleys: she does not "dare wander off" into their recesses any more than she would "open doors which might be bedroom doors, or sitting-room doors, or lead straight to the larder" in a "strange house" (*MD* 134). For Elizabeth, the "queer alley" and the "tempting bye-street" are transgressive spaces, connecting seemingly distinct and incompatible modes of life in order to imagine new spatio-social configurations. Within these "tempting" spaces, patriarchal categories of class, gender, and sexuality might be escaped or reimagined.

While Elizabeth may be able to consider material "bye-streets" and "queer alleys" as potential avenues of self-exploration—for, as Miss Kilman insists, things are different now that "every profession is open to women of [Elizabeth's] generation" (*MD* 133)—Clarissa's age and status as a well-known socialite and diplomat's wife hinder her ability to take such material detours. Her activity within the city is limited to the parks and the upper-class shopping districts of Bond Street in the neighborhoods of Westminster and Mayfair near St. James's Park. Yet Clarissa, like Elizabeth, yearns for roles beyond those that have been ascribed to her by the patriarchy: wife, mother, socialite, and hostess.

Although Clarissa might be limited in her ability to pursue socially transgressive material routes, she indulges counter-normative desires by taking detours of the mind and memory. Thus, this essay considers the "bye-street"—a physical urban space that was increasingly trodden by the middle and upper classes in modern London in the early decades of the twentieth century[1]—as a model for Woolf's evolving methods of female characterization in *Mrs. Dalloway*. Elizabeth's thoughts on the urban bye-street recall Woolf's own "tunneling process," which she developed as she drafted the novel and figures prominently in the characterization of its female protagonist, Clarissa. By interrogating the significance of Woolf's bye-street aesthetic, as well as its relationship to her representation of Clarissa's counter-normative subjectivity and lesbian desires, I add to the growing critical conversation about the centrality of space to modernist aesthetics.[2] In *Moving Through Modernity: Space and Geography in Modernism,* Andrew Thacker calls for the development of a modernist "literary geography" that places physical spaces in dialogue with their imagined, represented counterparts (58). Doing so reveals political and social critiques embedded within modernist representations of space. Following Thacker's lead, I consider how a specific type of urban space—the alley—contributed to Woolf's development of a distinctly modernist female subjectivity based on multiplicity and trans-spatial dialogue.[3] Woolf does not simply juxtapose the material and the imagined to express the politics structuring women's experiences; she interrogates the very nature of spaces and their influence on women's trans-temporal and trans-spatial identities.

"Tunnelling," Scenic Memory, and Dialogic Subjectivity: A "Bye-Street" Aesthetic

Virginia Woolf viewed the past, present, and future as integrally connected spaces. She explains in "A Sketch of the Past," for example, that "when the present

---

[1] The term "alley" came into usage in London in the fourteenth century, when the city was growing into a large metropolitan center, making it a distinctly modern, urban space (OED). As Sarah Wise points out in her book *The Blackest Streets*, Londoners traditionally viewed alleys as lower-class, criminal spaces, but this started to change at the turn of the twentieth century when main thoroughfares became so congested with traffic that middle- and upper-class pedestrians increasingly chose to take alleys as alternative routes.

[2] While Joseph Frank argued as early as 1945 that concepts of space were central to modernism, it has only been within the last two decades that modernist scholars have revisited his argument. Andrea Rummel, for example, has argued that modernists anticipated theories of space through their aesthetics of simultaneity (58). More recently, Rebecca Walsh has shown how influential early-twentieth-century scientific and popular discourses of geography were for American modernist poets. As Henri Lefebvre argues in *The Production of Space*, however, inquiry into the formative nature of spaces must be local and specific. This essay seeks to determine how a very concrete type of space and spatial practice may have influenced modernist form.

[3] While critics such as Jennie-Rebecca Falcetta and Savina Stevanato both discuss how modernist art techniques such as the use of montage and multiple perspectives influenced Woolf's formal approach to representing decentered subjectivities, I consider how types of urban space also served as models for her representation of Clarissa's subjectivity.

runs so smoothly that it is like the sliding surface of a deep river," "the past comes back" (98). It is in these moments, she continues, that "one sees through the surface to the depths" and "liv[es] most fully in the present" ("Sketch" 98). Woolf's choice of words suggests a spatial way of thinking about time and subjectivity: she views the past as a space in its own right, existing beneath the "surface" of present spaces in the "depths" of consciousness. Significantly, however, Woolf acknowledges that these layers of time and being can coexist in the present moment, leading to periods of intense vision, vitality, and becoming. By connecting past and present spaces, one "live[s] most fully in the present" ("Sketch" 98).

Woolf's trans-temporal, depth-model of subjectivity in "Sketch" is founded upon viewing the past and present as dynamic and fluid *spaces*, rather than as linearly progressing moments in time.[4] Arnold Weinstein observes that in her fiction, this spatialized understanding of time and subjectivity first manifests through what Woolf called her "tunnelling process" (203), a method of characterization Woolf developed as she drafted *Mrs. Dalloway*.[5] Woolf's "tunnelling" technique involves telling the "past by instalments, as [she has] need of it" (Woolf, *D2*, 272). In "The Tunnelling Process," Susan Dick argues that "tunneling" allows Woolf to dramatize and create character "selectively" (176). Dick's term "selectively" is critical since it illuminates tunnelling's association with revelation and the careful assemblage of identity across time and *space*; although Dick does not mention space explicitly, to "select" implies a range of selves that come together, from different places or positions, to create character.

The term "tunnelling" is itself a spatial metaphor that, as Edward Hungerford argues, is carefully chosen by Woolf as a means to create connections that lead to moments of "revelation" (165, 166). Woolf explains that the process involves digging "out beautiful caves behind my characters; I think this gives exactly what I want; humanity, humour, depth. The idea is that the caves shall connect, & each comes to daylight in the present moment" (*D2*, 263). Kristina Groover argues that Woolf's "image of the hidden cave connecting her characters ... creates a subversive subtext for the precisely mapped text of *Mrs Dalloway*," offering a substratum of

---

[4] My reading of memory in Woolf's novel builds on the works of Anne Fernald, Arnold Weinstein, Bonnie Kime Scott, Suzanne Nalbantian, Gayla Diment, and Makiko Minow-Pinkney, who note the significance of memory to her plots and conception of subjectivity. I extend the discussion to consider the role of space in memory.

[5] Thomas Docherty does link Woolf's use of memory and "tunnelling" to space. Although he does not discuss spatial time, he comments upon Modernism's, particularly Woolf's, "metaphorical approach to time," which aims to create a unified subject (146). While the "tunnelling" method is, indeed, metaphorical, I would add that Woolf's use of it to create fluidity between past, present, and future selves suggests that it is also quite literal. To "tunnel" is not simply to make time visible by representing temporalities as particular spatialities, but rather it is to demonstrate how time is, in fact, inherently linked to particular spaces; it is also to acknowledge that spaces and temporalities are more fluid than one might imagine.

"various liminal geographic spaces that transcend boundaries and create connections between characters who ordinarily inhabit disparate landscapes" ("Taking the Door off the Hinges"). In addition to creating connections between characters, I propose that "tunneling" creates new geographies of the self, connecting a variety of selves in the present moment of the text.

In the case of Clarissa, tunneling quite literally remaps the female subject. While Clarissa's walks can be conventionally traced on a map of London (as many online projects do well), this kind of mapping is inadequate to represent subjectivity. Woolf's inclusion of memories, and the tunnels between characters and places that these memories create, constructs a new kind of mapping, one that would need to include multiple places and times superimposed onto the present in order to capture the complexity of the modern subject's experience of space and self. Clarissa is no longer a woman walking through Bond Street, but a woman walking through multiple spaces at multiple periods in time as she simultaneously experiences the space of the present moment. The female subject is, in a sense, much more mobile than conventional mapping allows for.

Although Woolf was undoubtedly influenced by many avenues of thought, including, perhaps, psychoanalysis or sociology, which increasingly focused on depth models of subjectivity as well as the nature of human relationships in the early decades of the twentieth century, the spatial and geographic connotations of tunneling, especially as they are interpreted by Groover, recall the function of alleys and "bye-streets" in a modern city. In execution, tunneling operates aesthetically in a manner that is similar to the function of an urban alley. The "tunnels" that subjective memory creates within the text link seemingly disparate spaces, temporalities, people, and even ideologies, much as an alley serves as a liminal shortcut linking distinct parts of the city. Although it would be reductive to claim that Woolf's metaphor is entirely dependent upon material spatial practice, especially those that might be deemed transgressive for middle-to-upper-class women such as Clarissa, thinking of "tunneling" as an aesthetic version of taking a bye-street can help one to see how her method spatializes the text as well as models of subjectivity.[6] In *Mrs. Dalloway*, "tunneling" allows Woolf to represent subjectivity formation as trans-temporal *and* trans-spatial. Spaces of the past—spaces that come

---

[6] Similar to a bye-street, Woolf explains that the "caves [between and underneath characters] shall connect." Woolf's choice of the term "cave" combines the concepts of connection and depth, suggesting that, in reality, illuminating connections often lie hidden beneath or behind surface appearances. Since she links her method to notions of depth, claiming that tunneling "gives exactly what I want; humanity, humour, depth" (*D2*, 263), it makes sense that she would choose a space that typically exists underground beneath visible surfaces, as a cave suggests unseen depths of character or existence that the novelist brings to light. In terms of historical contexts, Woolf's choice of metaphor also resonates as it could be linked to developments in transport technology, particularly the Tube.

alive through the *scenic* act of remembering—are demonstrative of Woolf's need to develop character in such a way that illustrates and deconstructs how the events, feelings, and ideologies associated with particular spaces contribute to one's sense of identity across times and spaces.

The plot of *Mrs. Dalloway* is constituted as much by movement into the past as it is by action propelling characters forward. Woolf was conscious of the significance of memory for the plot and characterization, writing in her diary that she "found Clarissa in some way tinselly. Then I invented her memories" (*D3*, 32). Memories add depth to plot and character. Although many of the memories represented in the novel are narrated passively from the standpoint of the present as though they have already occurred, such as when Peter recalls that "as a child he had walked in Regent's Park" (*MD* 54), many memories take on a distinctly embodied and scenic quality. Scenic memories break through into the present moment, and they are often epiphanic. Woolf noted the illuminative quality of scenic memory in "Sketch." Although it was written later in her life, during World War II, Woolf's comments about scenic memory seem applicable to the way that scenic memory functions in her earlier novel. In "Sketch," she writes:

> I find that scene making is my natural way of marking the past. A scene always comes to the top; arranged; representative. This confirms me in my instinctive notion—it is irrational; it will not stand argument—that we are sealed vessels afloat upon what it is convenient to call reality; at some moments, without a reason, without an effort, the sealing matter cracks; in floods reality; that is a scene. ("Sketch" 142)

Similar to her description in "Sketch," scenic memories insert themselves into the present moment of *Mrs. Dalloway* in a dialogic manner: characters recall scenes from the past, and as they do so, the scenes recur within the spaces and temporalities of the present moment, creating passage-like conversations between past and present that result in breakdowns of spatio-temporal categories. In this manner, spatialized memories resonate with the function of "bye-streets," linking distinct spaces together in dialogues of connection.

It is critical to emphasize the conversational and dialogic nature of spatialized memory and "tunneling," a fact that many scholars have overlooked. For example, Ann Banfield discusses the ways that Modernist writers, especially Woolf, attempted to contextualize time within spaces in order to create "subjectivity... as a now in the past" (51). Similarly, Suzanne Nalbantian views memory in *Mrs. Dalloway* as a "full fledged transport to the past," thus arguing that through memory, characters become completely removed from the present (84). Banfield and Nalbantian's interpretation of spatial time suggests a complete removal from the present as the past imposes itself upon the present textual moment. Jean Love briefly mentions the relationship between time and space in Woolf's fiction and the significance of the movement between the two, but she does not go into great detail about the nature of this movement or how it contributes to the formation of character or the expression of subjectivity (61). I posit, however, that Woolf's spatialization of memory allows Clarissa to engage actively with her past self or selves (not just view it/them objectively from a distance), and that by doing so, she is able to "live most fully in the present." Past and present spaces (and the corresponding selves those spaces produce) are not isolated, but are in constant conversation and, therefore, reciprocal modification. This new conception of space allows Woolf to deconstruct and revise conventional notions of time, space, and identity as linearly evolving entities.

The dialogic, parallel positioning of past and present scenes begins early in the novel, when middle-aged Clarissa, speaking through the omniscient narrator from her London home, recalls memory-scenes from her past life as an adolescent girl at Bourton. Clarissa moves through her home in the present, noting that the "doors would be taken off their hinges" for her upcoming party (*MD* 3).[7] As she thinks about this, Clarissa crosses the threshold of her home's door on her way to buy flowers in Bond street, thinking "what a morning—fresh as if issued to children on a beach" (*MD* 3). The combination of doors, hinges, and the fresh June morning inspire an associative, scenic memory. Clarissa's thoughts continue: "What a lark! What a plunge! For so it had always seemed to her, when, with a little squeak of the hinges, which she could hear now, she had burst open the French windows and plunged at Bourton into the open air. How fresh, how calm, stiller than this of course, the air was in the early morning" (*MD* 3). Clarissa moves outside into the city, but her mind moves simultaneously into the physical, sensory spaces of Bourton. Her descriptions are embodied: she hears the "little squeak of the hinges" (although they are physically occurring in the present, she experiences them as though they are in the past and present simultaneously), and she feels the air, which is "fresh" like the air of the present, but "calm" and "stiller" (*MD* 3). Clarissa establishes London in the present and Bourton in the past as distinct spaces and times with their own intrinsic qualities, but her physical movements in present space and her psychological movements through memory-spaces become linked through association, creating a conversation between spaces that establishes meaning and a sense of self for Clarissa in the present moment.

Woolf's slippery use of verb tense in the passage formally underscores the blurring of lines between past and present. The passage begins in the future unreal conditional ("doors would be"), then switches from present simple ("what a

---

[7] Groover notes the significance of the threshold at this moment in the text, claiming that the French doors operate as a liminal space offering entry into the unknowable (para. 10). I would add that in addition to the "unknowable," the doors offer entry into disparate spaces and temporalities, creating a text and a female subject that are spatially and temporally multiple.

morning), to past continuous ("so it had always seemed to her"), to future unreal conditional ("she could hear now"), to past perfect ("she had burst open"), to past simple ("plunged"; "air was").[8] The slippage between tenses emphasizes movement between multiple spaces and temporalities that characterize Clarissa's identity and experience in the present; past, present, and future are fluid categories that shift and intersect. The use of tense suggests that Clarissa does not have to choose between a past Clarissa and a present Clarissa; she is simultaneously both, and both aspects of her identity are constructed dialogically in a spatio-temporal grid that lies outside of conventional linear notions of time and space. Hence, normative barriers of time and place are broken down via memory and narrative structure.

Moments later on Clarissa's walk, Woolf uses associative, scenic memories slightly differently to further destabilize spatio-temporal categories and represent the female subject as multiple. As she walks, Clarissa "could remember scene after scene at Bourton" (*MD* 6). Although these "scenes" are not related in any kind of detail, in the following paragraph, which seems to occur simultaneously with Clarissa's recollection of scenes, Woolf places Clarissa's experience of the present in parentheses:

> (June had drawn out every leaf on the trees. The mothers of Pimlico gave suck to their young. Messages were passing from the Fleet to the Admiralty. Arlington Street and Piccadilly seemed to chafe the very air in the Park and lift its leaves hotly, brilliantly, on waves of that divine vitality which Clarissa loved. To dance, to ride, she had adored all that). (*MD* 7)

The use of the parentheses registers the fluidity of past, present, and future at the formal level as the past is superimposed upon the present in a manner that makes the present secondary to, or underneath, the simultaneous presence of the past. The shifting tenses in the parenthetical passage are similar to those in my earlier example, if less varied. Tenses switch between past continuous and simple past, yet this passage relates primarily to the London of the material present (although the final line seemingly reverts to the distant or continuous past). Here, although technique is different, Woolf's result is the same: she establishes the past and present as dialogic, reciprocally informed spaces, and she locates the formation of subjectivity in the interstices of the two (or more) spatio-temporal categories that emerge out of their exchange.

These techniques, of which there are many examples across the duration of Clarissa's morning walk,[9] formally mirror the protagonist's resistant attitude about

---

[8] Although I have chosen to focus on this early portion of the "scenic" memory, it should be noted that the scene continues past this point and integrates a number of additional tenses, including past progressive, past conditional, and future real conditional.

[9] See, for example, Clarissa's inner monologue as she sits in St. James's Park on pages 6-7.

identity and life: "she would not say of herself, I am this, I am that" (*MD* 8). Although Clarissa walks along a main thoroughfare in the early pages of the novel, memory's function as a bye-street allows Woolf to aesthetically represent the plurality of subjectivity and experiences of time and place; she can experiment with modes of representation that operate outside of restrictive binaries as she maps a more mobile, fluid model of female subjectivity.

Exposing the Patriarchy: Scenic Remembering as Transgressive Spatial Practice

In addition to opening up and mobilizing female subjectivity, scenic memory operates to expose patriarchy's influence on Clarissa's identity formation across times and spaces, engaging the novel in political critiques of binary gender roles. The trans-temporal and trans-spatial aspects of scenic memory are a focal point in one of the novel's most extended retrospective passages, in which Clarissa recalls her past relationship with Sally Seton at Bourton after returning home from her trip to buy flowers in Bond Street.[10] The memories in this passage center upon Clarissa's rebellious and erotic adolescent relationship with Sally, who symbolizes an alternative way of life, love, and fulfillment that runs counter to Clarissa's patriarchal upbringing, which has prepared her only for the roles of daughter, "'perfect hostess,'"[11] and wife (*MD* 60).

The passage begins as passive narration of the past, with Clarissa remaining quite detached and distant from Sally and her past feelings. As she recalls many things about Sally, she thinks, "No, the words meant absolutely nothing to her now. She could not even get an echo of her old emotion" (*MD* 34). Suddenly, however, a scenic memory begins. The inspiration seems to be associative, as Clarissa's actions in the present—she is doing her hair—recall past actions:

> But she could remember going cold with excitement, and doing her hair in a kind of ecstasy (now the old feeling began to come back to her, as she took out her hair pins, laid them on the dressing table, began to do her hair), with the rooks flaunting up and down in the pink evening light, and dressing, and going downstairs, and feeling as she crossed the hall 'if it were now to die 'twere now to be most happy.' That was her feeling—Othello's feeling, and she felt it, she was convinced, as strongly as Shakespeare meant Othello to feel it, all because she was coming down to dinner in a white frock to meet Sally Seton!" (34)

---

[10] Clarissa's chain of memories occurs over the course of six full pages (*MD* 32-36). The only other scenic memory passage that exceeds this is Peter's reflections on Bourton and his rejection by Clarissa (*MD* 57-63). Together, these two passages provide the most comprehensive vision of Clarissa's past life

[11] It is Peter who refers to Clarissa as the "real hostess" and the "'perfect hostess'" (*MD* 60).

This memory is clearly embodied: "she could remember going cold with excitement, and doing her hair in a kind of ecstasy." Yet Clarissa is not entirely displaced from the space of the present. Although it is in parentheses, Clarissa's present actions are in dialogue with the space of the past: "(now the old feeling began to come back to her, as she took out her hair pins [... and] began to do her hair)." Clarissa moves into past spaces while also reliving her feelings in present space, and the two spatio-temporal dimensions interact and converse. As she begins to do her hair, for example, Clarissa remembers "wearing pink gauze" at Bourton, but quickly, in the present, questions this memory, asking, "Was that possible?" (*MD* 34). These two Clarissas coexist and speak to each other. The settings also seem immediate and co-present. In her scenic memory, it is "evening light," while in the present, it is late "on this June morning," a fact Clarissa sees reflected back at her through her looking glass, which sits opposite her bedroom window (*MD* 34, 36).[12] The two spaces exist simultaneously for Clarissa, and she is able to consider both and move fluidly between the two.

Woolf's use of spatial memory in this scene links Clarissa's interiority to the politics of the external environment, engaging the novel in a political critique of the patriarchy informing her sense of self. Clarissa is at once inside of herself, in the spaces of consciousness, and outside of herself, in a corporeal experience of material spaces. *Mrs. Dalloway* not only blurs boundaries between the public and private self,[13] as Annalee Edmondson has observed, but the transgressive nature of scenic memory also breaks down barriers between interiority and exteriority more generally, embedding both within ideological systems and hierarchies. The scenic, or embodied spatial nature of particular memories in *Mrs. Dalloway* is foundational to Woolf's critique of the patriarchy, as well as to her imagining of a more liberated subjectivity for women. This is because scenes, which are both temporal and spatial, are ideologically informed.

In "Politics of Retrospective Space," Georgia Johnston identifies the ideological nature of memory spaces within Woolf's autobiographical writing.[14] Spaces of the past, she explains, must work within the "ideologies of civilization" (Johnston 287). Johnston primarily focuses on the roles that the (female) autobiographical

---

[12] We know the time of day because Clarissa goes up to her bedroom after learning that Richard has gone to Lady Bruton's for lunch, and when she leaves her room to go down to the drawing room to mend her dress and Peter arrives, Big Ben strikes eleven (*MD* 39).
[13] Woolf acknowledges the collapse of public and private explicitly in *Three Guineas*, stating that "the public and the private worlds are inseparably connected; that the tyrannies and servilities of the one are the tyrannies and servilities of the other" is a "connection" that should be made (168). Although she mentions "worlds" in *Three Guineas*, *Mrs. Dalloway* implies that selves as well as worlds are implicated in ideological systems.
[14] Although Johnston deals strictly with the genre of autobiography, her ideas about the ideological nature of retrospective spaces can be applied to fiction.

subject takes on when retroactively creating spaces: "Other," "actor," and "spectator." She shows how these roles create in the female subject an "awareness" of ideological forces, an awareness that for Woolf is "based upon extraction from patriarchal society" (Johnston 289). Because of this extraction and the roles the female subject comes to fill through the creative acts of remembering and narrating, the spaces of the past, Johnston argues, are akin to "scenes."

By imagining the past and present as simultaneous, embodied scenes in *Mrs. Dalloway*, Woolf positions competing ideological frameworks that, together, inform Clarissa's sense of self in the present. Because of its associations with Sally, who defied convention and, according to Clarissa's father, was "untidy" and "shock[ing]" (*MD* 33), the past/pastoral space of Bourton contrasts with the sometimes stifling atmosphere of Clarissa's urban home, which is "cool as a vault" (*MD* 28). The relative freedom of the country for women as compared to London echoes throughout the text. Elizabeth, for example, reflects that she "so much preferred being left alone to do what she liked in the country, but they would compare her to lilies, and she had to go to parties, and London was so dreary compared with being alone in the country with her father and the dogs" (*MD* 131). Other characters imply that the country offered a similar space of fulfillment for Clarissa that seemed most expressive of her personality. Peter, for instance, sees Clarissa "most often in the country, not in London. One scene after another at Bourton" (*MD* 150). The country, because of its removal from the patriarchal institutions and social demands of London, which, as Elizabeth's comments observe, limit women's movements and objectify their beauty, offers a space that, while still patriarchal and male-dominated, holds the potential for fuller expression.

As this passage demonstrates, Woolf uses the ideological nature of memory scenes alongside scenes in the present to deconstruct how patriarchal ideology has shaped Clarissa's identity over time. Scenic memory not only functions as a narrative device which reveals the multiplicity of Clarissa, pointing to her differences and inconsistencies, but it also exposes the ways that ideology and social structures have forced Clarissa to adapt in order to survive within the patriarchy.[15] By remembering, Clarissa is "extracted" from the present as she enters spaces of the past, and she does become an "other," "actor," and a "spectator" of past selves. Assuming these roles enables Clarissa to become aware of the ideological forces that have shaped her in the past, and which are shaping her in the present moment. This awareness holds redemptive potential as Clarissa can begin to consider integrating past, fulfilled selves into her more restricted identity in the present. The scenic act of remembering operates as a transgressive spatial practice, just as

---

[15] See also Zwerdling, who, despite his claims of Woolf's "inward" aesthetics, discusses her criticism of patriarchy and her attempts to show the subject's process of "socialization" within the governing ideology in her novels (128-30; 137).

entering the "tempting bye-street" might operate for the younger Elizabeth; it provides Clarissa with the vantage point necessary to see the patriarchy and the oppressive roles it prescribes for women. However, it is not only vision that it provides; rather, scenic memory offers a new mode of being for contemporary women that is more inclusive and fulfilling. Women need not label themselves dichotomously, stating "I am this" or "I am that," but they may choose to be many selves at once.

The chain of scenic memories creates a conversation between multiple, very different Clarissas that exist in harmony rather than in stark opposition. The dialogic movement across time and space in this passage parallels Clarissa's current feelings of "lack" with past scenes of adolescent freedom, love, and fulfillment. In the present, Clarissa is in her "virginal" bedroom in London, where she has slept apart from her husband since her illness (*MD* 30). She has thoughts of isolation and deficiency and feels as if she has "failed" Richard (*MD* 31). She is aware that "what she lack[s]" is "something central which permeat[es]" (*MD* 31). These thoughts lead her to that "something central": her inability to resist "sometimes yielding to the charm of a woman" (*MD* 31). All of these thoughts of love, especially this "falling in love with women," lead to the recollection of Sally Seton (*MD* 32).

Vital characteristics emerge from Clarissa's memories of Sally. Clarissa remembers that, before Sally came, "she knew nothing about sex—nothing about social problems" (*MD* 32). She remembers "talking in her bedroom at the top of the house [with Sally], talking about life, how they were to reform the world" (*MD* 33). Clarissa associates the time she spent living with Sally with reading Plato, Morris, and Shelley, authors usually reserved for men, authors she had to hide from her aunt by covering them with "brown paper" (*MD* 32). These scenes directly contrast with Clarissa's former life at Bourton and her present life in London. In the present, for example, rather than roaming freely with Sally Seton, she is confined to "an attic room" (*MD* 30). Rather than reading and experiencing knowledge through the liberating texts of Plato and Shelley, authors studied in the traditional English male education but opened to Clarissa in her youth, she is reading Baron Marbot's *Memoirs*. This work provides her with no part in the action and places her outside the male occupations of revolution, conquest, and war (*MD* 30).[16]

---

[16] See Jean-Baptise-Antoine-Marcellin de Marbot, *The Memoirs of Baron de Marbot.* See also Linda Raphael, *Narrative Skepticism*, 126-67. Raphael interprets Marbot's *Memoirs* in *Mrs. Dalloway* differently, positing that Marbot represents "the human experience in war," as does the character of Septimus Smith, and as such, links Clarissa and Septimus as doubles. While I ultimately disagree with Raphael's interpretation of the *Memoirs*, it is possible to view the book's presence as a reminder of Clarissa's own inner turmoil, as she too, like Septimus and even Peter, is grappling with the aftermath of a crumbling culture and ideological system, and its implications for her as a woman. The book, however, when contrasted with the reading materials of her youth, seems to denote a regression into a state of passivity within the patriarchy and serves to materialize Clarissa's subjection to a limiting social and ideological system.

These memories and the contrasts they evoke with Clarissa in the present constitute an image of a past Clarissa: it is an image of a young woman coming to life for the first time through knowledge. Sally exposed Clarissa to everything from politics to literature to sexuality, and she inspired a passion for learning and a love and admiration of women. Clarissa's memories of her relationship with Sally represent a past Clarissa who embraced the possibility of breaking out of patriarchal social roles. This breaking out, this freedom from constraint, is contained ultimately in the kiss Clarissa shares with Sally, a kiss that, in accordance with society's expectations of a young woman such as Clarissa, *must be* and *is*, in fact, interrupted: "Peter faced them [....] It was like running one's face against a granite wall in the darkness! It was shocking; it was horrible! [....] she felt his hostility; his jealousy, his determination to break into their companionship. All this she saw as one sees a landscape in a flash of lightning" (*MD* 35). Joanne Trautmann Banks observes that Woolf's language in this passage—"she saw as one sees a landscape in a flash of lightning"—points to a "light-illuminated" flash of "reality" within the novel (22), or what Woolf describes as a "moment of being" in "Sketch" (73). As a "moment of being," Clarissa's scenic memory exposes the reality of patriarchal oppression, embodied by Peter, whose jealousy and hostility make love between women impossible. Woolf exposes how the patriarchy has shaped Clarissa over time, relocating her to a current position of "lack," by juxtaposing her patriarchal upbringing, moments of liberation with Sally, and reinsertion into patriarchal roles via Peter's interruption.

It is important to note that this same sequence of scenic memory and the dichotomies it illuminates—past Clarissa vs. present Clarissa, country vs. city, freedom vs. confinement, fulfillment vs. "lack," knowledge vs. convention, youth vs. middle age, and single life vs. marriage—establishes that Clarissa is equally and simultaneously *both* of each category, and that a binary way of imagining the self as either "this" or "that" is inadequate. For although her youth is tinged with nostalgic fulfillment, Clarissa also recalls its confinement: at Bourton she is "sheltered," nothing is discussed openly, and she moves within a world of parties, courtship, and convention despite Sally's recklessness (*MD* 32-3). This suggests that her youth is not merely the negative of her present reality, but is its own complex, layered space producing competing versions of Clarissa's "self" in the past, just as she is many selves in the present.

And while she grieves her inability to connect with Richard as she did with Sally and laments that in London "there [is] an emptiness about the heart of life," Clarissa is also fulfilled through marriage (*MD* 30). Prior to this scenic memory, Clarissa arrives home from shopping and is exceedingly happy to reenter her domestic sanctuary, reflecting that "it was her life, and ... she bowed beneath the influence, felt blessed and purified" (*MD* 28). She observes that "Richard, her husband, [is] the foundation of it—of the gay sounds, of the green lights, of the cook even whistling" (*MD* 28-9). Although Clarissa is passionate about Sally, she is also validated through her relationship with Richard, and she admires his "adorable, divine simplicity" (*MD* 117). The novel is clearly critical of the patriarchal institution of marriage and its oppression of women, but Clarissa's appreciation of her marriage suggests it is integral to her present identity. Portions of Clarissa's selfhood are established and maintained through her marriage, a notion perhaps best expressed just after her scenic memories of Sally and Bourton. Richard arrives home after lunch with Lady Bruton wishing to give Clarissa a gift to demonstrate his love for her. He presents her with roses, which Clarissa finds "absolutely lovely," understanding them to be a symbol of the marriage and Richard's love. She takes pleasure in the fact that, like the roses, "first bunched together; now of their own accord starting apart" (*MD* 116), her marriage allows her a brand of integrity and autonomy. She reflects:

> And there is a dignity in people; a solitude; even between husband and wife a gulf; and that one must respect ... for one would not part with it oneself, or take it, against his will, from one's husband, without losing one's independence, one's self-respect—something, after all, priceless. (*MD* 117).

Clarissa finds a new independence through her relationship with Sally, but she finds her marriage, with its conventions and fond detachment, to be a source of fulfillment and self-affirmation, as well. Woolf takes care to portray Sally's subjectivity in a similar manner. At the end of the novel at Clarissa's party, Sally is at once patriarchal dissenter and conventionalist; she is both Sally, the feminist, and Lady Rosseter, proud married mother of five sons. Importantly, Clarissa notes that Sally's "lustre" is gone, but she is still "Sally Seton" (*MD* 167). These two identities converse easily within Sally, as "Lady Rosseter ask[s] herself (who had been Sally Seton)" about old acquaintances she sees at the party (*MD* 176). Through Clarissa and Sally, Woolf proposes a female subjectivity based on inclusivity and multidimensionality, rather than one based on the adherence to debilitating patriarchal binaries.

Recalling the past at Bourton and contrasting it with both the strengths and limitations of her marriage in the present provides Clarissa with a sense of completeness. Her past and present selves have connected, resulting in a moment of vision. By experiencing past and present spaces in dialogue as actor, participant, and spectator, Clarissa realizes the extent to which patriarchal ideology and institutions—which rely upon binary categories—have oppressed and repressed her as a subject. She can then look to the future with a new ability to connect various aspects of her identity; as a result, she can experience a sense of completeness and permanence, of substantiality. Because she has touched and reinstated parts of herself she thought gone or unacceptable, Clarissa can finally collect "the whole of her at one point" and see the face of "Clarissa Dalloway; of herself" in "the very heart of the [present] moment" (*MD* 36).

Importantly, however, Clarissa realizes that to be whole in the sense that her patriarchal society prescribes is in itself a debilitating fiction. She reflects:

> That was her self when some effort, some call on her to be her self, drew the parts together, she alone knew how different, how incompatible and composed so for the world only into one center, one diamond, one woman who sat in her drawing room and made a meeting-point, a radiancy no doubt in some dull lives, a refuge for the lonely to come to, perhaps; she had helped young people, who were grateful to her; had tried to be the same always, never showing a sign of all the other sides of her. (*MD* 36)

Clarissa recognizes the unity the patriarchy demands of her, to be "this" or "that," yet she recognizes this kind of "center" is an oppressive illusion. As her memories have made clear, she contains "other sides" that complicate her identity. Clarissa is at once the radical and the "perfect hostess" (*MD* 60), the wife and the lover of women. And these positions are not presented as exclusive binary categories, but rather as varying aspects of the same, multiplicitous female subject. Through the scenic act of remembering, Clarissa realizes that to be "whole" is impossible, and perhaps undesirable. Transgressive spatial practice via the act of scenic remembering, however, offers a means of celebrating and redeeming one's incompatible selves rather than repressing them; it breaks down oppressive dichotomies. This passage of scenic memory not only exposes how the patriarchy has shaped Clarissa's current subjectivity, it also explores how trans-spatial dialogue can lead to transformative vision, and it posits a model of female subjectivity that is multiple and divergent rather than singular and unified.

Scenic Memory: Spatial Transgression and Lesbian Desire

One of the predominant elements of Clarissa's scenic recollections is her desiring and allowing for eroticized friendships with women. In fact, it is a desire for women in the present that activates Clarissa's memories of the past. Scholars have established the lesbian connotations of the kiss, and have discussed the novel's sexual politics.[17] Little has been said, however, about how desire enacted

---

[17] See, for example, the works of Tonya Krouse, Tuzyline Jita Allan, Eileen Barrett, Theresa de Lauretis, Jeremy Tambling, and Judith Roof, "The Match in the Crocus." I owe my reading of the kiss as a moment of lesbian eros to these critics' various discussions of the subversive sexual politics of the novel.

via memory alters Clarissa's understanding of identity and perception of herself as a subject.[18] In *Modernism, Memory, and Desire: T.S. Eliot and Virginia Woolf,* Gabrielle McIntire argues that "to remember *is* to desire [and] to desire *is* to remember" (9). Memory and desire in this reading are mutually constitutive, and they both demand a certain level of awareness, or engagement, on the part of the remembering and desiring subject. McIntire's reading of the interaction between desire and memory helps clarify that, as Clarissa remembers, she becomes aware of what it is she desires. Remembering creates Clarissa as an active participant in her desires, engaging a component of her subjectivity that is repressed under the patriarchy, which demands marriage and heterosexual desire. Hence, to remember scenically is to transgress spatially *and* sexually; it is also to reimagine a subject position for women that exists outside of heterosexual roles.

In "'Here was One Room, There was Another': The Room, Authorship, and Feminine Desire in *A Room of One's Own* and *Mrs. Dalloway*," Christina Stevenson argues that the space of Clarissa's attic bedroom "both works to disrupt the fantasy of autonomous individuality and provide space for the expression of a desire outside of masculine demand" (122-23). She claims that "the room emerges in the novel both as a representation of and compensation for femininity's superficiality; not as a space of unplumbable depths but as a network of possible connections" (Stevenson 123). Stevenson's discussion of the bedroom provides a convincing analysis of Clarissa's subjectivity as multiple and divergent, rather than singularly composed and bounded. This kind of model of subjectivity allows for the possibility of "the desire outside of masculine demand" (Stevenson 123). Stevenson's argument that Woolf "Conceiv[es of] the room as a space of surfaces" rather than impenetrable depths (121), however, does not account for the critical movement between past and present spaces and temporal zones that integrate Clarissa's sexually deviant desire into the patriarchal spaces of the present. I propose that scenic memory, which allows for both surface and depth, past and present, and the roles of spectator *and* actor, is what enables Clarissa to begin to comprehend her identity as something that exists beyond the realm of patriarchal definitions in a new space of multiplicity. Clarissa is not "nothing at all" or mere surface (Stevenson 127); rather, she is a myriad of contradicting selves that do, at least to some extent, form a sense of redemptive, if socially and sexually deviant, identity in the present.

Clarissa's realizations about the past lead her to reassess her relationship with her husband and her position within the heterosexual institution of marriage in the

---

[18] The exception is Judith Roof's reading of the kiss and Clarissa Dalloway in *A Lure of Knowledge*. Although she does not discuss memory, Roof argues that moments of same-sex desire are not always meant literally in *Mrs. Dalloway,* but instead function abstractly as "a desire for desire" (14). Roof reads Clarissa's feelings for Sally as symbolic of agency; by recognizing her desire through awareness of a "lack," Clarissa gains insight into her identity.

present, which then gives her the ability to move on with her life and party as a transformed subject. Although, as I have noted, Clarissa's marriage is a source of happiness, enabling her to be in the midst of what she loves most, life and society (*MD* 117-18), and although she loves Richard in her own way, the novel makes it clear that the marriage is not sexually fulfilling. Clarissa states "she [has] failed" Richard and that she has a "cold spirit" (*MD* 31). She cannot comprehend feeling for him that "something warm which broke up surfaces and rippled the cold contact of man and woman" (*MD* 31). Thus, Clarissa's current relationship with her husband, while affectionate, is sexually detached, and at times even ridiculous. For example, Clarissa often hears Richard coming up to his room at night "in his socks" dropping "his hot-water bottle and [swearing]," causing her to break out in laughter at the idea of him and of their marriage (*MD* 31). Clarissa can only perceive sexual "warmth" with women, and hence her memories of Sally integrate a sexual identity into Clarissa's present social role of wife, adding additional dimensions to her sense of self (*MD* 33).

While the language used to describe Clarissa's relationship with her husband is devoid of sexual passion ("nun," "attic room," "virginal," "cold"), Clarissa's language describing women is erotic and corporeal. For women, Clarissa feels "something central…something warm which broke up surfaces" (MD 31). She describes her connection with women as:

> A sudden revelation, a tinge like a blush which one tried to check and then, as it spread, one yielded to its expansion, and rushed to the farthest verge and there quivered and felt the world come closer, swollen with some astonishing significance, some pressure of rapture, which split its thin skin and gushed and poured with an extraordinary alleviation over the cracks and sores! (*MD* 31)

The contrast between the two spaces and relationships serve as a foundation for the competing identities, or subjectivities, which emerge in this scene. While patriarchal marriage is sexually unfulfilling, erotic female companionship is orgasmically liberating.

Clarissa endows her kiss with Sally with "religious feeling" (*MD* 35), but unlike her marriage to Richard, which is also described using religious terms—it "blesse[s] and purifie[s]"—this kiss must be "wrapped up" (*MD* 35). Woolf uses kisses in the text to illustrate how lesbian desire and love between women exist outside of patriarchal authority. In a parallel kiss, Hugh Whitbread locks Sally in a closet at Bourton and forces himself upon her. Both Sally and Peter recall this second kiss at various points throughout the novel (*MD* 71-72, 177, 185). While Clarissa's kiss with Sally is a "religious" moment of beauty, Hugh's kiss with Sally, as Makiko Minow-Pinkney has argued, is an example of a male patriarch using sexual force as a means of dominating female subjectivity. The kiss occurs shortly after Hugh and Sally have had an argument about women's rights. Sally claims that the kiss was meant "to punish her for saying that women should have votes" (*MD* 177). This kiss does not stem from a desire for love, acceptance, and freedom; it stems, on the contrary, from the need to exert control and assert dominance. Both the interruption of Clarissa and Sally's kiss by Peter and the kiss forced upon Sally by Hugh ultimately create Clarissa and Sally as patriarchal subjects. These kisses create moments of movement in the text, illuminating when the female characters become positioned as subservient to men within hierarchical social systems. Transgressing via scenic memory, however, can reintegrate lesbian desire and inclusive relationships into women's lives in positive ways. It also makes their oppression visible in ways that can empower them to conceive of alternative positions and roles. Desire is a pivotal point in patriarchal society: what one desires gives insight into one's position within the over-arching system, since it determines whether one is a wife, a mother, or something outside of these accepted categories. Consequently, Clarissa Dalloway's memories and desires function as subversive spaces in the novel. By juxtaposing memory spaces with present spaces, Woolf imagines a process of remembering for women that is redemptive and inclusive, rather than repressive. Women need not limit themselves to these categories, but can fill social roles even as they acknowledge and celebrate other vital parts of their identities and desires.

Conclusion

Mrs. Dalloway's bye-street aesthetic and use of spatial memory makes the personal political by offering women a new way of existing in the present moment that is not based on the repression or negation of counter-normative selves and desires. Within the novel itself, spatial memory allows Clarissa to escape restrictive roles associated with the patriarchy; she does not have to identify as "this" or "that," but can instead simply *be*, as the novel's closing line implies: "For there she was" (*MD* 190). Memory is used not only to propose a new model of female subjectivity, but also an ontology of trans-spatial, trans-temporal inclusiveness, a mode of living that would eradicate binary oppositions and instead create new, freer spaces for women (and perhaps men) to exist on their own plural terms. The subversive, ontological effects of spatial memory in the novel lend new meaning to Clarissa's description of her party as an "offering" (*MD* 118). The party is not hosted out of social duty, but rather is the celebration of "life" that Clarissa so much loves, and that, to a large extent, defines her (*MD* 118). It is a celebration of life in general, but also of Clarissa's multifaceted identity and vitality.

The ontological impact of Woolf's bye-street aesthetic has real-world consequences for future generations of women, who might choose to live outside of debilitating categories in a new landscape of mobility and social progress.

Paralleling her daughter, Clarissa enjoyed taking omnibus rides through London in her youth, accompanied by Peter. Clarissa loved the top of the bus, as it made her feel "everywhere," supporting her "theory" that "since our apparitions, the part of us which appears, are so momentary compared with the other, the unseen part of us, which spreads wide, the unseen might survive, be recovered somehow attached to this person or that, or even haunting certain places after death" (*MD* 149). Woolf's use of spatial memory enacts Clarissa's theory at the level of form; scenic memory "recovers" the "unseen" but still vital parts of Clarissa, allowing her to remain alive in the face of death.

Yet Woolf's inclusion of Elizabeth's omnibus ride contrasts with her mother's, suggesting faith in political change. While Clarissa rides with Peter companionably, Elizabeth "step[s] forward and most competently board[s] the omnibus, in front of everybody," in an act of political defiance against convention and patriarchal expectations (*MD* 132). At Clarissa's party, Sally notes that Elizabeth is "unlike Clarissa at her age," again suggesting that Elizabeth may, in fact, be destined for more than a brief, youthful interlude of freedom (*MD* 188). Elizabeth's mobility and her "oriental" demeanor suggest that Woolf was optimistic that more inclusive models of female subjectivity may alter social as well as personal landscapes. While Clarissa gains self-awareness and fulfillment through the transgressive bye-streets of memory, Elizabeth and women of her generation may enact this new subjectivity as they move through a shifting, more inclusive political landscape. Whether at the level of the personal or the political, Woolf makes it clear that to transgress spatially—to tread the "queer alleys" and "tempting bye-streets" of memory—is to strive, at the most basic level of everyday lived experience, for political, social, and individual freedom, and for models of female subjectivity that invite fuller self-expression.

I would like to thank Dr. Georgia Johnston for her guidance as I drafted this essay. Her input was invaluable.

Works Cited

Allan, Tuzyline Jita. "The Death of Sex and the Soul in *Mrs. Dalloway* and Nella Larsen's *Passing*." *Virginia Woolf: Lesbian Readings*, edited by Eileen Barrett and Patricia Cramer, New York UP, 1997, pp. 95-113.

Banfield, Ann. "Remembrance and Tense Past." *The Cambridge Companion to the Modernist Novel*, edited by Morag Shiach, Cambridge UP, 2007, pp. 48-64.

Banks, Joanne Trautmann. "Through a Glass, Longingly." *Trespassing Boundaries: Virginia Woolf's Short Fiction*, edited by Kathryn N. Benzel and Ruth Hoberman, Palgrave Macmillan, 2004, pp. 17-24.

Barrett, Eileen. "Unmasking Lesbian Passion: The Inverted World of Mrs. Dalloway." *Virginia Woolf: Lesbian Readings,* edited by Eileen Barrett and Patricia Cramer, New York UP, 1997, pp. 146-64.

de Lauretis, Teresa. *The Practice of Love: Lesbian Sexuality and Perverse Desire.* Indiana UP, 1994.

Dick, Susan. "The Tunelling Process: Some Aspects of Virginia Woolf's Use of Memory and the Past." *Virginia Woolf: New Critical Essays,* edited by Patricia Clements and Isobel Grundy, Vision P, 1983, pp. 176-99.

Diment, Galya. *The Autobiographical Novel of Co-Consciousness: Goncharov, Woolf, and Joyce.* UP of Florida, 1994.

Docherty, Thomas. *Reading (Absent) Character: Towards a Theory of Characterization in Fiction.* Oxford UP, 1983.

Edmondson, Annalee. "Narrativizing Characters in *Mrs. Dalloway*." *Journal of Modern Literature* vol. 36, no. 1, 2012, pp. 17-36.

Falcetta, Jennie-Rebecca. "Geometries of Space and Time: The Cubist London of Mrs. Dalloway." *Woolf Studies Annual* vol. 13, 2007, pp. 111-36.

Fernald, Anne E. *Virginia Woolf: Feminism and the Reader.* Palgrave Macmillan, 2006.

Frank, Joseph. "Spatial Form in Modern Literature: An Essay in Three Parts." *The Sewanee Review* vol. 53, nos. 2-4, Spring-Autumn, 1945.

Groover, Kristina. "Taking the Door off the Hinges: Liminal Space in Virginia Woolf's *Mrs. Dalloway*." *The Literary London Journal*, vol 6, no. 1, March 2008, Literarylondon.org.

Hungerford, Edward A. "'My Tunnelling Process': The Method of *Mrs. Dalloway*." *Modern Fiction Studies* vol. 3, no. 2, 1957, pp. 164-7.

Johnston, Georgia. "Politics of Retrospective Space in Virginia Woolf's Memoir 'A Sketch of the Past.'" *Mapping the Self: Space, Identity, Discourse in British Auto/Biography,* edited by Frederic Regard. Saint-Etienne UP, 2003, pp. 285-96.

Krouse, Tonya. *The Opposite of Desire: Sex and Pleasure in the Modernist Novel.* Lexington Books, 2009.

Love, Jean O. *Worlds in Consciousness: Mythopoetic Thought in the Novels of Virginia Woolf.* U of California P, 1970.

Marbot, Jean-Baptiste-Antoine-Marcelin, Baron de. *The Memoirs of Baron de Marbot, Late Lieutenant-General in the French Army,* translated by Arthur John Butler. 5th ed. Longmans, Green and Co., 1903.

McIntire, Gabrielle. *Modernism, Memory, and Desire: T.S. Eliot and Virginia Woolf.* Cambridge UP, 2008.

Minow-Pinkney, Makiko. *Virginia Woolf & the Problem of the Subject.* Rutgers UP, 1987.

Nalbantian, Suzanne. *Memory in Literature: From Rousseau to Neuroscience.* Palgrave Macmillan, 2003.

Raphael, Linda S. *Narrative Skepticism: Moral Agency and Representations of Consciousness in Fiction.* Fairleigh Dickinson UP, 2001.

Roof, Judith. *A Lure of Knowledge: Lesbian Sexuality and Theory.* Columbia UP, 1991.

———. "The Match in the Crocus: Representations of Lesbian Sexuality." *Discontented Discourses: Feminism/Textual Intervention/Psychoanalysis*, edited by Marleen S. Barr and Richard Feldstein, U of Illinois P, 1989, pp. 100–116.

Rummel, Andrea. "People in the Crowd: British Modernism, the Metropolis, and the Flâneur." *Literature in Society,* edited by Regina Rudaityte, Cambridge Scholars Publishing, 2012, pp. 57-76.

Scott, Bonnie Kime. "Introduction." *Mrs. Dalloway by Virginia Woolf,* edited by Bonnie Kime Scott, Harcourt, 2005, pp. xxxv-lxvii.

Stevanato, Savina. *Visuality and Spatiality in Virginia Woolf's Fiction.* Oxford UP, 2005.

Stevenson, Christina. "'Here was One Room, There was Another': The Room, Authorship, and Feminine Desire in *A Room of One's Own* and *Mrs. Dalloway*." Pacific Coast Philology vol. 49, no. 1, 2014, pp. 112-32.

Tambling, Jeremy. "Repression in Mrs. Dalloway's London." *Essays in Criticism* vol. 39, no. 2, 1989, pp. 137-155.

Thacker, Andrew. *Moving Through Modernity: Space and Geography in Modernism.* Manchester UP, 2003.

Walsh, Rebecca. *The Geopoetics of Modernism.* UP of Florida, 2015.

Weinstein, Arnold. *Recovering Your Story: Proust, Joyce, Woolf, Faulkner, Morrison.* Random House, 2006.

Wise, Sarah. *The Blackest Streets: The Life and Death of a Victorian Slum.* Bodley Head, Random House, 2008.

Woolf, Virginia. "A Sketch of the Past." *Moments of Being: A Collection of Autobiographical Writing*, edited by Jeanne Schulkind. 2nd ed. Harcourt, 1985, pp. 61-159.

———. *The Diary of Virginia Woolf,* edited by Anne Olivier Bell. Vols. 1-3 Harcourt Brace Jovanovich, 1977-1980.

———. *Mrs. Dalloway.* 1925. Harcourt, 2005.

———. *Three Guineas.* 1938. Harcourt, 2006.

Zwerdling, Alex. *Virginia Woolf and the Real World.* U of California P, 1986.

Textbook Greek: Thoby Stephen in *Jacob's Room*
Amanda Golden

When Virginia Woolf's narrator first invites readers into Jacob's room, she concludes her survey of its contents by noting that he had "all the usual textbooks" (38). Contemporary readers of *Jacob's Room* (1922) may have known academic publishers like George Bell & Sons, with offices in Covent Garden, selling books in Cambridge, New York, and Bombay. But Woolf's twenty-first century readers might overlook the final reference in her catalogue. Woolf's sense of a typical assortment of student books may have been based on those that filled some of the shelves in her home, from the Clarendon Press student editions of Greek plays that she translated to the texts that her brother Thoby Stephen inscribed at Clifton College and Cambridge University. These volumes, now in Virginia and Leonard Woolf's library at Washington State University, shaped the academic landscape that Jacob inhabited. Beginning with the genre of the textbook, the books in Woolf's library allow us to see that her depiction of modern life depended upon the materiality of handling, translating, and publishing of classical texts.[1]

When Woolf and other members of her family translated Greek, they used their personal copies as workbooks, underlining words and adding their own translations in the margins (figures 1-3). While she wrote in books as she translated, Woolf did not tend to do so as she read other kinds of texts, and scholars are familiar with the notebooks that provided what Hermione Lee has called Woolf's "system of annotation" (406). In an early sketch on ["writing in the margin"], Woolf expressed her well-known dislike of writing in books, primarily those that others owned (Golden, "Woolf's Marginalia").[2] Woolf's response to writing in books has led scholars to investigate whether she did so and what her library can tell us about her handling, collecting, and constructing of books.[3] Critics have also addressed the significance of Woolf's own travels in Greece and the plays to which she alludes.[4] Turning to

---

[1] Shifting to the academic publishing industry draws new attention to the marketing and distribution of Greek texts, even as Fernald points out that in Woolf's time that "knowledge of Greek [was] cultural capital" (17) and "Greek in particular was seen as a suitably impractical genteel pursuit" (20). Regarding Woolf and material culture, see also Brown.
[2] The text of Woolf's "[writing in the margin]" sketch was published in Golden, "Virginia Woolf's Marginalia Manuscript."
[3] Daugherty has considered the contents of Woolf's library before she married Leonard Woolf, noting volumes she learned to stamp in gold leaf. Sparks has addressed London's presence in Woolf's library, and Gillespie addresses Woolf's writing in, and her family members' drawings in books in her introduction to *The Library of Leonard and Virginia Woolf: A Short-Title Catalog.*
[4] Regarding Woolf's travels, see Dubino; for the plays Woolf translated, see Fernald, and Prins, "OTOTOTOI"; on the influence of Jane Harrison and Janet Case, see Marcus, Prins,

Woolf's Greek texts, this essay argues that academic practices and materials, from her approach to translating to the editions she read, contributed to the development of *Jacob's Room*.[5]

Print culture studies have led to new considerations of publication history, ranging from Lise Jaillant's *Modernism, Middlebrow and the Literary Canon: The Modern Library Series, 1917-1955* (2016) to studies of the Hogarth Press.[6] Turning our attention to the marketing, publishing, and distributing of late nineteenth and early twentieth century classical texts illuminates the significance of academic presses for Woolf and her contemporaries. Even early in her career Woolf was familiar with the publishing industry, perhaps due to her half-brother Gerald Duckworth's firm, and she noted in "Venice," her 1909 review of *Pompeo Molmenti's Venice: Its Individual Growth from the Earliest Beginnings to the Fall of the Republic* (1906-1908), that "The Greek and Latin classics came from the Aldine Press; scholars from Constantinople lived in Venice and taught the wonderful dead languages; private people began to store books in 'cupboards and on shelves of carved walnut' and the State founded the great library in the magnificent building of Sansovino" (E1 245). Beginning in 1494, Woolf recounts, the Aldine Press's efforts led to the teaching, exchanging, and preserving of classical texts.

In *The Death of the Book: Modernist Novels and the Time of Reading* (2016), John Lurz gives new treatment to Woolf's attention in her fiction to books as such, but does not take into account Woolf's use of her own library or her annotating strategies. After considering Clarissa Dalloway's reading of *Cymbeline* in a shop window, Lurz argues that the whole of *Mrs. Dalloway* "views the mental world of linguistic deciphering and imagination as bound up with, indeed dependent on the physical or perceptual relationship Clarissa has with that language's material support" (2). Lurz emphasizes the production, publication, and circulation of texts (10); apart from the "the format of the book," he focuses on "the book facing the reader," without attending to the ways that readers alter books (7). These factors shaped Woolf's encounters with Greek texts, but she also underlined and annotated texts as she translated them, adding layers to their pages in the process of determining their meaning.[7]

---

and Mills; on academic institutions, see Cuddy-Keane; regarding Jacob, war, and the implications of the Greeks regarding sexuality, see Neverow, and Moffat (focusing on Forster).

[5] Annotating itself is an academic practice, as Jackson notes: "Writing notes in response to a text appears to be a habit acquired at school . . . Under instruction, children learn to mark the text conservatively, and to use the endpapers for institutionally approved, standard kinds of note-taking" (21).

[6] For considerations of the Hogarth Press, see Hammill and Hussey and Southworth.

[7] Regarding Woolf's *Agamemnon* notebook, see also Golden, "A Brief Note in the Margin."

Yopie Prins, by contrast, focuses on Woolf's construction of an *Agamemnon* notebook, pasting published text of the play onto her own bound pages, and annotating the text as she translated. In design, Prins observes that while Woolf "had chosen to transcribe Verrall's text, the layout of her notebook looks more like Trevelyan's translation. Instead of placing Greek on the left page and English on the right, she followed the format of the acting editions of the Cambridge Greek play, with Greek on the right page and English on the left" ("OTOTOTOI" 180). Prins sees this change as leading to a more complicated reading practice as Woolf translated on the opposing blank page and in the margins of the Greek text. It also shows her decisions as she constructed an edition, which, even if Prins imagines it was "private," could have been composed with an audience in mind as Woolf herself had become a publisher (173).[8] When she first worked with Janet Case, Prins notes, Case "was preparing her own translation of *Prometheus Bound* for publication in 1905: an inexpensive pocket-sized edition . . . With Greek and English text on facing pages" ("Sexual Politics" 171). The dual language format of Woolf's notebook also resembled the editions "that Woolf loved to read in the Loeb Classical Library. . . . With ancient Greek text and modern English translation on facing pages" ("OTOTOTOI" 181). Prins's comparison of Woolf's efforts to those of the Cambridge and Loeb series allows us to see her potential edition as an intervention in the form and content of the classics publishing industry. In different ways, Lurz also cites the ways that typographical and stylistic experimentation coincide in *Jacob's Room*, with its "unconventional page layout in which empty spaces of varying sizes separate the scenes of the narrative, a printing decision that was significantly tied to the inauguration of the [Hogarth] press in 1917" (23).

Jacob's Room is an attempt to render the living of life during the first two decades of the twentieth century. Its narrative leaves much unexplained, yet the novel depicts scenes and sensations from new vantage points. Because of modernist attempts to imagine the life of the mind, Dirk Van Hulle has argued in *Modern Manuscripts: The Extended Mind and Creative Undoing from Darwin to Beckett and Beyond* (2014) that many examples from literary modernism make the material

---

[8] Prins demonstrates the extent to which Woolf was informed about different approaches to translating, and yet Prins may not be giving Woolf enough credit for her response to these contexts: "when Woolf returned to Aeschylus a decade later, the translation she chose to transcribe for her *Agamemnon* notebook was not by Headlam, but by Professor Verrall. Known as 'the Great Verrall', he was praised . . . for a poetic sense of Aeschylean language[.] . . . In her notebook Woolf drew on Verrall's authority to enlarge her conception of Greek, and 'extend her reach' into English as well. Choosing Verrall over Headlam, she seems to have taken sides in a notorious debate between the two scholars about editing Aeschylus, in which Headlam claimed philological expertise and Verrall literary sensibility. . . . In contrast to Headlam and Verrall and their public debates about editing Aeschylus, she made this private 'edition' for herself to transpose their self-authorizing glosses into the unauthorized *glossolalia* of Ladies' Greek" ("OTOTOTOI" 173).

records of composition and reading, including drafts and marginalia, vital to understanding a writer's "extended mind" (149). He clarifies that because "manuscripts reflect the process of thinking and writing there is a connection between the act of preserving these traces of the production of stories . . . and methods of evoking the characters' consciousness" (4). We can see the outcome of this process in *Jacob's Room's* stream-of-consciousness. Woolf scholars have long been interested in her composition practices, but Van Hulle's description of what manuscripts can capture should also inspire us to study the contents of Woolf's and her brother's libraries.

Van Hulle underscores that when readers write in books, "marginalia are not so much a copy of the mind but rather . . . a *part* of the mind" (153). Inscribing her books as she translated, Woolf practiced what Emily Dalgarno characterizes as "an approach that reveals . . . [Woolf's] dependence on a now outdated model that envisions the substitution of one word for another" (3). Woolf's translations in her Greek texts resemble Edward Pargiter's process of translating Antigone at Oxford University in *The Years* (1937). Edward

> read; and made a note; then he read again. . . . He caught phrase after phrase exactly, firmly, more exactly, he noted, making a brief note in the margin, than the night before. Little negligible words now revealed shades of meaning, which altered the meaning. He made another note; *that* was the meaning. His own dexterity in catching the phrase plumb in the middle gave him a thrill of excitement. There it was, clean and entire. But he must be precise; exact; even his little scribbled notes must be clear as print. (47)[8]

Woolf's example of annotating in *The Years* demonstrates what Van Hulle sees as a more basic interaction between writers' minds and their physical surroundings. Compared with *The Years, Jacob's Room* has a sparser narrative economy. *The Years* fills in gaps where Woolf wished that she "could have screwed Jacob up tighter" (*D2* 210). In *Jacob's Room*, the narrator's gaze rests on items for an instant before turning its attention elsewhere.

Considering Woolf's handling of her library sheds light on the material contexts that informed her aesthetic choices and development of character in her fiction. In "A Sketch of the Past," Woolf distinguished Thoby as "not, as I am, a breaker off of single words, or sentences, not a note taker. He was more casual, rough and ready and comprehensive" (*MOB* 138). Gesturing here to her reading notebooks, Woolf's phrasing also evokes her practice of isolating words as she translated Greek. Focusing on Woolf's "major texts from the mid-1920s," after the publication of *Jacob's Room* in 1922, Anne Fernald has argued that "During these years, Woolf emphasized our distance from Greece: how little we know of the ancient Greek language and culture and the mystery of our continued fascination and attraction with it nonetheless. Her metaphor for this

---

[9] For further treatment of *Antigone* in *The Years*, see Saloman.

imperfect knowledge was the distinctly modernist one of the fragment" (18). Woolf did not just, as Fernald finds, use "images of cutting and slicing to describe Greek" (29-30), "breaking off" and altering texts was part of her engagement with language.[10]

While Woolf's sense of Greek and Greece was inherently incomplete, her library presents a landscape to which we can return. But even as a wealth of materials can provide depth and continuity, archival materials remain glimpses of what we can never access in its entirety. In *The Boundaries of the Literary Archive: Reclamation and Representation*, Lisa Stead introduces Paul Voss and Marta Werner's understanding of "the archive" as "both a physical site—an institutional space enclosed by protective walls—and an imaginative site—a conceptual space whose boundaries are forever changing" (2). Stead points out that "Archives are incomplete sites of knowledge, necessarily fragmentary and changeable" (2). In the reading room at Washington State, one can consider Woolf's and Thoby's libraries together, gaining a sense of the ways both siblings navigated language differently, despite their similar tools and techniques.

Woolf would have honed her translating practices as she studied with Case, whom, critics have noted, Woolf described as "no sentimentalist: she had her grammar at her fingertips – she used to pull me up ruthlessly in the middle of some beautiful passage with 'Mark the ar'" (*PA* 182).[11] "Mark" evokes the act of making and the result of a physical impression, as in the title of Woolf's later story, "The Mark on the Wall" (1917), or those Woolf added to pages as she translated.[12] It is likely that she was referring to what Prins calls "the Victorian denigration of 'Lady's Greek, without the accents'" ("OTOTOTOI" 170). In an obituary for her tutor, Woolf elaborated that "'If the pupil were destined to remain an amateur, Janet Case accepted the fact' and then 'the grammar was shut and the play opened. Somehow the masterpieces of Greek drama were stormed, without grammar, without accents, but somehow, under her compulsion, so sane and yet so stimulating, out they shone, if inaccessible still supremely desirable'" (qtd. in "OTOTOTOI" 170). Following Case's lead separated Woolf from the readers who inspired Case to put the grammar aside.[13]

---

[10] Woolf also cut pages from an existing play to form her *Agamemnon* notebook; a stack of discarded paper strips remains between its pages in the Berg Collection. See Golden, "A Brief Note in the Margin."

[11] Fernald sees this passage as demonstrating that Woolf "strove to find a balance between her love of poetry and the accuracy demanded by tutors and translators" (19-20).

[12] See Van Hulle's reading of the way that the speaker of Woolf's "The Mark on the Wall" shifts between her thoughts and the wall.

[13] Prins points out that "While girls might not have been trained to write ancient Greek with the proper accents or to pronounce it with the proper accentuation, an amateur's understanding made it seem even more desirable, accentuating the passion of Lady's Greek beyond a (merely) scholarly reading" ("OTOTOTOI" 170). Elsewhere, Prins notes that Woolf "recalled

Even as she adopted the practice, Woolf's reference to Edward's "little scribbled notes" in *The Years* may also suggest that her dislike of writing in books extended to doing so to translate.[14] Emily James has argued that Woolf's use of the word "scribbling" does not tend to be positive, and is reminiscent of Nathaniel Hawthorne's "scribbling women" (281). James finds that "Scribbling, for Woolf, is an early stage in the writing process, before revising, editing, or publishing. A publisher herself, Woolf does not glorify this stage of writing; she refers dismissively to the 'scribbling' of female writers" (280). James stresses that "scribbling implies haste and sloppiness; such undisciplined script lacks the clarity and reproducibility of type. Accordingly, scribbled texts reside in the margins of word production; untyped and unpublished, they include jotted notes, marginalia, and first drafts" (280). Edward's youth, as well as Woolf's and Thoby's early translations of Greek, resonate with James's proposal that "If scribbling and scrawling are early stages of writing, then they are also suggestive of childhood or childishness" (281). The contrast that Woolf draws between her approach and her brother's "rougher" style in "A Sketch of the Past," for instance, is visible at times in their Greek texts. But annotators are also subject to the difficulty of writing clearly in the spaces of pages filled with lines of text. Woolf's and Thoby's translations (Figures 1-3) respond to this spatial challenge, preserving what may be early thoughts in a small hand.

Thoby also often added sketches to the inside covers of his books, like those of birds in his copy of Pindar (Figure 4), and shared his father's inclination to draw in the margins of his reading (see Gillespie). In "A Sketch of the Past," Woolf recalled Thoby as

> not clever; but gifted. And his gifts were natural to him, naturally it came
> to him to look distinguished; to be silent, to draw. He would take a sheet
> of paper, hold it at an odd angle and begin easily, naturally drawing a bird,

---

in her early journals how Miss Case 'procured a Grammar, & bade me start with the very first exercise' and 'never failed to point out, with perfect good humour that my exercises were detestable'" ("Sexual Politics" 171). Prins adds that "Although Miss Case never seemed to miss a case (grammatically speaking), Woolf also describes how 'she would spend a whole lesson in defining the relation of Aeschylus towards Fate' and proved herself 'a really valiant strong minded woman. . . . We strayed enough from grammar to let me see this'" (171)

[14] Colleen Lamos explains that "Woolf's relation to Greek seems paradoxical. On the one hand, she inherited it as a masculine tradition against which she fought bitterly throughout her life. On the other hand, Greek was a mode of intimacy with her teachers, lovers, friends, and brother—the means through which she formed and articulated some of her most passionate attachments. Rachel Bowlby describes this 'ambiguous' relation as Woolf's "'double vision' of Greek" (154-5). Fernald also "offer[s] a new way to understand how Woolf retained and transformed a tradition she loved into a source of resistance to patriarchy" (12-13) and notes that "her female tutors introduced her to a counterhistory of Greek heroines while providing a living model of how the discipline of Greek can be open to all" (18).

> not where I expected, but at some queer place, so that I could not guess how the bird would become a bird. He was not precocious; but won prizes now and then, yet failed to win a scholarship at Eton. His Latin and Greek were very rough, I think the masters said. But his essays showed great intelligence. Yet it was through him I first heard about the Greeks. (125)

In the novel, we see Clara Durrant's admiration of the fact that Jacob "gives himself no airs" (*JR* 72). And we learn that "Jacob knew no more Greek than served him to stumble through a play" (78). Both Jacob and Thoby combine aesthetics and impulse. In his volume of John Donne's poetry, Jacob "had marked the things he liked . . . and they were savage enough" (170). But in his sketch of a bird, Thoby questioned how one might go about depicting life, which materializes in Woolf's approach to *Jacob's Room*.

In *Jacob's Room*, texts capture remnants of readers' inclinations. Jacob becomes frustrated in the Scilly Isles with "those little thin paper editions [of Shakespeare] whose pages get ruffled, or stuck together with sea-water" (46). And we get a sense of his taste when "Sometimes Jacob, choosing a very fine pen, made a correction in the margin" (21). While Woolf had critiqued kinds of annotators, in *Jacob's Room* she granted them greater discrimination. Jacob possesses more restraint than his predecessor in "[writing in the margin]" whose corrections in his books suggested that he was "conscientious & possibly useful, but, we conceive, of a precise & pedantic spirit" ("Woolf's Marginalia" 117). The narrator of *Jacob's Room* later draws our attention to "Mrs. Durrant, [who] sleepless as usual, scored a mark by the side of certain lines in the *Inferno*" (*JR* 78). In her late night reading of Dante, Mrs. Durrant presents a refined version of Woolf's reader in "[writing in the margin]" who drew lines beside stanzas of "minor poets" "to give expression, to some transient emotion" ("Woolf's Marginalia" 117). In doing so, Mrs. Durrant leaves a physical imprint on her reading of the classics.

If *Jacob's Room* is an elegy for Thoby Stephen, then his library would have provided vestiges of his intellectual life. And when Woolf wanted to understand the education that she was not able to receive, Thoby's books and other books in her home would have provided an introduction.[15] Thoby's focus on the classics, however, might have lacked elements that Woolf desired to study and that she continues to envision for the future of education in *A Room of One's Own* (1929). It was when crafting *Jacob's Room* that she began to articulate some of

---

[15] One copy of Aeschylus includes a message in the back: "Thoby Stephen was a magnificent fellow . . . He was before me at Trinity." The book has a bookplate from Henry C. Adams of Magdalene College. The annotations and drawings in the book may have been Thoby's and the book's owner may have given it to the Woolfs. MASC.

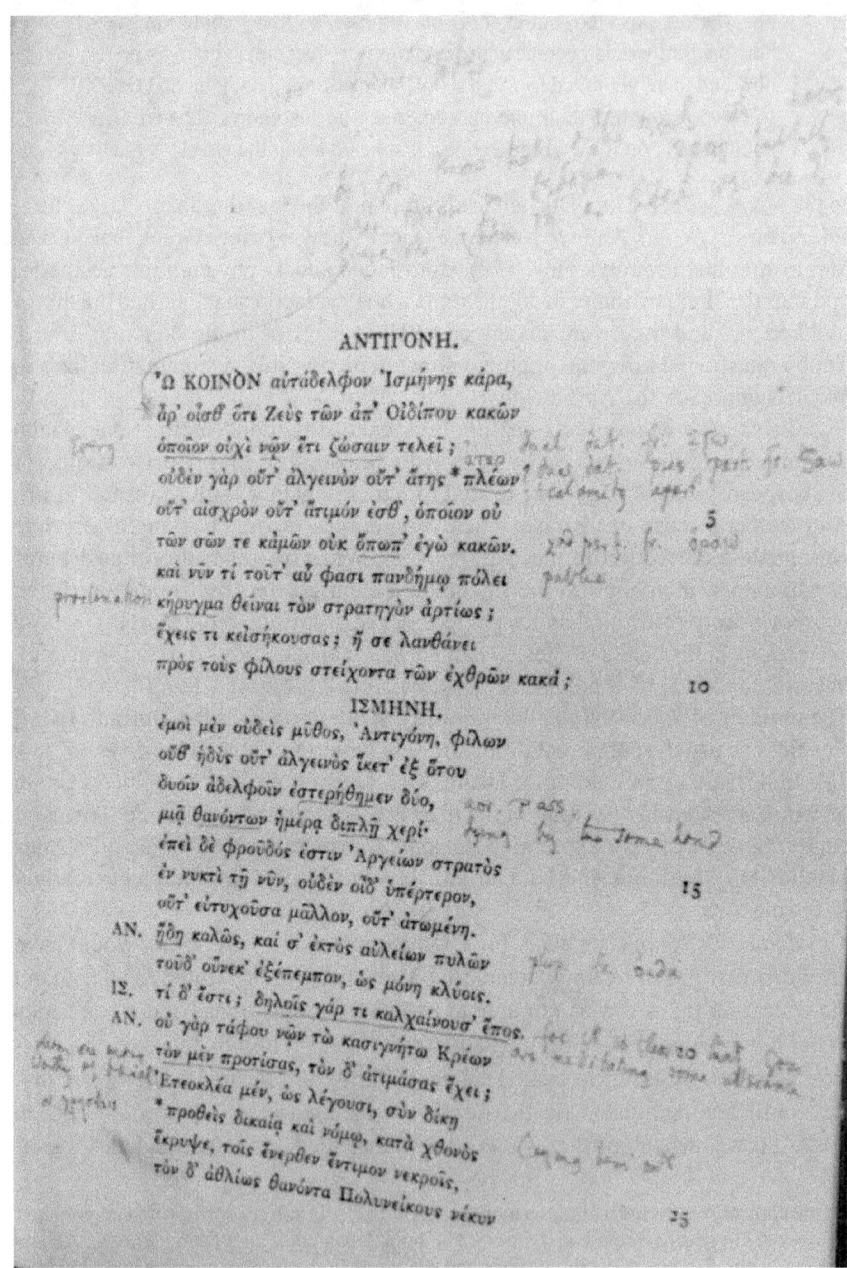

Figure 1: Virginia Woolf's annotations in Antigone. *MASC.*

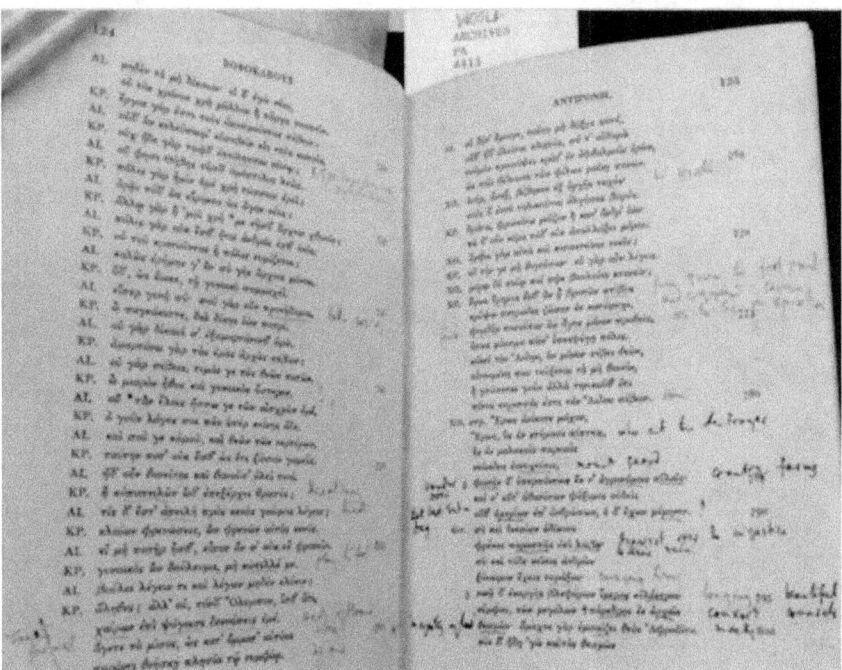

Figure 2: Woolf's copy of Antigone. *MASC.*

these sentiments, shifting from the "extended mind" to the "enormous mind" (*JR* 113) of the canon that Julia questions in the British Museum.[16]

Jacob's Room connects the physicality of books with the experience of reading, as "Each has his past shut in him like the leaves of a book known to him by heart" (65). Understanding some of the ways that Woolf's own reading existed in conversation with the strategies of those with whom she lived allows us to broaden our sense of the materials shaping her life narratives.

Textbooks

When Woolf introduces the books in Jacob's library, they appear at first to stand in the place of a more traditional introduction to facets of his character. In reality, they are eclectic and somewhat inexplicable, not unlike a reader or writer's own library.[17] Woolf even interrupts her catalogue with an observation to this effect,

---

[16] Jane Goldman observes in a recent review: "*Hellenism and Loss* thereby also shows that Greek studies fueled in Woolf 'a deep-rooted intellectual preoccupation with asymmetrical educational opportunities at the turn of the twentieth century'" (391).

[17] This evasion presents an extension of Quigley's sense that "Rather than providing 'clear,

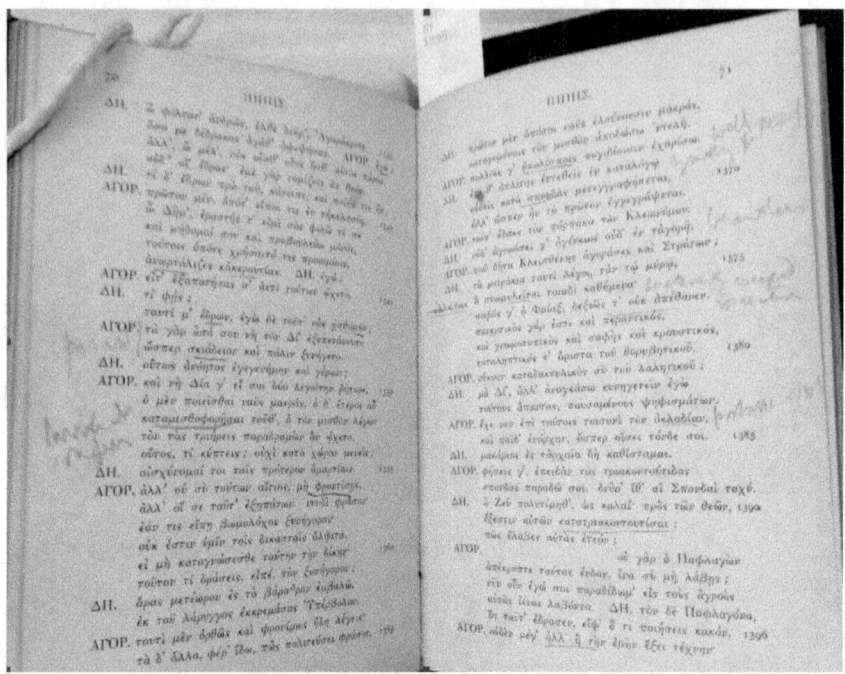

Figure 3: Thoby Stephen's annotations in Aristophanes, The Knights. *MASC.*

suggesting that Jacob should be of interest to readers because his tastes are of his own design.¹⁸ His shelves contained

> books enough; very few French books; but then any one who's worth anything reads just what he likes, as the mood takes him, with extravagant enthusiasm. Lives of the Duke of Wellington, for example; Spinoza; the works of Dickens; the *Faery Queen*; a Greek dictionary with the petals

---

definite' and impartial answers to these questions . . . Woolf's next novel [*Jacob's Room*], through its fragmentation, gaps and narratorial asides, demonstrates the impossibility of ever finding objective answers" (90). While Quigley cites Woolf's observation in "On Not Knowing Greek," "[I]t is to the Greeks that we turn when we are sick of the vagueness" (qtd. in Quigley 84), Jacob's Greek books are part of an unclear sketch.

¹⁸ Lurz sees Woolf's observation about reading as a statement that she is going to introduce Jacob's characteristics by means of his books, but does not do so: "The narrator's claim that 'any one who's worth anything reads just what he likes' suggests that a list of Jacob's reading preferences offers a window into the type of person he is. As such, however, she essentially looks past Jacob and any particularity of character that he might have in her drive to 'read' him" (111).

Figure 4: The birds in Thoby's copy of Pindar. MASC.

> of poppies pressed to silk between the pages; all the Elizabethans. . . . The works of Jane Austen too, in deference, perhaps, to someone else's standard. Carlyle was a prize. There were books upon the Italian painters of the Renaissance, a *Manual of the Diseases of the Horse*, and all the usual textbooks. (37-38)

Woolf's image of a reader following his or her own inclinations, however, reminds us of Thoby's "more casual, rough and ready and comprehensive" (*MOB* 138) style. In "A Sketch of the Past," she imagines he might have become "Justice Stephen . . . with several books to his credit; one or two on law; some essays exposing humbugs; perhaps a book on birds, with drawings by himself" (140). Thoby's library, then, would reflect the passions of his writing life. After encountering James Strachey's books in 1919, Woolf remarked that "He has all the right books, neatly ranged, but not interesting in the least—not, I mean, all lusty & queer like a writers [sic] books" (*D1* 305). While Woolf might be imagining her own interests as a writer here, her description makes Jacob's tastes seem bland.

In constructing Jacob's library, several of the books that appear to be more revealing of his character and interests were not among those in Thoby's library, but were owned by Woolf's Cambridge-educated father and brother. Lurz argues that Jacob represents "a manifestation of a general, established type, what we might call the 'Cambridge gentleman'" (111). By investigating the books to which Woolf had access, we can see some of the variability that this "type" may have encompassed and the extent to which she manufactured her depiction of it. Like Jacob, Thoby received a copy of Carlyle's *French Revolution* as a prize when he was a student at Clifton College, but it was Leonard who possessed a copy of Spinoza. Similarly, Thoby's Spenser does not remain in the Woolfs' library, but Leonard and Leslie Stephen's do. One of the more telling moments earlier in the novel, when Jacob selected "the works of Byron in one volume" (19), also may have grown out of Woolf's familiarity with her father and Leonard's annotated copies, as a copy does not remain in Thoby's library.

The rest of the volumes on Jacob's shelves contribute to its eclectic selection. Austen and the Italian painters might have been predictable choices for Jacob, as Woolf also gestures toward his admirers and his appreciation for aesthetics. Lurz sees the inclusion of Austen as "meant to explain what might seem an anomalous choice for a young man otherwise interested in titles of a more 'masculine' bent, though it also indicates that the narrator approaches Jacob's books with some preconceived notions, a set of expectations she is looking to the books to fulfill" (111). We can see vestiges of the equestrian passions that a student like Jacob might possess in his *Manual of the Diseases of the Horse*. In Thoby's library, a similar book is his copy of *British Birds* (1892). This hardcover volume, however, provided a form of diary that Thoby carried, adding details from his encounters with birds, including their dates and locations. Two entries in Thoby's small, careful hand refer to birds he spotted in London and Cambridge (Figure 5).

A "Greek dictionary" is a predictable book for a classics student like Jacob to have, but, as we have seen in her memory of Case, similar resources take a prominent position in Woolf's memories of her own education. In "A Sketch of the Past," Woolf remembers how her "mother's finger with the opal ring I loved pointed its way across French and Latin Grammars" (177).[19] On the table in Woolf's room at Hyde Park Gate "stood my open Greek lexicon; some Greek play or other" (122). While the Greek lexicon Woolf read in her youth does not remain in her library at Washington State, Thoby and Leonard Woolf both owned volumes edited by Henry George Liddell and Robert Scott. Woolf refers to their well-known lexicon from Oxford University Press as she reminisces: "Left alone in the great house . . . I mounted to my room; spread my Liddell and Scott upon the table, and settled

---

[19] In "Professions for Women," Woolf had also proposed that the amount of time in which the speaker was occupied in killing the "Angel in the House" "had better have been spent upon learning Greek grammar" (*DM* 238), presenting an opposition between intellectual pursuits and the home that her own mother, in teaching Woolf Greek grammar, prepared her daughter to make.

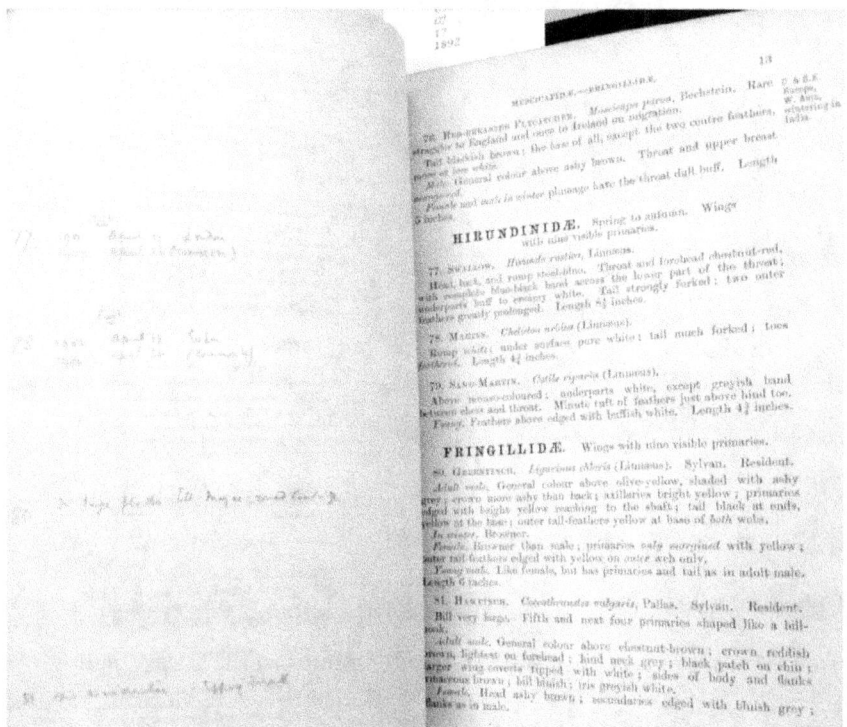

Figure 5: Thoby's notes in Leonard Howard Lloyd Irby's British Birds: Key List. MASC.

down to read Plato, or to make out some scene in Euripides or Sophocles for Clara Pater, or Janet Case" (148). Woolf is addressing an audience who would have recognized the shorthand, and while it was from Thoby that Woolf "first heard about the Greeks" (125), she was also nodding to the academic world to which Pater and Case had introduced her.

When she envisioned Jacob's room, with its tools for classical study and shades of his fate in the war, Woolf may have remembered Case's room, which contained "the photographs of young soldiers, & the silhouettes, & Janet's books, which never seem to be read, & the greek [sic] dictionary with the piece of paper sticking out of it" (*D1* 213). Filling Jacob's Greek dictionary with poppies, Woolf updates a third type of reader from "writing in the margins," for whom, after reading, "a whole botanical collection is returned to the library, pressed between the leaves" ("Woolf's Marginalia" 117). Woolf's choice of poppies, Vara Neverow has argued, foreshadows Jacob's death (ixxxv). The pages of Thoby's

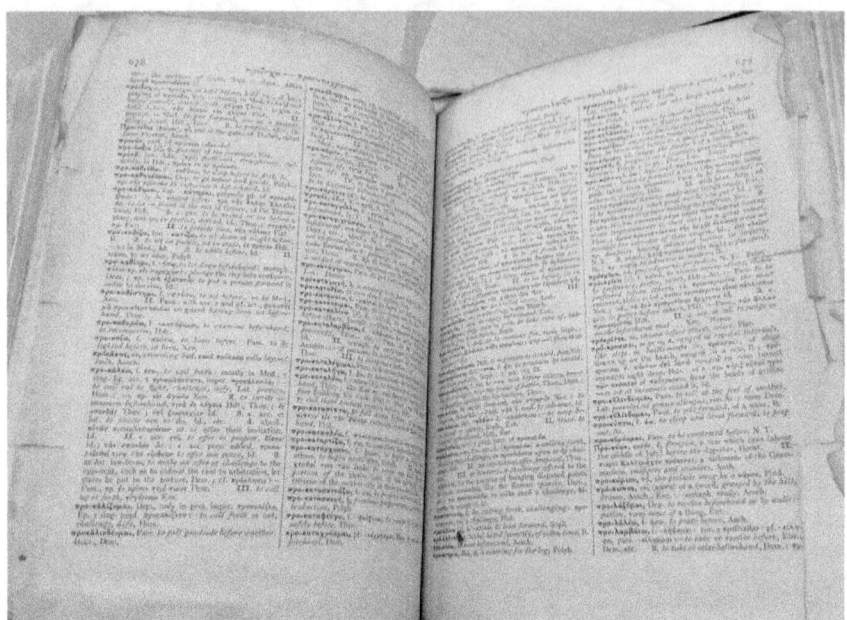

Figure 6: Thoby's copy of Liddell and Scott, An Intermediate Greek-English Lexicon. *MASC.*

Greek-English Lexicon are tattered (Figure 6), but it is Woolf's copy of Baedeker's *Northern France* (1899) that contains a dry leaf, now in an envelope that accompanies the volume, that Woolf may have encountered as she plotted Jacob's travels in Paris (Figure 7). Like the Baedeker guides that Woolf and Jacob consult, the Greek plays that Woolf translated were part of a series of educational texts.

    In listing "the usual textbooks," Woolf may have been referring to introductory manuals or guides, like those listed in the catalogue descriptions for the introductory courses in which Woolf enrolled at King's College London.[20] For Jacob and his contemporaries, the "text-book" may have referred to an instruction book for any discipline.[21] The *Oxford English Dictionary* defines "text-book" as "A book used as the standard work for the study of a particular subject; now usually one written specifically for this purpose; a manual of instruction in any science or branch of study, esp. a work recognized as an authority" (*s.v.* 2). Its earliest reference dates

---

[20] The only textbook in the Woolfs' library is *Cockerell, Bookbinding and the Care of Books: A Textbook for Bookbinders and Librarians* (1901). MASC.
[21] Mid-nineteenth and early twentieth century text-books include Graham, Jamieson, and von Georgievics.

Figure 7: Baedeker's Northern France *from the Library of Leonard and Virginia Woolf. MASC.*

from *Mirror* in 1779: "The letters of the immortal Earl of Chesterfield, which I intend to use as my text-book on this occasion."[22] This definition of the text-book as guide appears consistent with our sense of the term in the twenty-first century.

Woolf and Thoby shared some of the same academic landscape and texts. Working with tutors, however, Woolf lacked the camaraderie that she mythologized in *Jacob's Room* and that she encountered when meeting Thoby's college friends. As she imagined in *Jacob's Room*, "If any light burns above Cambridge, it must be from three such rooms; Greek burns here; science there; philosophy on the ground floor. Poor old Huxtable can't walk straight;—Sopwith, too, has praised the sky any night these twenty years; and Cowan still chuckles at the same stories. It is not simple, or pure, or wholly splendid, the lamp of learning" (38). Late into the night there would be "Talking, talking, talking—as if everything could be

---

[22] The *OED*'s example is from *Mirror* No. 38. The OED's previous reference to N. Bailey *Dict. Britannicum* (folio), 1730, to an obsolete meaning of the term suggests students' composition of a text to which the instructor would add comments: "*Text-Book* (in Universities is a Classick Author written very wide by the Students to give Room for an Interpretation dictated by the Master, &c. to be inserted in the Interlines" (*s.v.* 1). This presents a version of a student's notebook.

talked—the soul itself slipped through the lips in thin silver disks which dissolve in young men's minds like silver, like moonlight" (39). The image is material and communal, but restricted in gender.

Woolf's reference to "the usual text-books" could mean introductory texts for a range of subjects.[23] It is unclear what this would have meant for Thoby, as he had studied the classics at Clifton College before arriving at Cambridge, and would not necessarily have taken introductory courses there. Lurz argues that in this reference Woolf "points explicitly to a predetermined standard by which she is judging him. She limits him, that is, to a manifestation of . . . the 'Cambridge gentleman'" (111). The contents of a textbook, like the disks of ideas that dissolve, are likely to have been those that a student will surpass, as neither Woolf nor Thoby saved any books with "textbook" or "text-book" in the title that they may have acquired.

The Latin and Greek courses in which Woolf enrolled at King's College, London, often separated "text-books" from other central readings in the catalogue which Woolf may have acquired for the course or already owned. Woolf registered for Elementary Greek from 1897 to 1898 (Jones and Snaith 15) and the "Textbooks" included *Greek for Beginners* by Joseph Bickersteth Mayor and *Stories in Attic Greek* by Morice, neither of which Woolf kept, if she acquired them (Jones and Snaith 19). The latter, if Woolf read it, resembles an anthology with some introductory materials. In October of 1897 (L1 10), Woolf enrolled in Pater's "Intermediate Reading" Greek, which included Sophocles's *Antigone* (Jones and Snaith 24). Woolf inscribed her heavily annotated "Clarendon Press Series: Sophocles: For The Use of Schools" edition of Sophocles, "AVS 1898."[24] This copy contains additions in ink and pencil, suggesting that she added notes on different occasions, perhaps even returning to it over time (figure 2). At the back of the volume, the publishers included a list of the "Clarendon Press Series Latin Educational Works."[25] This list and others like it would have presented a canon of sorts; a place to access and order the range of editions edited by scholars and commissioned by Oxford University Press.[26]

---

[23] Shifting from classical texts to literary ones, Woolf refers to a textbook as a reference guide in *Orlando* (1928), 167.

[24] Dalgarno explains that "Woolf read *Antigone* throughout her life and in three languages, in the process frequently noting her reservations about translation. She read the play with her first tutor, Clara Pater, between May and July 1900, and in 1901 wrote to her brother Thoby of the experience. . . . In 1919 Woolf read *Antigone* again, as her reading notes comment, "'in Greek'" (39).

[25] Between Woolf's study of Greek and her composition of *Jacob's Room,* she and Leonard founded the Hogarth Press, which might have brought the distribution of textbooks to her attention.

[26] In the Oxford University Press archives, files remain addressing the production of new editions of French lexicons and other texts. Oxford University Press archives. Oxford, UK.

Oxford's publication of the student editions followed the growth of British schools during the second half of the nineteenth century. As Christopher Stray observes, "A search of textbooks . . . before 1865 gathers a very thin crop" ("Educational Publishing" 3). The number of "public," "proprietary," and "middle-class schools" increased during the 1860s, and Oxford University Press directed its efforts toward "a school and university market for instructional books" ("Educational Publishing" 1). As we have seen, Woolf and Thoby read books from "the Clarendon Press Series (CPS), an imprint rather than a series proper [of Oxford University Press] whose first title appeared in 1865" ("Educational Publishing" 1-2). Woolf's wide-ranging books reflect the fact that "The CPS was intended to include 'educational' rather than 'academic' books, but it ranged from elementary to higher education" ("Educational Publishing" 16).

For Woolf, classical texts provided access to the world of scholarship that influenced university and secondary education. Greek and Latin were among her primary sources of formal education and her access to some of the same resources through her tutors and courses at King's College allowed her to participate in larger conversations. Drawing on her own reading in her depiction of Jacob's study and travels, Woolf is also making a larger argument that understanding the world for many at the time was filtered through the study of the classics, and this ultimately also included the First World War.[27]

As later portions of Woolf's novel turn to Jacob's travels, guide books take the place of textbooks. They provide quick reference points, underscoring their role as texts with which travelers were familiar. And like Liddell and Scott's *Greek-English Lexicon*, Baedeker's guides were identifiable in part because they sold well (Geppert 236). Liddell and Scott's *Greek-English Lexicon* was a "best seller" in the late nineteenth century, one of two Oxford University Press books to turn a profit, the other being the Bible ("Educational Publishing" 6 and Sutcliffe 15).[28] Liddell and Scott's *Lexicon* and Baedeker's guides are emblematic of the changing impact of academic and popular publishing on readers' understanding of Greek and Greece, and more broadly, translation and travel.

Guide Books

As she drafted Jacob's travels, Woolf probably consulted her own Baedekers or other guide books. The concept of the "guide" or "guide-book" is not unlike that of a textbook, and the earliest instance of the use of "guide-book" in the *OED*

---

[27] For further treatment of the roles of Greek and World War One in the novel, see Neverow's introduction to *Jacob's Room*.
[28] Stray adds, "In the 1870s in classics, the only books in the CPS with runs of more than 2,000 were Liddell and Scott's lexicons and Charles Wordsworth's Greek grammar and primer" ("Educational Publishing" 29). Liddell's daughter was the Alice who inspired Lewis Carroll's *Alice in Wonderland*, which contributes to his recognition (Curthoys 47-48). See Larabee regarding the history of Baedeker guides.

dates from 1830, coming after their first reference to "text-book." Mark Larabee has noted the ways that Baedeker's guides provide a less substantial guide than living life in novels like E. M. Forster's *A Room with a View* (1908). Woolf returns to these guides in her diaries, acknowledging their reputation and limitations. In 1918, she remarked that there were "pictures in French papers of English tourists, only wanting spectacles & Ba[e]dekers to finish them" (*D*1 195-196).[29] Larabee notes the recognizable "red covers" of the Baedeker in Forster's novel (64), and this element presents a visual parallel to the Oxford editions of Greek texts that Woolf annotated, later referred to as "Oxford Reds" (Henderson 1).[30]

Jacob visits France and Greece; the latter, as it had for Woolf, provides a modern context for his studies. Woolf explored these connections in an early segment of her journal, "Greece, 1906," and story, "[A Dialogue Upon Mount Pentelicus]," in which, Jeanne Dubino has argued, Woolf brought new dimensions to what she had encountered in language:

> Though she transforms the details of the real journey that "[A Dialogue]" is based on, she used these details to underscore what Dimitris Tziovas calls *topos*, or topicality, in opposition to the *logos*, or the way Westerners have typically represented Greece, as a country of the mind. Tziovas proposes a *heterotopia*, or a topology that privileges neither the *topos* nor the *logos*, but rather "sustain[s] the tensions between the two" (189). In Woolf's writing, *logos*, try as it might, cannot escape *topos*. (22-3)

Woolf's books themselves present another kind of landscape, casting light on, but differing from, her visit to Greece. From the translations in her Greek texts to the condition of her Baedekers, each book would have altered Woolf's impression of its contents as she returned to it.

Virginia and Leonard Woolf's library includes numerous copies of Baedeker's guides and items related to their travels or others' use of the volumes. The maps in these guide books are folded and refolded, suggesting their handling. Acquired after Thoby's death, this edition could have provided a reference when Woolf was composing *Jacob's Room*. Tickets and hand drawn maps that once rested within their copy of Baedeker's *Greece* (1909) are now preserved in an envelope and a folder. The tickets may not have been from the Woolfs' travels, but the Athens

---

[29] Bulson notes that Woolf critiques "literary tourists" in a 1902 review and reviewed "a literary guidebook to Dickens" in her 1905 essay, "Literary Geography" (31).

[30] I thank Nathan Uglow for bringing *Oxford Reds* to my attention. Mills also points out that Jane Harrison's *Mythology and Monuments of Ancient Athens* (1890) "was known colloquially as 'The Blue Jane' for its blue cover and quickly became a standard travel guide for British travelers to Greece at the turn of the century" (21). If Woolf or other members of her family consulted this guide, they did not keep a copy as one does not remain in her library.

Figure 8: Five items enclosed in the Woolf library copy of Baedeker's Greece. *Four tickets and a schedule. The schedule is turned over and photographed on recto and verso. The first two sets of tickets are from "Antiquities of Greece." MASC.*

tickets are from sites that the Woolfs would have been inclined to visit. Two sets of tickets with stamped images of a female relic and birds are labeled "Antiquities of Greece," and were probably from archaeological ruins, such as the Acropolis, Parthenon, and Temple of Dionysus (figure 8). In addition to the tickets, the Woolfs' Baedeker included a schedule; figure 8 depicts photographs of both the recto, with an image that looks as if it were printed after 1906, and the verso, with a schedule that lists sites in Athens, such as the National Archaeological Museum and the Acropolis, which Woolf and Jacob visited (*PA* 327-8, *JR* 158).

When she visited Greece in 1906, Woolf contemplated the relationship between the ruins and the creative process. She began "[A Dialogue Upon Mount Pentelicus]" with an aside, "Mount Pentelicus[,] as we who read Baedeker know yet bears on her side the noble scar that she suffered at the hands of certain Greek stone masons" (63, bracket in original). She soon returns to the classics, imagining the view as "Plato looked up from his page on sunny mornings" (63). The physicality of texts, like those she translated, is not far from her imagination: "You might have heard the voice of Theocritus in the plaint that it made on those stones, and certain of the English did hear it, albeit the text was dusty on their shelves at home" (64). The Woolfs also visited Greece in 1932 with Roger Fry and his sister Marjorie (Glendinning 269),[31] and their tickets may date from this trip, when they visited the Acropolis, the Parthenon, and, Woolf reflects, the "theatre [of Dionysos], with its curved marble seats . . . Here L. sat & we said that Sophocles Euripides & Aristophanes must have sat here & seen—Anyhow the hills were before them, as before us" (D4 91, 98). In the process, Woolf imagines the impact of this view on the development of the texts that she had studied.

Jacob's response to the ruins is not one for which a guide book could have prepared him. We see Jacob "up very early, looking at the statues with his Baedeker" (JR 153). Consulting his guide book, "he was accurate and diligent; but profoundly morose. Moreover he was pestered by guides" (157).[32] It is atop the Acropolis with a different book, however, that "Jacob read on again. And laying the book on the ground he began, as if inspired by what he had read, to write a note upon the importance of history—upon democracy—one of those scribbles upon which the work of a lifetime may be based; or again, it falls out of a book twenty years later, and one can't remember a word of it. It is a little painful. It had better be burnt" (158). As Jacob's "scribbles" take the shape that James argued marginalia also demonstrate, his epiphany may capture an early moment in which his aspirations shift toward a future in the law. Jacob's insecurity also recalls Leslie Stephen's fears. But preservation is also subject to chance. One's books will contain

---

[31] In 1961, Leonard also traveled to Greece with Trekkie Parsons (Glendinning 396), and it is possible that the tickets could date from this trip. In 1932, the Woolfs' Baedeker became a place to conceal their currency: "We had been advised to hide all except 600 drachmas—where? . . . we disposed them all over—in the pockets of Baedeker, in an envelope" (*D4* 99). Woolf also visited a museum in Athens with Roger Fry that may have been included on this schedule (99)

[32] Lurz compares Jacob's impressions to the Omega Workshop's aesthetic, including the geometric shapes as a reflection of "the novel's larger attentiveness to the object world, it participates in the sensitivity to the material features of objects that was a major facet of the artistic and intellectual milieu in which Woolf composed her novel" (110).

remnants of thoughts and memories, like the poppies in Jacob's *Lexicon* or the tickets in the Woolfs' Baedeker.

Returning to Textbooks

When she returns from Greece in 1932, Woolf revisits translation as she depicts Edward annotating *Antigone* at Oxford in *The Pargiters* (*D*4 129).³³ Compared with her overview of Jacob's shelves, Edward's "one bookcase . . . was . . . arranged with rows of old books . . . which he had bought almost as much as for the subdued ripple of brown & gold that their backs made as for their contents. His [*work*] <text> books, his note books, his . . . shabby dictionaries [*& textbooks*] were concealed beneath a curtain on the lower shelves" (*Pargiters* 59). He is motivated by aesthetics, concealing the books that were subject to greater use, not unlike Thoby's *Lexicon*. As Woolf revises this scene, she gives reference books greater prominence than she had in *Jacob's Room*.

By the time Woolf completes the "1880" section of *The Years*, Edward's texts are no longer concealed, but sitting on his table as he prepares to work. Edward "looked at the textbooks, at the dictionaries lying before him. He always had some doubts before he began" (46). Edward's translation anticipates her own account of translating with "Liddell and Scott" on her desk in "A Sketch of the Past." Woolf acknowledged in "On Not Knowing Greek," "Sophocles['s] reputation for restraint and mastery has filtered down to us from the scholars" (27). Some of these scholars informed the editions that Woolf read, and in her inclusion of textbooks in *The Years* she gestures toward the fact that Edward is learning to enter this conversation.

From *Jacob's Room* to *The Years*, we can see the extent to which Woolf's engagement with Greek was intertwined with the academy and the publishing industry, from the books she read to her annotating of them. In "On Not Knowing Greek," Woolf proposed that in reading Greek "A fragment of their speech broken off would, we feel, colour oceans" (27). As we observed in "A Sketch of the Past," Woolf described herself as "a breaker off of single words, or sentences." The similarity in these statements takes on new meaning when we consider that Woolf's reading of Greek involved physically marking texts. In her library, we can observe the results of these practices, adding to our understanding of Woolf's attention to language and its role in *Jacob's Room*.

---

[33] Dalgarno notes that Woolf's "final notes on *Antigone* are among those in a notebook that Silver dates 1931-9, and are keyed in the margin to the first 161 pages of the Jebb translation. . . . In October 1934, she noted in her diary: 'Reading Antigone. How powerful that spell is still – Greek. . . . (*D*4: 257)" (40).

I am grateful to Emily James, Margaret Konkol, and Randi Saloman for their feedback on versions of this article. I would also like to thank Trevor J. Bond and my student Savina Ruppaner for their assistance, and Manuscripts and Special Collections (MASC) at the Pullman Library, Washington State University, and the Society of Authors as the Representative of the Literary Estate of Virginia Woolf for permissions.

Works Cited or Consulted

Aeschylus, *Aischylou Agamemnon = Aeschyli Agamemnon ad fidem manuscriptorum emendavit notas et glossarium adjecti* Carolus Jacobus Blomfield. 4th ed. B. Fellowes, 1832. MASC.

Baedeker, Karl. *Northern France, from Belgium and the English Channel to the Loire, Excluding Paris and its Environs: Handbook for Travellers.* 3d ed. K. Baedeker, 1899. MASC.

——. *Greece: Handbook for Travellers.* 4th rev. ed. K. Baedeker, 1909. MASC.

Brown, Bill. "The Secret Life of Things (Virginia Woolf and the Matter of Modernism)." *Modernism/modernity*, vol. 6, no. 2, 1999, pp. 1-28.

Bulson, Eric. *Novels, Maps, Modernity: The Spatial Imagination, 1850-2000.* Routledge, 2010.

Byron, George Gordon, Baron. *The Life, Letters, and Journals of Lord Byron*, edited by Thomas Moore. J. Murray, 1866. MASC.

——. *The Works of Lord Byron.* J. Murray, 1842. MASC.

——. *The Works of Lord Byron.* J. Murray, 1828-31. 6 vols. Vol. 4 only. MASC.

Carlyle, Thomas. *The French Revolution: A History.* Chapman and Hall, 1898. 3 vols. MASC.

Catullus, Gaius Valerius. *Catulli Veronensis Liber*, edited by Arthur Palmer. Macmillan, 1896. MASC.

Cockerell, Douglas. *Bookbinding and the Care of Books: A Textbook for Bookbinders and Librarians.* The Artistic Crafts Series of Technical Handbooks, no. 1. J. Hogg, 1901. MASC.

Cuddy-Keane, Melba. *Virginia Woolf, the Intellectual, and the Public Sphere.* Cambridge UP, 2003.

Curthoys, Mark. "The Press and the University." *The History of Oxford University Press: Volume II: 1780-1896,* edited by Simon Eliot. Oxford UP, 2013, pp. 1-78, Oxford Scholarship Online, August 2014, DOI: 10.1093/acprof:oso/9780199543151.001.0001

Dalgarno, Emily. *Virginia Woolf and the Migrations of Language.* Cambridge UP, 2011.

Daugherty, Beth Rigel. "A Library of Her Own: Virginia Stephen's Books." Modern Language Association Convention, Chicago, IL. January 10, 2014. Conference Presentation.

Dubino, Jeanne. "From 'Greece 1906' to '[A Dialogue upon Mount Pentelicus]': From Diary Entry to Traveler's Tale." *Virginia Woolf Miscellany,* vol. 79, Spring 2011, pp. 21-23.

Fernald, Anne E. *Virginia Woolf: Feminism and the Reader.* Palgrave Macmillan, 2006.

Fowler, Rowena. "Moments and Metamorphoses: Virginia Woolf's Greece." *Comparative Literature,* vol. 51, no.3, 1999, pp. 217-242.

Friedman, Ariela. "Did it Flow?: Bridging Aesthetics and History in Joyce's *Ulysses.*" *Modernism/modernity,* vol.13, no.1, 2006, pp. 853-868.

Georgievics, Georg von. *A Text-Book of Dye Chemistry (The Chemistry of Dye-Stuffs),* translated by Eug. Grandmougin, and rev. from the 4th German ed. (with additions) by Frederick A. Mason. Scott, Greenwood, 1920.

Geppert, Alexander C. T. *Fleeting Cities: Imperial Expositions in Fin-de-Siècle Europe.* Palgrave Macmillan, 2010.

Gillespie, Diane F. "Introduction." *The Library of Leonard and Virginia Woolf: A Short-Title Catalog,* edited by Julia King and Laila Miletic-Vejzovic. Washington State UP, 2003.

Glendinning, Victoria. *Leonard Woolf: A Biography.* Counterpoint, 2006.

Golden, Amanda. "'A Brief Note in the Margin:' Virginia Woolf and Annotating." *Contradictory Woolf: Selected Papers from the Twenty-First Annual Conference on Virginia Woolf,* edited by Derek Ryan and Stella Bolaki. Clemson U Digital P, 2012, pp. 209-214.

——. "Virginia Woolf's Marginalia Manuscript." *Woolf Studies Annual* vol. 18, 2012, pp.109-117

Goldman, Jane. "Virginia Woolf: Prophet of 'Pure Loss.'" Review of *Hellenism and Loss in the Work of Virginia Woolf* by Theodore Koulouris. *Modernism/modernity* vol. 22, no.2, 2015, pp. 389-395.

Graham, John. *The Compositor's Text-Book, or, Instructions in the Elements of the Art of Printing.* John Joseph Griffin & Co., 1848.

"Guide-book," n. *Oxford English Dictionary,* www.oed.com, Accessed 24 February 2016.

Hammill, Faye and Mark Hussey, *Modernism's Print Cultures.* Bloomsbury Academic, 2016.

Henderson, John. *"Oxford Reds": Classic Commentaries on Latin Classics.* Gerald Duckworth & Co. Ltd., 2006.

Irby, Leonard Howard Lloyd. *British Birds: Key List.* 2d ed. Porter, 1892. MASC.

Jackson, H. J. *Marginalia: Readers Writing in Books.* Yale UP, 2001.
Jaillant, Lise. *Modernism, Middlebrow and the Literary Canon: The Modern Library Series, 1917-1955.* 2014. Routledge, 2016.
James, Emily. "Virginia Woolf and the Child Poet." *Modernist Cultures* vol. 7, no. 2, 2012, pp. 279-305.
Jamieson, Andrew. *A Text-Book of Applied Mechanics and Mechanical Engineering* C. Griffith & Co., Ltd., 1918-.
Jones, Christine Kenyon and Anna Snaith. "'Tilting at Universities': Woolf at King's College London." *Woolf Studies Annual* 16, 2010, pp. 1-44.
King, Julia and Laila Miletic-Vejzovic, editors. *The Library of Leonard and Virginia Woolf: A Short-Title Catalog.* Washington State UP, 2003.
Lamos, Colleen. "Virginia Woolf's Greek Lessons." *Sapphic Modernities: Sexuality, Women and National Culture,* edited by Laura Doan and Jane Garrity.: Palgrave, 2006, pp. 149-164.
Larabee, Mark D. *Front Lines of Modernism: Remapping The Great War.* Palgrave, 2011.
Lee, Hermione. *Virginia Woolf.* Random House, 1996.
Liddell, Henry George. *An Intermediate Greek-English Lexicon Founded upon the Seventh Edition of Liddell and Scott's Greek-English Lexicon.* Clarendon Press, 1889. MASC.
———. and Robert Scott, comp. *A Greek-English Lexicon.* 6th ed., rev. Clarendon Press, 1869. MASC.
Lurz, John. *The Death of the Book: Modernist Novels and the Time of Reading.* Fordham UP, 2016.
Marcus, Jane. *Virginia Woolf and the Languages of Patriarchy.* Indiana UP, 1987.
Martin, Linda. "Elegy and the Unknowable Mind in *Jacob's Room.*" *Studies in the Novel* 47.2 (Summer 2015): 176-192.
Mills, Jean. *Virginia Woolf, Jane Ellen Harrison, and the Spirit of Modern Classicism.* Ohio State UP, 2014.
Moffat, Wendy. *A Great Unrecorded History: A New Life of E. M. Forster.* Farrar, Straus and Giroux, 2010.
Morice, F. D. *Stories in Attic Greek: Forming a Greek Reading Book.* Rivingtons, 1883, https://archive.org/details/storiesinatticg00unkngoog. Accessed 26 Nov. 2016.
Neverow, Vara. "Introduction." Virginia Woolf, *Jacob's Room.* Harcourt, 2008, pp. lxxxvii-xciv.
The Periodical, vol. IV. December 1897. Oxford University Press Archive, Oxford, UK.
Pollock, Frederick. *Spinoza, His Life and Philosophy.* 2d ed. Duckworth, 1899. MASC.

Prins, Yopie. "OTOTOTOI: Virginia Woolf and the 'Naked Cry' of Cassandra." *Agamemnon in Performance 458 BC to AD 2004*, edited by Fiona Macintosh, et al. Oxford UP, 2005. pp. 163-185.

——. "The Sexual Politics of Translating *Prometheus Bound*." *Cultural Critique* vol. 74, 2010): pp. 164-180.

Quigley, Megan. *Modernist Fiction and Vagueness: Philosophy, Form, and Language.* Cambridge UP, 2015.

Reiman, Donald H. *The Study of Modern Manuscripts: Public, Confidential, and Private.* Johns Hopkins UP, 1993.

Saloman, Randi. *Virginia Woolf's Essayism.* Edinburgh UP, 2012.

Southworth, Helen, editor. *Leonard and Virginia Woolf, The Hogarth Press and Networks of Modernism.* Edinburgh UP, 2010.

Sparks, Elisa Kay. "Leonard and Virginia's London Library: Mapping London's Tides, Streams and Statues." *Virginia Woolf's Bloomsbury: Volume 1 Aesthetic Theory and Literary Practice,* edited by Gina Potts and Lisa Shahriari. Palgrave Macmillan, 2010, pp. 64-74.

Spenser, Edmund. *Works of Edmund Spenser,* edited by J. Payne Collier. Bell and Daldy, 1862. 5 vols. MASC.

——. *The Works of Edmund Spenser*, edited by R. Morris. Macmillan, 1899. MASC.

Spinoza, Benedictus de. *The Chief Works of Benedict de Spinoza*, translated by R. H. M. Elwes. Rev. ed. Bohn's Philosophical Library. G. Bell, 1903. 2 vols. Vol. 2 only. MASC.

Stead, Lisa. Introduction. *The Boundaries of the Literary Archive: Reclamation and Representation,* edited by Carrie Smith and Lisa Stead. Ashgate, 2013, pp. 1-14.

Stray, Christopher. "Classics." *The History of Oxford University Press: Volume III: 1896 to 1970,* edited by Wm. Roger Louis. Oxford University Press, 2013, pp. 1-28. Oxford Scholarship Online, August 2014, DOI: 10.1093/acprof:oso/9780199568406.001.0001

——. "Educational Publishing." *The History of Oxford University Press Volume II: 1780 to 1896,* edited by Simon Eliot. Oxford University Press, 2013, pp. 1-66. Oxford Scholarship Online, August 2014,DOI:10.1093/acprof:oso/9780199543151.003.0012

Sutcliffe, Peter. *The Oxford University Press: An Informal History.* Oxford UP, 1978. "text-book, n.," s.v.1 and 2, Oxford English Dictionary, www.oed.com, Accessed 24 Feb. 2016.

Van Hulle, Dirk. *Modern Manuscripts: The Extended Mind and Creative Undoing from Darwin to Beckett and Beyond.* Bloomsbury, 2014.

Woolf, Virginia. "[A Dialogue Upon Mount Pentelicus]." *Complete Shorter Fiction*, edited by Susan Dick. Harcourt Brace, 1989, pp. 63-68.

——. *Agamemnon* Reading Notebook. Berg Collection. New York Public Library, New York, NY.
——. *The Diary of Virginia Woolf: Volume One 1915-1919*, edited by Anne Olivier Bell. Harcourt Brace, 1977.
——. *The Diary of Virginia Woolf: Volume Two: 1920-1924*, edited by Anne Olivier Bell, assisted by Andrew McNeillie. Harcourt Brace, 1978.
——. *Jacob's Room*. 1922. Edited by Vara Neverow. Harcourt, 2008.
——. *The Letters of Virginia Woolf: Volume One 1888-1912*, edited by Nigel Nicolson and Joanne Trautmann. Harcourt Brace, 1975.
——. "On Not Knowing Greek." *The Common Reader: First Series Annotated Edition,* edited by Andrew McNeillie. Harcourt Brace, 1984.
——. *Orlando: A Biography.* 1928. Harcourt Brace, 1956.
——. *The Pargiters: The Novel-Essay Portion of The Years,* edited by Mitchell A. Leaska. Harcourt Brace, 1977.
——. *A Passionate Apprentice: The Early Journals 1897-1909,* edited by Mitchell A. Leaska. Harcourt Brace, 1999.
——. "Professions for Women." *The Death of the Moth*. 1942. Harcourt Brace, 1970, pp. 235-242.
——. "A Sketch of the Past." *Moments of Being*, edited by Jeanne Schulkind. Harcourt Brace, 1985, pp. 64-159.
——. "Venice." *Essays: Volume One: 1904-1912,* edited by Andrew McNeillie. Harcourt Brace, 1986, pp. 243-348.
——. *The Years.* 1937. Edited by Eleanor McNees. Harcourt Brace, 2008.

It's You I Adore: On the Odes of Virginia Woolf
Jacqueline Shin

> If I fall on my knees, if I go through the ritual, the ancient antics,
> it's you, unknown figures, you I adore; if I open my arms,
> it's you I embrace, you I draw to me—adorable world!
> — Woolf, "An Unwritten Novel," 21

Virginia Woolf begins her first typescript draft of *Pointz Hall*—dated the 2nd of April, 1938—with an address to a lamp. The setting is a summer night. The unnamed narrator, in a single labyrinthine sentence that I will quote here in full, apostrophizes and pays tribute to this nondescript object. As formatted by Mitchell A. Leaska, the square brackets indicate Woolf's deletions and the angle brackets show insertions:

> Oh beautiful and bounteous light on the table; oil lamp; ancient and out-of-date oil lamp; upholding as on a tawny tent the falling grey draperies of the dusk; seen across the valley; not a wandering light like the car's; but steady; assurance to the next house over there in the darkness that the [fleet] <ships> have reached harbor after the day's toil; circled by gaitered legs; slippered feet; and dogs couchant; <lamp that> presides over truth; when the active and the urgent slip their vestments and become disapparelled; rid of the five fingers; five toes; money in the pocket; and brooches and watches; when the whole emerges [at top like a many-scaled fish,] all its parts now visible, not evanescent and vanishing and immortality broods; and death disappears; and the moment is for ever; yet sleep has not leathered the eye; nor the body to knock at this door, to observe that fur, that rag, that window, that grating, this, that and the other, surveys the whole unembarrassed by the part; unimpeded; oil lamp, that calls out the colour in the faded, [matches] <unifies> the discordant [in unity; God or Goddess;] accept the praise of those dazzled by daylight; drowned by uproar; oil lamp. (33)

The entirety of this opening is cut in the later typescript draft as well as in the novel's published version, which was printed posthumously as *Between the Acts* (1941).[1] Remnants, however, of the "Prayer to the Night Bird" that follows a few

---

[1] As Mark Hussey notes in his preface to *Between the Acts*, the novel was never finished. Woolf "began to write her last novel, *Between the Acts*, in the spring of 1938, but by early 1941 was dissatisfied with it. Before completing her final revisions, Woolf ended her own life, walking into the River Ouse on the morning of March 28, 1941" (xvii).

pages after this address to the lamp, do remain. Here the humble creature—not a glamorous nightingale, associated with poetry and death—flits, a "wise and honest bird; not afraid of saying, snails, shells, pebbles, little bits of parsley; worms; slugs; slime! They have, he chuckles and chatters, still their substance and succulence, even at midnight" (*Pointz* 34).[2] The bird is addressed directly: "Oh sensible and ironic bird," and is invited, with a Shakespearean ease and swift shift in tone, to "come, and tweak and twitter and free our long ears clutted up with fur," to "tweak us awake this jocund night of early summer and remind us of the [cold] <grass> under our feet; [of our nakedness;] how the sole of the foot and all the skin is bare, and the hairs are still capable of sensation; while our tongues shape the smoke in our brains into talk about herrings and cesspools" (34-35).

As Woolf was beginning what was to be her final work of fiction, she was playing with forms of praise and apostrophe, musically circling this nocturnal moment when the vestments of civilization are dropped, when our bodies return to pure sensation once we put away our clothing, conventions, and individual identities: a moment revisited in the conclusion of the published novel, set as it is in the "heart of darkness" and the "fields of night" (129). Elevating the mundane and "out-of-date" oil lamp and "some anonymous little bird of daylight" to ironically great heights, ceremonially asking the former to "accept the praise of those dazzled by daylight" (while crossing out the appellation of "God or Goddess"), Woolf, I would suggest, composes two brief and essentially ephemeral odes.[3] The ode is a notoriously tricky term to define; in its long history, rivalling that of the epic and hymn, the ode, as G.N. Shuster playfully notes, "can be said to have been all things to all men" (3).[4] I argue that throughout her career Woolf responded to, repurposed, and was in conversation with the classical Pindaric ode in particular, known for its difficulty, swiftness, loftiness, and triadic structure, as well as with other ancient and related forms of praise including the hymn and prayer.[5] Woolf's experiments

---

[2] The published version reads: "A bird chuckled outside. 'A nightingale?' asked Mrs. Haines. No, nightingales didn't come so far north. It was a daylight bird, chuckling over the substance and succulence of the day, over worms, snails, grit, even in sleep" (5).

[3] I call them ephemeral in the sense that they only survive in this draft form, not in the novel as published.

[4] Several other scholars note the vagueness of the term "ode" and the difficulty of defining it. See for instance Carol Maddisson's *Apollo and the Nine: A History of the Ode*, Paul H. Fry's *The Poet's Calling in the English Ode*, John Heath-Stubbs's *The Ode*, and Robert Shafer's *The English Ode to 1660: An Essay in Literary History*. Shafer notes that the best odes generally have a "majestical and ceremonious air, a largeness not merely quantitative, which suggests to their readers something formal and public in nature" (3).

[5] Shafer contends that Pindar merges "lyric enthusiasm" with "the restraining limits of a difficult and complicated verse form" (28): "Thus it is difficult to see how any poet of any age could attain Pindaric qualities without adopting a rapid and compressed style, predominantly allusive in character; without in consequence achieving the constant variety and

with the ode—including her seldom discussed, elaborately titled "Ode Written Partly in Prose on seeing the name of Cutbush above a butcher's shop in Pentonville" (1934)—express, as do most poetic odes, "deep lyrical enthusiasm" that often leaps into "fervor, reflection, and jubilation" (Shuster 22, 10). Ceremonial, yet playful in tone, they can be seen as part of what Jane Goldman describes as the author's broader "experimentations with the poetical," especially with the elegy, which are "bound up with her feminist interventions with the politics of gender, class and empire" (50). In their establishment of a realm of plenitude rather than scarcity, her prose odes can also be read in the light of what Pericles Lewis, in *Religious Experience and the Modernist Novel*, refers to as Woolf's "re-enchantment of the world," offering "a new form of spirituality independent of the Christian God and appropriate for the twentieth century" (144). They offer "sacramental moment[s]" rooted in what Lewis aptly calls a "sublime of the quotidian," as well as opportunities for communion (Lewis 160, 169), but register, near the close of her career, a shift from celebration to a more troubling and troubled aesthetic.

Woolf's novels have often and rightfully been associated with elegies and the elegiac, with loss and trauma, both personal and historical. The calling of Jacob Flanders's name ("Ja-cob! Ja-cob!"), for instance, echoes throughout *Jacob's Room*, tinged with an "extraordinary sadness," "[p]ure from all body, pure from all passion, going out into the world, solitary, unanswered, breaking against rocks—so it sounded," until we learn that Jacob has died in the First World War, leaving his room empty (5).[6] Mrs. Dalloway, after contemplating her consoling belief in an afterlife—"somehow in the streets of London, on the ebb and flow of things, here, there, she survived"—observes how "This late age of the world's experience had bred in them all, all men and women, a well of tears" (9). Scholars have read several of Woolf's works, especially *To the Lighthouse* and *The Waves*, as novel-elegies, pushing, as does John B. Vickery in *The Prose Elegy*, this traditionally poetic genre into the realm of the novelistic.[7] Indeed, as Woolf was "making up" *To the Lighthouse*, she famously noted that she had "an idea" that she would "invent a new name" for her books "to supplant 'novel.' A new— by Virginia Woolf. But what? Elegy?" (D3 34). I will propose that another term Woolf could have suggested is *Ode*.

---

brevity essential to lyrical fervour; and without the use of certain devices, almost wholly emotional in their effect, such as Pindar's recurrent words" (27).

[6] Hermione Lee suggests that the death of Virginia's brother Thoby in 1906 "intensified her sense of life as a threatened narrow strip between 'two great grindstones,' 'something of extreme reality.' The novels she would now write would almost all be elegiac" (223).

[7] See, for instance, essays by Gillian Beer, Maria DiBattista, Christine Froula, David Kennedy, Peter Knox-Shaw, Sean Latham, Alex Oxner, Erin Kay Penner, Karen Smythe, Randall Stevenson and Jane Goldman, John B. Vickery, and Alex Zwerdling.

In her essay "Poetry, Fiction and the Future" (1927), Woolf asks whether prose can "chant the elegy, or hymn the love, or shriek in terror, or praise the rose, the nightingale, or the beauty of the night?" (82).[8] Her immediate answer, which she goes on to qualify and explain, is *no*, yet most readers of her work would agree that her novels are superbly adept at chanting the elegy, conveying a powerful sense of loss, melancholy, and ghostliness while grappling with the reality of death. Most readers would likely also concur that her novels are equally adept at hymning love and praising "the rose, the nightingale, or the beauty of the night"; yet this odic or encomiastic strain (two oddly awkward and insufficient terms) within her work and within modernism more generally has for the most part been overlooked, or, if it has been attended to, has not been theorized as such. Perhaps this element is simply taken for granted; without a sense of love or attachment, after all, loss would be meaningless. One of the most beloved lines in *Mrs. Dalloway* comes right before Clarissa's reflection on her version of an afterlife and on the world's "well of tears"; we are told that, "what she loved was this, here, now, in front of her; the fat lady in the cab" (9). Both the elegy and the ode, loss and praise, appear to be different sides of the same coin; we know that the eulogy, an address to survivors left behind in a world bereft of a loved one, is almost always accompanied by praise.[9] Yet discussions of the elegiac impulse within modernism have far eclipsed those of the odic or encomiastic, to the neglect of these strains in Woolf's body of work. Throughout her career, not just at its end, Woolf gave voice to an adoration of the world—of people, places, and things—that moved parallel to yet also separately from her investment in sorrow and the language of mourning. There are elements of the hymn, the prayer, the rhapsody, and the love letter in her work, from *The Voyage Out* onwards; moments in her writing that glow with praise, gratitude, wonder, admiration, and exuberance—affects that have often been regarded by scholars of modernism and post-modernism with some degree of suspicion and skepticism, or simply with boredom and disinterest. Given the intense focus on the elegy within modernist studies in particular, it seems at times that to be modern means to be an elegist, wrestling with meaning in the liminal zone between the living and the dead, sending one's voice out into the darkness and imagining the voices that speak back, or else raging against the resounding silence.[10]

---

[8] Goldman offers a perceptive discussion of this essay in "From *Mrs. Dalloway* to *The Waves*."
[9] Max Cavitch argues that the "Elegy is a way of dealing with being left behind and thus often yields resentment and ideological violence along with consolation and beauty" (32). See also Jahan Ramazani, *Poetry of Mourning: The Modern Elegy from Hardy to Heaney*, and Diana Fuss, *Dying Modern: A Meditation on Elegy*.
[10] Ramazani notes that the elegy, "Among the oldest and richest of poetic genres," "survives the twentieth century's challenge to inherited forms. Indeed, the poetry of mourning for the dead assumes in the modern period an extraordinary diversity and range, incorporating anger and skepticism, more conflict and anxiety than ever before" (1).

The ode, compared to the elegy, can seem like a relic of the past. John Heath-Stubbs, in his concise overview of the ode, published in 1969, asserts that the genre "has been out of key with contemporary tendencies" and "can scarcely be said, either in its Pindaric or its Horatian form, to be any longer a vehicle which contemporary or future poets are likely to employ" (109, 111). Like the medium of sculpture, which was viewed by some in the early twentieth century as a dead form, no longer able to speak to a contemporary population, the ode seems worthy of study but not elastic enough (unlike the elegy) to adapt to the times.[11] Heath-Stubbs sees Gerard Manley Hopkins's *The Wreck of the Deutschland* (composed in 1875-76) as perhaps "the last truly great" ode, although it is not formally labeled as such, insisting that the "poets of the present century have gone further in experimentation, and for them the traditional genres have largely become meaningless" (108-109).[12] I suggest that the ode, rather than dying out in the early twentieth century, or merely being relegated to "public and academic occasions," instead took other forms, a fact that has not yet been fully explored. A vital reason for this oversight is the persistence of a dominant narrative about modernism that valorizes the irreverent, the transgressive, the nihilistic, and the skeptical, and that is wary of vertical rather than horizontal structures of power. Forms of praise can seem too stiffly conservative and hierarchical, not to mention sentimental, with their emphasis on commemoration or worship coming uncomfortably close to the tainted realms of propaganda on the one hand and advertising on the other. Once an artist humbles himself or herself by expressing veneration for an object and especially for another person, becoming entangled in questions of value and worth, a reader might begin to suspect the motives for such praise. There is, moreover, a general critical suspicion of categories such as the "beautiful" (often celebrated by odists), that views them as outmoded at best or dangerous at worst, with "beautiful objects and aesthetic experiences" potentially "complicit with the forces of oppression" and becoming the means of "ideological obfuscation" (Rothman). In terms of beauty

---

[11] Arturo Martini, in "Sculpture Dead Language," described sculpture as an outmoded form: "Poetry, music, architecture, like ancient languages, have been translated into new idioms, by clinging to life. Only sculpture has remained immobile across the centuries, a courtly language, the language of the liturgy, a symbolic writing, incapable of making its mark on daily acts" (176).

[12] It seems odd to categorize Hopkins's poem as an ode when it commemorates the death of five nuns, yet Heath-Stubbs's brief discussion focuses on the poem's praise of God, as "giver of breath and bread; / World's strand, sway of the sea; / Lord of the living and dead," who "has bound bones and veins in me, fastened me flesh, / And after it almost unmade... / Over again I feel thy finger and find thee" (qtd. 108). Heath-Stubbs's account of the ode of course only goes up to 1969, yet his assumption is that the ode as a relevant form has been long dead. There has been a contemporary revival of odes, but for the most part the form has not found the same popularity or been granted the same weight as the elegy throughout the twentieth and into the twenty-first century.

specifically, Elaine Scarry has noted how the political critique directed towards it is composed of two arguments, one of which argues that "beauty, by preoccupying our attention, distracts attention from wrong social arrangements," making us inattentive and indifferent, while the second argument "holds that when we stare at something beautiful, make it an object of sustained regard, our act is destructive to the object," "reifying" it as "the very object that appears to be the subject of admiration" (58). Praise can blind us to a number of wrongs and, for some, can constitute a wrong in itself.

In what follows, I propose to catalogue, unabashedly, Woolf's engagements with the ode, as part of a larger study of the encomiastic within British modernism.[13] I contend that for Woolf the ode is inseparable from the quotidian, the ludic, as well as the elegiac. She begins her writing career by democratizing the ode (as does Walt Whitman), and continues to respond to and adapt the Pindaric form, drawing on its mobility and structure while seeking out opportunities for exaltation, reverence, address, and tribute within the realm of prose. More than attempting to "clutch its object," struggling, as in an elegy, to let things go or to gain mastery by wresting meaning from death, Woolf's odes are generously "meant to be spread over the world and become part of the human gain" (TTL 47).[14]

I. Mending and Democratizing Odes in *The Voyage Out*

> I CELEBRATE myself, and sing myself,
> And what I assume you shall assume,
> For every atom belonging to me as good belongs to you.
> —Walt Whitman, *Song of Myself*, 63

In Woolf's first novel, *The Voyage Out*, Rachel Vinrace's uncle, Ridley Ambrose, works studiously to "restore" and "mend" the odes of Pindar: the classical Greek "poet, priest, and prophet" whose poems were taken as one of the primary models for English odes (Maddisson 2-3). In their villa in South America—a South America, as E. M. Forster put it, "not found on any map"—there are "many rooms," but in particular "one room ... possessed a character of its own because the door was always shut, and no sound of music or laughter issued from it" (172):

---

[13] I am alluding here to the title of Ross Gay's celebrated collection of poems, *A Catalog of Unabashed Gratitude* (Pittsburgh: U of Pittsburg P, 2015). My work-in-progress, *Encomium: Forms of Praise in British Modernism*, includes a chapter on "The Charm of Virginia Woolf's Face," which takes up *Orlando* along with other love letters and portraits. I also explore E. M. Forster's parodic "Anniversary Ode," the genre of "city symphonies," rhapsodies, and other twentieth-century forms of the encomiastic.

[14] "It was love, she thought ... love that never attempted to clutch its object; but, like the love which mathematicians bear their symbols, or poets their phrases, was meant to be spread over the world and become part of the human gain."

> Every one in the house was vaguely conscious that something went on behind that door, and without in the least knowing what it was, were influenced in their own thoughts by the knowledge that if they passed it the door would be shut, and if they made a noise Mr. Ambrose inside would be disturbed. Certain acts therefore possessed merit, and others were bad, so that life became more harmonious and less disconnected than it would have been had Mr. Ambrose given up editing *Pindar*, and taken to a nomad existence, in and out of every room in the house. As it was, every one was conscious that by observing certain rules, such as punctuality and quiet, by cooking well, and performing other small duties, one ode after another was satisfactorily restored, and they themselves shared the continuity of the scholar's life. (170)

This account of what "every one" in the household knows is filtered through Rachel's youthful perspective; her uncle's work, along with her own and her aunt Helen's, are strictly gendered. The women weave their domestic activities around the needs of Mr. Ambrose, feeling that they are playing a (limited) part in the "restoration" of Pindar's odes, which themselves are known for their sense of decorum and order. (In *Olympian 1* the poet writes: "it is proper that a man should speak well of the gods; / thus he is less likely to incur blame" [3]). It is as if the life of the household helps shape these odes as they are translated and pieced together, with one kind of work enabling the other and all forming a harmonious whole. As in *To the Lighthouse*, the male scholar depends on the sustaining order of the domestic realm to function properly (TTL 37, 65).

Woolf seems to gently mock the reverence that Rachel exhibits towards her uncle's work. Her reverence echoes the encomiastic nature of Pindar's odes, which were composed (those that survived) to "honour the victors in the Greek public games," praising "not only the victor but also his ancestors and his cities" (Heath-Stubbs 3). We see this veneration, for example, in Pindar's *Nemean* 9, written for Chromius of Aetna, winner of the chariot race: "There is a saying among men, that a noble accomplishment / should not be hidden on the ground in silence; / what is needed is a divine song of heroic verse. / Let us then lift high the deep-voiced lyre / and lift up the pipe, for this very pinnacle of horse-races, / founded by Adrastus for Phoebus by the waters of Asopus. / Mindful of this, I shall celebrate the hero / with honours that bring him renown" (111). Ensconced in his study, Mr. Ambrose is set apart, absorbed in a realm that the females of the household cannot access, sitting "hour after hour among white-leaved books, alone like an idol in an empty church, still except for the passage of his hand from one side of the sheet to another," restoring such odes to their original glory. The narrator's tone seems both genuinely respectful of the work being carried out and also slightly satirical, as we sense that Mr. Ambrose himself is fully aware of his own importance, his work conducted in complete silence "save for an occasional choke, which drove him to extend his pipe a moment in the air" (170). When Rachel enters his room and "hailed him twice, 'Uncle Ridley,' before he paid her any attention," we can see Woolf delicately playing with the form of the ode, deliberately choosing the word "hail," with its sense of formality and hierarchy, to describe Rachel's address (an element of many odes, including Woolf's "Ode Written Partly in Prose," which I discuss below) rather than selecting a more commonplace word such as "called" (170). Rachel's "hail" transposes the ode into the realm of the everyday, gently mocking the ode's formality and leveling out the traditionally hierarchical structure embedded in its reverential expressions of praise.

Helen Ambrose takes the narrator's quiet subversion even further when she teasingly notes how her "husband spends his life digging up manuscripts which nobody wants," "amused by Ridley's expression of startled disapproval" (198).[15] Ridley Ambrose's scholarship may seem incidental to this bildungsroman, focused as it is on Rachel's mental and emotional voyages of discovery as she luxuriates in the newfound possibility of doing "exactly as she liked" (173-74). Yet I would argue that *The Voyage Out*, as part of its own venture, takes his work, and the Pindaric ode, down from their great heights—shifting them from a secluded, male, sanctified, and exclusive realm to a level defined by the everyday yet transformative experience of love. There is a democratizing impulse at play in the novel that carries through to Woolf's subsequent works. Indeed, she directly takes up Pindar near the end of her career in *Three Guineas*: according to Woolf's speaker, for "the sons of educated men" to be asking "the daughters to help them to protect culture and liberty" in the year 1938 is akin to the Duke of Devonshire "step[ping] down into the kitchen" to ask the maid peeling potatoes to help him "construe" a "difficult passage in Pindar" (277-78). In both texts, Pindar is a stand-in for an elite realm that excludes women, the less educated, and especially less educated women. *The Voyage Out* can be seen as performing its own subtle mending of Pindar's odes insofar as it rewrites them on another level. As she does with her complex responses to other male poets such as Percy Bysshe Shelley, Woolf takes Pindar as a point of departure, an object of criticism, and a source of inspiration, as part of her feminist literary intervention.[16]

---

[15] Verity notes the reverence with which Pindar was viewed by other odists. Horace wrote that "Whoever strives to rival Pindar, Iulus, is relying on wings joined with wax by the skill of Daedalus and is destined to give his name to the glassy sea" (Pindar xx); in the eighteenth century, Thomas Gray writes a Pindaric ode that acknowledges "that Pindar is inimitable" (xxi). Pindar's odes "provided, and continue to provide, an aesthetic and intellectual challenge" (xxi).

[16] James Holt McGavran, Jr. notes that "References to Shelley abound in Woolf's fiction, and from the start she involves them in confrontations between the comic and the lyric, politics—both national and sexual—and the arts, realism and idealism, life and death" (58). Shelley's influence on Woolf is "made even more complex" due to "her strong consciousness

Rachel, aged twenty-four, gains self-knowledge and self-awareness throughout the novel (until, that is, her untimely death), particularly as she encounters love for the first time. In the same chapter that we learn of her uncle's work on Pindar, we see Rachel out walking along a nearly dried out river bed, viewing the trees on a bank "which Helen had said it was worth the voyage out merely to see" (173). She views the blossoms and is "filled with one of those unreasonable exultations which start generally from an unknown cause, and sweep whole countries and skies into their embrace" (173). Soon after this, she sits outside reading, and her mind drifts to seek out "the origins of her exaltation" (175). Her thoughts dwell on the young men she has met the night before, St. John Hirst and Terence Hewet, feeling "a kind of physical pleasure such as is caused by the contemplation of bright things hanging in the sun. From them all life seemed to radiate; the very words of books were steeped in radiance" (175); Rachel demands to herself, to the world, "What is it to be in love?" (175). Her commonplace yet exhilarating discovery of love is expressed through an odic idiom of exultation, splendor, and radiance.[17] Robert Shafer notes of Pindar that he "drains the Greek vocabulary dry of words for light and bright, shine and shimmer, glitter and glister, ray and radiance, flame and flare and flash, gleam and glow, burn and blaze" (23); this emphasis on light is apparent in the way that the young men seem to Rachel like twin suns, generating radiance as well as an almost abstract pleasure such as one feels regarding bright objects shining in the sunlight. The forms of praise that we find in odes such as those of Pindar are here shifted from a heroic realm to a very prosaic, youthful, and embodied register.

The connection between odes and love—in *To the Lighthouse*, Lily Briscoe notes how "from the dawn of time odes have been sung to love" (103)—is made more explicit in the novel, again lightly and teasingly, in the sanctified space of a church.[18] The narrator dips into the mind of Susan Warrington, who feels peaceful

---

of herself as a woman writer and of Shelley as a man who, on the one hand, 'fought for reason and freedom in private life' but who, on the other, continually used and victimized women in his life" (64).

[17] This idiom is vividly apparent in *Olympian 1*, which famously begins: "Water is best, / while gold gleams like blazing fire in the night, / brightest amid a rich man's wealth; / but, my heart, if it is of games that you wish to sing, / look no further than the sun: as there is no star / that shines with more warmth by day from a clear sky, / so we can speak of no greater contest than Olympia" (Pindar 3).

[18] Lewis points out the fact that "the works of several major modern novelists include scenes in which lone wanderers—usually male, often with touristic inclinations—visit churches and brood over the question of just what sort of power remains when, in Larkin's words, even disbelief no longer motivates their view of religion" (5). Earlier we saw Ridley Ambrose compared to "an idol in an empty church"; here, the church is a space for the erotic and illicit, where "the erotic encounter has quasi-spiritual value as a type of communion, a sign of the 'truth about this vast mass we call the world'" (159).

and calm in this setting: "Her emotions rose calmly and evenly, approving of herself and of life at the same time" (226). Even the priest's reading of a psalm, which calls out desperately to "Break their teeth, O God, in their mouths; smite the jaw-bones of the lions, O Lord," does not shake her serene mood. Her mind is "really occupied with praise of her own nature and praise of God—that is of the solemn and satisfactory order of the world" (227). This stable, serene realm of the encomiastic echoes that of the scholarly space in which Ridley Ambrose mends his odes by Pindar; there is an element of self-praise and self-satisfaction mingled with praise of another. At the back of the chapel, Mrs. Flushing sits with Hirst and Hewet, "in a very different frame of mind" (229) from Susan Warrington. Hewet is preoccupied with thoughts of Rachel, "almost painfully disturbed by his thoughts as she was by hers" (230). Meanwhile, Hirst is reading from a "thin pale-blue volume," which Mrs. Flushing inquires about, surprised at seeing on one side of the page a Greek poem and on the other its translation:

> "What's that?" she whispered inquisitively.
> "Sappho," he replied. "The one Swinburne did—the best thing that's ever been written."
> Mrs. Flushing could not resist such an opportunity. She gulped down the Ode to Aphrodite during the Litany, keeping herself with difficulty from asking when Sappho lived, and what else she wrote worth reading, and contriving to come in punctually at the end with "the forgiveness of sins, the Resurrection of the body, and the life everlastin'. Amen." (230)

Hirst is most likely reading Charles Algernon Swinburne's "Anactoria" (1866), which many readers agree is "pornographic" as well as sadomasochistic in its depiction of homosexual love between women (Cook 77).[19] Like the psalm that the priest earlier read out, Sappho's address to a deity also calls for help and a kind of vengeful retribution. Sappho, spurned by the woman she hotly desires, sees Aphrodite (called *Love* in Swinburne's version) in a vision, "as burning flame from crown to feet, / Imperishable, upon her storied seat" (ll. 67-68). The goddess asks Sappho who wrongs her and promises:

> "Even she that flies shall follow for thy sake,
> And she shall give thee gifts that would not take,
> Shall kiss that would not kiss thee" (yea, kiss me)
> "When thou wouldst not" [...] (ll. 81-84)

[19] Lewis notes that Woolf recalls this ode in *To the Lighthouse* and elsewhere, and that her "sublime erotic moments resemble Sappho's in their interpersonal emphasis, in their illustration of the way that love transcends the boundaries of the self and that this transcendence closely resembles self-destruction." Other elements also "suggest continuities from Sappho's sublime to Woolf's" (158, 163).

In this sly reference and brief moment of illicit reading, Woolf is further overturning the ode as a genre that is set apart in a male, elite, and scholarly realm that women need to tiptoe on the outskirts of. She gives Sappho her due as another classical ode-writer who has influenced the history of the form as much as Pindar, Horace, or Alcaeus. Swinburne's version of Sappho's ode is sensual and full of pained desire, shocking to read in a quiet colonial church where women like Susan Warrington feel safe in the "solemn and satisfactory order of the world" and where the priest reads from a psalm that asks about righteousness and the "mischief" of the "ungodly" (Psalm 58:1). Mrs. Flushing (again, we see Woolf being tongue-in-cheek here in the choice of name) cannot resist temptation; we can imagine her flushing as she "gulps" the erotic ode, addressed to a female deity, needing to hold back her torrent of questions, then managing to cover over her excitement by reciting the end of the Litany along with the rest of the congregation, ending with a pious "Amen." *In The Voyage Out,* the odic is brought (as Sappho brings it) to the level of the body; to shared readings, to the shouting of nonsense words as one is filled with the confused pain and excitement of love. It is transposed to the realm of prose, and becomes illicit and alive rather than sanctified and remote.

In referencing Swinburne's translation of Sappho, Woolf may also have been alluding to his poem "Sapphics," with which she must have been familiar. This poem, according to Joyce Zonana, subverts rather than simply translates the "Ode to Aphrodite" (41). Whereas in the original, as we saw, "Sappho had appealed for the aid of an Olympian Goddess, Aphrodite, imploring her to descend from heaven to Lesbos," in Swinburne's work "the Goddess is on earth, pleading with the poet to look at and listen to her" (Zonana 41). In this "inverted" text, Swinburne composes his own ode to Sappho as the "tenth Muse" who strikes the other (divine) muses silent with the power of her songs—songs that "move the heart of the shaken heaven, / Songs that break the heart of the earth with pity, / Hearing, to hear them" (ll. 78-80). In so doing, as Zonana argues, he "radically redefines the nature of poetic inspiration," offering a "steady celebration of humanity" over divinity (39). Swinburne's Sappho turns away from Love and the divine in "Sapphics," and in this repudiation finds the inspiration for powerful songs. As we shall see in "An Unwritten Novel," Woolf takes to heart, in a more playful register, this celebration of the aesthetic over the romantic, turning from the realm of love to the dazzling play of the mind.

II. A Mobile Aesthetic: "An Unwritten Novel"

> All things counter, original, spare, strange;
> Whatever is fickle, freckled (who knows how?)
> With swift, slow; sweet, sour; adazzle, dim;
> He fathers-forth whose beauty is past change:
> Praise him.
> —Gerard Manley Hopkins, "Pied Beauty"

"Glory be to God for dappled things," begins Gerard Manley Hopkins's "Pied Beauty," a poem of praise that celebrates the irregular and variegated aspects of the beauty of the world. Woolf never offers praise to a Christian god, yet expresses a similar adoration of the world in "An Unwritten Novel" (1921). "An Unwritten Novel," according to Hermione Lee, "gave [Woolf] an idea of further possibilities" after completing her second novel, *Night and Day*. Writing to her friend Ethel Smyth ten years after its composition, Woolf notes how "The Unwritten Novel was the great discovery," which:

> in one second showed me how I could embody all my deposit of experience in a shape that fitted it—not that I have ever reached that end; but anyhow I saw it, branching out of the tunnel I made, when I discovered that method of approach, Jacobs Room, Mrs. Dalloway etc—How I trembled with excitement; and then Leonard came in, and I drank my milk, and concealed my excitement, and wrote I suppose another page of that interminable Night and Day (which some say is my best book). (qtd. Lee 370-71)

Here, Woolf seems akin to Mrs. Flushing, excited by her discovery of Sappho, yet falling in line and concealing her excitement by seeming to engage with another text. Woolf's almost accidental discovery of a particular aesthetic approach branches out, as she puts it, into her more experimental writing as she finds a means of embodying her experience in a style and shape of her own. One element of what she discovered or brought to the fore is a merging of the odic register with the ludic and quotidian, the celebratory and ceremonial with the playful and the everyday. Her prose ode continues the work of *The Voyage Out* in mending and democratizing the ode; it equates the odic with movement and motion, using a lightness of touch that does not grasp at its subject or object, and that praises in particular the swift agility of the writer's mind.[20]

---

[20] Pindar, as I noted above, is often celebrated for the swiftness and mobility of his odes. Horace famously described Pindar's poetry as "Like a stream running down from a mountain, a stream which the rains have swollen over its familiar banks"; "Pindar boils and rushes without measure with unrestrained voice" (qtd. Pindar xxi)

The conclusion of "An Unwritten Novel" is the epigraph to my article, and clearly indicates a feeling of adoration, with the narrator of this short story (which seems also part essay) imagining falling on her knees and going through the "ancient antics" of veneration and praise in response to what she sees. What she sees is a woman who had been sitting across from her on the train, whose circumstances and life she had vividly conjured, disembarking and meeting a young man with whom she walks away. Upon first noticing her in the carriage, the narrator had been struck by the woman's misery; after some brief conversation, she feels (like a detective) that she has read this stranger's "message, deciphered her secret, reading it beneath her gaze" (11). Putting together the clues, she imagines Minnie Marsh, as she names her, as a spinster visiting her condescending and belittling sister-in-law. She envisions an awkward dinner with Millie's niece and nephew, but skips over it, "Skip, skip, till we reach the landing on the upper floor." As if she were skimming the pages of a book (one written by a "materialist" Edwardian) or had invented the "fast forward" button before such technology existed, she skips through the scenes, until she comes to Minnie alone in the guest room:

> Three o'clock on a December afternoon; the rain drizzling; one light low in the skylight of a drapery emporium; another high in a servant's bedroom—this one goes out. That gives her nothing to look at. A moment's blankness—then, what are you thinking? (Let me peep across at her opposite; she's asleep or pretending it; so what would she think about sitting at the window at three o'clock in the afternoon? Health, money, hills, her God?) Yes, sitting on the very edge of the chair looking over the roofs of Eastbourne, Minnie Marsh prays to God. That's all very well; and she may rub the pane too, as though to see God better; but what God does she see? Who's the God of Minnie Marsh, the God of the back streets of Eastbourne, the God of three o'clock in the afternoon? (12)

Moving nimbly between the train carriage and this conjured scene of thought and prayer, Woolf gets closer to what she elsewhere calls "Life itself," or to the elusive figure of "Mrs. Brown" ("Mr. Bennett and Mrs. Brown" 388). She discovers a playful, net-like narrative mobility that had been absent from *The Voyage Out* as well as *Night and Day*, but that would be present in various forms in her later works.

Woolf dips into this woman's consciousness and tries out different possibilities for her life, attempting to fit the pieces together. Her willingness to play with a wealth of options and not settle on any one truth runs counter to the demands of realist fiction. "A parting, was it, twenty years ago? Vows broken?" "No—more like this": perhaps one night Minnie was tempted by a shop display, losing track of time. She rushed home only to find "[n]eighbors—the doctor—baby brother—

the kettle—scalded—hospital—dead—or only the shock of it, the blame? Ah, but the detail matters nothing!" The truth is elusive and inconsequential; the beauty is in the elusiveness, the speculation, the play. Woolf's narrator describes people as being like butterflies or moths (a familiar metaphor for Woolf, of course) perched on flowers: when a writer grasps the stem of the flower, "the butterfly's off—the moth that hangs in the evening over the yellow flower—move, raise your hand, off, high, away." She apostrophizes:

> Hang still, then, quiver, life, soul, spirit, whatever you are of Minnie Marsh—I, too, on my flower—the hawk over the down—alone, or what were the worth of life? To rise; hang still in the evening, in the midday; hang still over the down. The flicker of a hand—off, up! then poised again. Alone, unseen; seeing all so still down there, all so lovely. (15)

This breathtaking, odic passage is later echoed in a passage from *Between the Acts* that I will discuss below, as well as one in *Jacob's Room*, where the narrator insists that although Jacob cannot really be known or his character fully grasped, "something is always impelling one to hum vibrating, like the hawk moth, at the mouth of the cavern of mystery, endowing Jacob Flanders with all sorts of qualities he had not at all" (97). Much of what Jacob says is "unintelligible" or "mostly a matter of guess work," yet "over him we hang vibrating" (98). In both *Jacob's Room* and "An Unwritten Novel," the narrative presence hovers, hangs still, and rises, with complete freedom of movement, not really interested in pinning down what she sees. The essay is a virtuosic exercise that revels in the ease and power of the artist who is able to conjure a life and several possible lives from what is presented to her: a woman whose identity and life she will never know the truth of.

The centrality of a Keatsian negative capability within Woolf's aesthetic has long been recognized: we can see it strikingly at play in the essay (which seems also part short story) "Street Haunting: A London Adventure" (1930), in the speaker's delight that "[i]nto each of these lives one could penetrate a little way, far enough to give oneself the illusion that one is not tethered to a single mind, but can put on briefly for a few minutes the bodies and minds of others. One could become a washerwoman, a publican, a street singer" (35).[21] "An Unwritten Novel" in particular also celebrates failure. Once the narrator realizes that her version of

---

[21] Maria DiBattista, in *Virginia Woolf's Major Novels*, notes how Woolf saw her own writing as a "species of mediumship" (in Woolf's words). DiBattista discerningly describes how the "mimetic power and imaginative authority of Woolf's narrative presence derives from her negative capability in penetrating, becoming, and ordering the human and inhuman reality she contemplates. Hers is a species of mediumship descending from Keats's formulations concerning the chameleon poet who has no identity," part of an inheritance that goes back to "the memory of Shakespeare" (14-15).

"Minnie's" life is inaccurate—she discovers that the woman has a son and is thus no spinster dependent on a cruel sister-in-law—rather than expressing disappointment or devastation, the narrator is first "confounded" and then experiences exaltation. She feels, "Well, my world's done for! What do I stand on? What do I know? ... Who am I? Life's bare as bone." As she takes a final look at the two figures, never to see them again, she is filled with wonder, which "floods [her] anew":

> Mother and son. Who are you? Why do you walk down the street? Where to-night will you sleep, and then, to-morrow? Oh, how it whirls and surges—floats me afresh! I start after them. ... Wherever I go, mysterious figures, I see you, turning the corner, mothers and sons; you, you, you. I hasten, I follow.

The mystery of the unknown, rather than calling for mastery, is instead celebrated in a kind of hymn that revels in *not* knowing and not needing to know. It is "you, you, you" that the speaker sees, apostrophizes, and mentally follows. The classical ode, as well as later odes, explore the unique individuality of that which they praise; here, as elsewhere, Woolf instead seems to sweep her arms open with a net to pull towards her the entire world, only to let it all flow through the mesh. This gesture is essential to her odic impulse, and is fully realized in *To the Lighthouse*.

III. (Ode) *To the Lighthouse* and Mrs. Ramsay

> Could loving, as people called it, make her and Mrs. Ramsay one?
> for it was not knowledge but unity that she desired, not inscriptions on
> tablets, nothing that could be written in any language known to men,
> but intimacy itself, which is knowledge, she had thought,
> leaning her head on Mrs. Ramsay's knee.
> —*To the Lighthouse*, 51

To the Lighthouse, while certainly a prose elegy for Woolf's parents and for an entire lost generation of young men, can also, like Shelley's "To a Skylark," or Keats's "To Autumn," be read as an ode *to* the lighthouse—and to Mrs. Ramsay, who is connected with it—representing the height of the odic impulse in Woolf's works.[22] Mirroring the three-part structure of the Pindaric ode (returning in a more formal sense to Pindar as opposed to her subversive play in *The Voyage Out*), which paralleled the movements of the classical chorus, moving as it did

---

[22] As Gillian Beer notes: "All Virginia Woolf's novels brood on death, and death, indeed, is essential to their organization as well as their meaning. Death was her special knowledge: her mother, her sister Stella, and her brother Thoby had all died prematurely. But death was also the special knowledge of her entire generation, through the obliterative experience of the First World War" (31).

"in a dance rhythm to the left," chanting "the *strophe*; moving to the right, the *antistrophe*; then, standing still, the *epode*" (Abrams and Harpham 262), Woolf's novel tacks back and forth and then stands, focused throughout on an adoration of Mrs. Ramsay. The fluid movement of "An Unwritten Novel" and "Street Haunting," which unpredictably dip in and out, is here structured far more rigidly. The novel's triadic structure, like that of Pindar's odes, offers a "peculiar majesty and stateliness" that prevents monotony as well as sentimentality (Shafer 28). I argue that the powerful love towards Mrs. Ramsay expressed by various characters in the novel, particularly in its first section, not only gives force to Woolf's elegiac impulse in the second, but also enables her to make such economic and experimental use of parentheses in the "Time Passes" segment. Exploring the encomiastic impulses in this novel, and reading the work as (in part) a prose ode, allows us to trace the yearning behind the odic for Woolf more generally: that is, the desire for an intimacy that is not grasping, but instead specific and impersonal, unique and diffused. If the elegy, as Gillian Beer and others have noted, is essentially about learning "how to let go"—about "let[ting] go of the past, formally transferring it into language, laying ghosts and confining them to a text and giving them its freedom"—the ode offers another form of non-attachment that is rooted in praise, offering a compensation of its own (Beer 31).

At the heart of the novel is the "archetypal mother, Mrs. Ramsay," who, as Maria DiBattista describes her, is "the primary focus of all feeling in the prewar idyll of 'The Window,' an iconic figure of idealized desire whose 'royalty of form' derives not from the authority commanded by her moral being, but from the power of her extraordinary beauty" (75). The unpopular and generally despised Charles Tansley, who takes a walk with Mrs. Ramsay, is at one point struck by this beauty, realizing that "she was the most beautiful person he had ever seen." He feels, "for the first time in his life," an enormous pride walking alongside her. Others are unexpectedly moved by her as well; Lily Briscoe, the painter, and William Bankes, the scientist, both also outsiders to the family group, share a mutual regard for her. We see her powerful effect on others in Lily's observations and reflections (Lily, who wonders if she might be in love with Mrs. Ramsay). While painting and discussing Mrs. Ramsay with Mr. Bankes, Lily notices his "rapture," which is equivalent, she feels, "to the loves of dozens of young men":

> That people should love like this, that Mr. Bankes should feel this for Mrs. Ramsay (she glanced at him musing) was helpful, was exalting. She wiped one brush after another upon a piece of old rag, menially, on purpose. She took shelter from the reverence which covered all women; she felt herself praised. (48)

Lily's response to her friend's feelings for Mrs. Ramsay encapsulates the odic element within this novel. Bankes's adoration is not a desire to in any way possess Mrs. Ramsay, to make her his own, or to tie her identity to his. Instead, his feelings are more like a source of light that radiates outwards, offering shelter and praising not just one woman but all women. It is a "heavenly gift," and of its bounty the whole world can share; it is love "distilled and filtered," love such as a poet feels for their phrases or a scientist for their problems. Again, there is reverence without hierarchy, and plenitude rather than lack. Lily's focus on rapture and benediction offers her a sense of solace and ease from the "perplexity of life"; however, this does not last, and her revelation is soon followed by a feeling of horror at the inadequacy of her own work. Adoration turns to disgust, then reflection. Anger turns to elation, then relief. First one way, then another, then a pause. We see this three-part movement in Lily's musings on Mr. Bankes himself, as she offers tribute while disavowing personal praise: first all of her feelings pour forth "in a ponderous avalanche" ("That was one sensation"); then she addresses him silently and with reverence; then she simultaneously thinks of his faults. Her silent address to him is a kind of ode: "I respect you ... in every atom; you are not vain; you are entirely impersonal; you are finer than Mr. Ramsay; you are the finest human being that I know; you have neither wife nor child (without any sexual feeling, she longed to cherish that loneliness), you live for science ...; praise would be an insult to you; generous, pure-hearted, heroic man!" (24). Through such moments of tacking, as of a sailboat or a chorus, the novel zig zags its way closer and closer to the lighthouse.

The painting that Lily works on throughout the first section of the novel and that she completes in the novel's final lines transforms Mrs. Ramsay and her youngest son, James, into the shape of a purple triangle, and is a "tribute," if, "as she vaguely supposed, a picture must be a tribute" (52-53). While discussing the painting with her, Bankes expresses his fascination with the notion that one could depict a mother and child—"objects of universal veneration, and in this case the mother was famous for her beauty"—and reduce them to "a purple shadow without irreverence" (52). If realism in representation entails grasping a subject in an attempt to pin it down on the canvas or page, Lily's abstract rendering of her subjects allows her, as an artist, to escape that grasp. Mrs. Ramsay sees herself, too, as "a wedge of darkness," "[l]osing personality," able to live many lives, finding rest, not as herself, but as this other shape (63). The abstraction of a simple geometric form (such as the cylinder of a lighthouse or the triangle of its beam or the shape of "two blocks joined by a corridor," as Woolf envisioned her novel [*TTL: Holograph* 44]), offers a means of escaping the entanglements of the particular.[23] In addition

---

[23] Woolf's sketch of the shape of her novel is accessible at www.Woolfonline.com or in the Harcourt annotated edition of the novel, in addition to the *Holograph* edited by Susan Dick.

to the wedge of darkness, Mrs. Ramsay identifies herself with one of the beams of light emanating from the lighthouse. As she sits and thinks, she looks out "to meet that stroke of the Lighthouse, the long steady stroke, the last of the three, which was her stroke, for watching them in this mood always at this hour one could not help attaching oneself to one thing especially of the things one saw; and this thing, the long steady stroke, was her stroke" (63). Her stroke is, significantly, the "last of three," reflecting the novel's triadic structure.

The narrator observes how Mrs. Ramsay "praised herself in praising the light, without vanity, for she was stern, she was searching, she was beautiful like that light" (63). Then there is a predictable shift in tone, a tacking in a different direction, and Mrs. Ramsay looks at the light, now with "some irony in her interrogation":

> ...the steady light, the pitiless, the remorseless, which was so much her, yet so little her, which had her at its beck and call (she woke in the night and saw it bent across their bed, stroking the floor), but for all that she thought, watching it with fascination, hypnotised, as if it were stroking with its silver fingers some sealed vessel in her brain whose bursting would flood her with delight, she had known happiness, exquisite happiness, intense happiness, and it silvered the rough waves a little more brightly, as daylight faded, and the blue went out of the sea and it rolled in waves of pure lemon which curved and swelled and broke upon the beach and the ecstasy burst in her eyes and waves of pure delight raced over the floor of her mind and she felt, It is enough! It is enough! (64-65)

With this labyrinthine, breathless sentence, which builds, on a wave of conjunctions, to a climax of plenitude, Woolf offers a sense of repletion, which then shifts to stand on a platform of stability. At dinner, Mrs. Ramsay thinks of how "there is a coherence in things, a stability; something, she meant, is immune from change, and shines out … in the face of the flowing, the fleeting, the spectral, like a ruby; so that again tonight she had the feeling she had had once today, already, of peace, of rest. Of such moments, she thought, the thing is made that endures" (105). This thing that endures provides an enormous force of love and emotion in the novel, which, because of its zig zagging, avoids the sentimental while conveying deep sentiment. The odic as a force unites, rather than setting the living against the dead, separating the bereft from the departed. As adapted by Woolf, the ode's gift is the intimacy of impersonality. As Mrs. Ramsay makes her way to bed, she feels "that community of feeling with other people which emotion gives as if the walls of partition had become so thin that practically (the feeling was one of relief and happiness) it was all one stream, and chairs, tables, maps, were hers, were theirs, it did not matter whose, and Paul and Minta would carry it on when she was dead" (113-14). This is a moment of communion between the living and between the living and the dead, that is elevated to an almost religious level. According to Lewis, "[w]hile Mrs. Ramsay rejects what she evidently sees as the ideological consolations offered by religion, she does contemplate a different sort of quasi-religious ecstasy" in such moments of reflection and vision (163); in the "disenchanted world of *To the Lighthouse*," the "hoped for re-enchantment takes the form of communion that only intense privacy can achieve" (169). I would add that the means of accessing such intense feelings in this novel is by way of the ode.

When, in "Time Passes," we learn in a brief parenthetical that Mrs. Ramsay has died ("[Mr. Ramsay, stumbling along a passage one dark morning, stretched his arms out, but Mrs. Ramsay having died rather suddenly the night before, his arms, though stretched out, remained empty]" (128)), the force of this death is all the greater because of the plenitude of the odic in the previous section. In the contrast, or tacking, from the richness of love and adoration in "The Window" to the crushing inadequacy of language that comes with death, the odic merges into the elegiac. The novel's previous willingness to not grasp at or try to possess those around us, its insistence upon the impersonality of love, is set against Mr. Ramsay's empty arms, reaching blindly for his wife who is no longer there. One impulse does not negate the other, but rather both balance out the other, and in the third segment, the stand, or *epode*, of "The Lighthouse," there is a turn to both. The parenthetical account of Mr. Ramsay's grief and Mrs. Ramsay's death is able to be so powerfully concise and seemingly incidental because we as readers have also been swept up in adoration for Mrs. Ramsay, and can thus read between the spaces of the words the vast sense of loss and the terror and fragility of life that Mrs. Ramsay (like Mrs. Dalloway) had always felt. There is no need to say more; there is no more that can be said without irreverence. Prue Ramsay, we are also informed in a parenthetical aside, has died in childbirth, when all "had promised so well" (132); Andrew Ramsay, "whose death, mercifully, was instantaneous" (133), was blown up in the war, along with twenty or thirty other young men (and, we know, millions of others). There is a mercy in brevity, as earlier we saw an exhilaration in stretching a sentence to its utmost limits.

In "The Lighthouse" section, as Lily and others return to the summer house after several years have passed and face the reality of Mrs. Ramsay's absence, Lily remembers Mrs. Ramsay "bringing them together; Mrs. Ramsay saying, 'Life stand still here'; Mrs. Ramsay making of the moment something permanent (as in another sphere Lily herself tried to make of the moment something permanent)—this was of the nature of a revelation":

> In the midst of chaos there was shape; this eternal passing and flowing (she looked at the clouds going and the leaves shaking) was struck into stability. Life stand still here, Mrs. Ramsay said. "Mrs. Ramsay! Mrs. Ramsay!" she repeated. She owed it all to her. (161)

Like the regular beam of the lighthouse, counted out in threes, or the reliable structure itself, Mrs. Ramsay provides a sense of protective stability, an impersonal shape that can be filled with and emptied of meaning. James, who finally arrives at the lighthouse with his father and sister at the end of the novel, sees it as "stark and straight," "glaring white and black, and one could see the waves breaking in white splinters like smashed glass upon the rocks" (203). The "window" of Section I has broken to pieces; yet James also acknowledges that his previous vision of the lighthouse as "silvery, misty-looking" with a "yellow eye, that opened suddenly, and softly in the evening," is also true. "For nothing is simply one thing. The other Lighthouse was true too" (186). If *To the Lighthouse* can be read, as I am proposing, as a prose ode as well as an elegy, it is one that encompasses and brings together twin visions of love and loss, offering twin consolations. The novel is an attempt to let go (we know that Woolf felt a sense of release after composing the novel, as if laying the ghosts of her parents to rest [*MOB* 81]), yet it also suggests the possibility of not grasping in the first place, of celebrating impersonality. It envisions loss as leading to despair but also, if Mrs. Ramsay is indeed a triangle, or like the triangular beam of light from the lighthouse, she is also part of an "eternal passing and flowing" that does not know death. Woolf is able to adapt the structure of the Pindaric ode to convey a rich emotional and psychological complexity. Her novel *Orlando*, published a year after *To the Lighthouse*, is another form of tribute, a "love letter" to Vita Sackville-West that also challenges the limits of a life. I will now turn to two of Woolf's later works, both of which might prompt us to ask Mr. Oliver's question from *Between the Acts:* "Had it—he was ignorant of musical terms—gone into the minor key?" (72).

IV. Going into the Minor Key: "Ode Written Partly in Prose" and *Between the Acts*

> We must somehow take a wider view, look at the whole landscape, really see it, and describe what's going on here. Then we can at least wail the right question into the swaddling band of darkness, or, if it comes to that, choir the proper praise.
> —Annie Dillard, *Pilgrim at Tinker Creek*, 11

Woolf's "Ode Written Partly in Prose" and *Between the Acts* are written in a tone and style remarkably different from *To the Lighthouse*. After completing her first draft of *The Pargiters* in 1934, which, after much revision and struggle, would become *The Years*, Woolf wrote her "strange prose Ode," as Hermione Lee calls it (647). Lee briefly mentions this ode in her magisterial biography of Woolf, suggesting that it was composed during a dark time in the author's life and in response to Wyndham Lewis's critique of her and the Bloomsbury set as feebly "peeping" at the world from a position of safety. As a rebuttal to Lewis, Woolf (according to Lee) imagines "the whole life of a London butcher from a sign glimpsed in the street, but recognized in some despair the limitations of her view" (647). I would like to suggest that we might also read this work in the context of Woolf's other odes, and in relation to the encomiastic impulse in her works. This is the only text of hers that Woolf directly labels as an ode, yet in some ways it is, I would argue, one of the least odic of her works; it foregrounds the mismatch between lyric elevation and prosaic mundanity as well as the potential violence of imagining the lives of others, particularly those of a lower class. Within this work we can trace the beginnings of a larger, late modernist, shift away from what Marina MacKay calls the "optimistic liberal humanism of Virginia Woolf in the 1920s" (and early 1930s), towards the darker, more nightmarish visions of authors including Samuel Beckett, Jean-Paul Sartre, and Albert Camus ("Going Nowhere" 1610). What was once celebratory and jubilant—a modernism that was "expansive," full of "expressive possibility, of mobility and liberation" (1602)—becomes more diminished, yet I would maintain in no way defeated.

By forcing the encomiastic into the shape of a poem that is also part prose (the genre that has traditionally "taken all the dirty work on to her own shoulders; has answered letters, paid bills, written articles, made speeches, served the needs of businessmen, shopkeepers, lawyers, soldiers, peasants" [Woolf, "Poetry" 79]), Woolf creates a disjunctive text that leaves no room for sentimentality and very little for sentiment. She explores the push and pull between poetry and prose, as she goes on to do in her draft of *Pointz Hall* and *Between the Acts*, hinting that what might be needed to express the encomiastic in the future is something more like a rhapsody, sudden and violent. Her "Ode" returns to "An Unwritten Novel" as well as "Street Haunting," celebrating as they do the play of the mind and the wealth of available narrative possibilities, and in a sense underscoring what she had been doing so far in her career: placing the modernist ode firmly in the realm of prose. However, in this work and in her final novel, dissonance overcomes any expression of exuberance or exaltation, and the tenuousness of one's hold on life, while still a cause for celebration, also potentially stirs up a sense of discomfort.

The typescript of Woolf's "Ode" is dated the 28th of October, 1934 (less than four years before she composed the opening of *Pointz Hall*), and begins with an address: "Oh Cutbush, little John, standing glum between / your father and mother, the day they decided what / to make of you, should you be florist or butcher ... / Shall John be florist or butcher?" (ll.1-5, 10) [Figure. 1]. Although the ode's title notes that it is written "partly in prose," and while Lee calls it a "prose Ode," the entire text of the typescript is lineated, although with very little

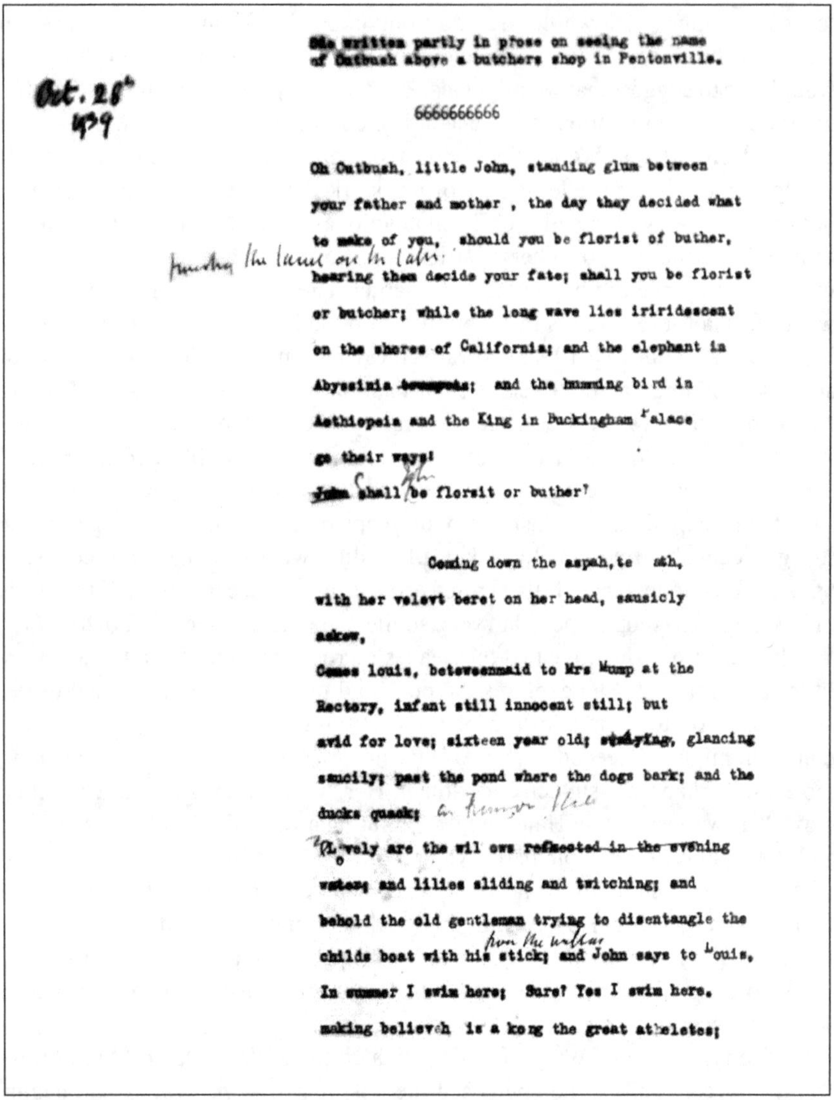

> Ode written partly in prose on seeing the name
> of Outbush above a butchers shop in Pentonville.
>
> 6666666666
>
> Oh Outbush, little John, standing glum between
> your father and mother , the day they decided what
> to make of you, should you be florist of buther,
> hearing them decide your fate; shall you be florist
> or butcher; while the long wave lies iriridescent
> on the shores of California; and the elephant in
> Abyssinia trumpets; and the humming bird in
> Aethiopeia and the King in Buckingham Palace
> go their ways!
> John shall be florsit or buther?
>
> Coming down the aspah,te ath,
> with her velevt beret on her head, sausicly
> askew,
> Comes louis, betweenmaid to Mrs Mump at the
> Rectory, infant still innocent still; but
> avid for love; sixteen year old; studying, glancing
> saucily; past the pond where the dogs bark; and the
> ducks quack;
> Lovely are the will ows reflected in the evening
> waters; and lilies sliding and twitching; and
> behold the old gentleman trying to disentangle the
> childs boat with his stick; and John says to Louis,
> In summer I swim here; Sure? Yes I swim here,
> making believeh is a kong the great athelates;

Figure 1: Typescript of Woolf's "Ode" with Holograph Revisions. Monk's House Papers B9. With the permission of the Society of Authors as the Representative of the Literary Estate of Virginia Woolf.

rhyme or meter to speak of.[24] The work thus *appears* to be a poem, yet has no other strong markers of the poetic, and is instead enmeshed in the prosaic realm of the quotidian. The speaker pays attention—an attention that seems unique within the realm of the poetic (or part-prose) ode—to the "cold meat, / shrouded in white nets borne on men's shoulders; / meat from the Argentines; from haired and red pelted / hogs and bullocks" (ll. 58-61). With a kind of anthropological precision, the speaker alsonotes the "stark and frozen corpses that shall lie like / mummies in the ice house till the Sunday fire revives / them and they drip juice into the big plate to / revive church goers" (ll. 64-67). Woolf is forcing together the elevated style of the classical ode with the realities of working class life, drawing out the "pied beauty" of the everyday while revealing at the same time a detached distaste for her subjects that almost verges on repugnance. The encomiastic impulse within her work—and perhaps, she is suggesting, within modernist works more broadly—seems to find its proper expression in prose, not poetry. Woolf's "Ode" begins to register a faltering of the odic register even as it continues the author's playful experiments and repurposing of the classical form.

After introducing us to John Cutbush as a child whose life will be determined by his parents, Woolf describes, "Coming down the asphalt path, / with her velvet beret on her head, saucily / askew," a young woman named "Louie, betweenmaid to Mrs. Mump and the Rectory, infant still innocent still; but / avid for love; sixteen years old; glancing / saucily; past the pond where the dogs bark; and the / ducks quack" (ll. 11-18). Woolf's description here is reminiscent of Jane Austen's juvenilia, and as Louie comes down the street, eager for love, we see the predictable story that will unfold. Girl meets boy. Boy (John Cutbush of Pentonville) talks of swimming and Lord Byron. The pair cuddle, kiss, and press together; they lie on the grass of Primrose Hill. John of Pentonville dreams of swimming and Byron, but then sets aside these dreams when he opens his own shop. What follows is a choppy shift in register and tone that Woolf employs throughout *Between the Acts:*

> John Cutbush stands at the
> door of his shop.
> He stands at the door of his shop.
> Still he stands at the door of his shop.
> But time has run its wheels over him. (ll. 103-107)

Caught in a cycle of Gertrude Stein-like repetitions, time passes (as it does in *To the Lighthouse*), and suddenly John has aged, run over by the wheels of time, his

---

[24] While my claim that the text is lineated can be contested given the appearance of other typescripts of Woolf's works, this claim seems corroborated by the fact that Susan Dick chose to retain the line divisions in publishing this text—the only one in *CSF* to have such lineation.

face "red; his eyes bleared" (l. 110). He has competition from a butcher's across the street, and "Louie in the room behind the shop is broad / thighed, sullen eyed; and the little boy died; / and the girl is a worry, always after the boys" (ll. 118-20). In this rhyming singsong, of "thighed," "eyed" and "died," the slant rhyme of "Louie" and "worry," the difficulties of working class lives seem handled too lightly for comfort. It is when rhyme is used explicitly that the mismatch between the poetic form and the work's content seems most apparent; one can imagine the older Louie as Mrs. Dempster in *Mrs. Dalloway*, the tired woman who reflects that "really, what with eating, drinking, and mating, the bad days and the good, life had been no mere matter of roses," and who plaintively asks for "Pity" for this loss of roses (27). Yet this working class woman, whose life we briefly glimpse in the novel, has a dignity denied to Louie, as though the traditionally elevated ode shuts out this possibility in the comic mismatch between subject and form.

Like "Street Haunting," this ode "deviate[s] into those footpaths" in "the heart of the forest where live those wild beasts, our fellow men," yet does so without a strong sense of "delight and wonder" (35). In Pentonville and Islington, we are told, there are flares lit "over barrows"; "meat blazes"; the "lumps are tossed and wrapped"; "[b]ags bulge on / women's arms" (ll. 89-94). The children "gaze up at the flares and the / coarse light and the red and white faces burn them / selves for ever on the pure eyeballs" (ll. 95-97). There is something both celebratory and discomfiting in these details (the lumps, bulges, coarse light, and eyeballs), as though the speaker is both fascinated and repulsed by what she sees.[25] After describing how life has been difficult for John and Louie, the speaker again shifts tone to note:

> These are semblances of human faces seen in passing
> translated from a foreign language.
> And the language already makes up new words.
> For next door there are urns and slabs of marble in an
> undertaker's window; next door are musical instruments
> next a home for cats and dogs; and then the Convent
> and there on that eminence stands
> sublime the tower of the Prison .... (ll. 124-131)

Echoing the conclusion of "An Unwritten Novel," this passage seems to celebrate, with a stately ceremony, a sense of plenitude and wealth, yet is written in a far less exuberant and almost a fatigued key. The speaker notes how the "flower of life ever shakes free from the / bud," and how we "give thanks to the armies / and

---

[25] This unsettling attention to corporeality can be seen in the description of Mrs. Haines in *Between the Acts*: "Mrs. Haines, the wife of the gentleman farmer, a goosefaced woman with eyes protruding as if they saw something to gobble in the gutter" (3).

navies and flying men and actresses / who provide our nightly entertainment" (ll. 143-47). When we hold the pages of the newspaper, we little:

> think of the wealth we can gather between the
> palms of two hands; how little we can grasp
> how little we can interpret and read aright
> the name John Cutbush but only as we pass his
> shop on Saturday night, cry out Hail Cutbush,
> of Pentonville, I salute thee; passing. (ll. 148-54)

It is the elusive and the speculative that Woolf salutes and hails here, passing; it is her power as a writer to conjure a life and a world from a shop sign randomly passed on the street that she celebrates. There is again an appreciation for a kind of dappled beauty and a willingness to not grasp at the subjects whose lives one is imagining. Yet there is also a more melancholy (if not wholly despairing) acknowledgment of what might get left out in sweeping one's net over the city, a more subdued sense of the violence of the "wheels of time," of the grinding realities of life and lust and loss. Woolf seems conscious of the more uncomfortable politics of the odic impulse employed so exuberantly elsewhere in her works—to question and ironize the belief that any individual, especially of the lower classes, could provide a wealth of imaginative opportunities for an author, who is free to dip into a life and speculate about it and then easily move on, hastening, following, "you, you, you." The imagined John Cutbush and his wife Louie can be ceremonially elevated by Woolf's speaker (as she later elevates an oil lamp and a daylight bird), yet do not share the same opportunities to become untethered from their lives and identities.

Woolf's later excision of her two brief prose odes from all but the first typescript draft of *Pointz Hall* suggests a further embrace of and turn away from the classical ode. Like the "ancient and out-of-date oil lamp" celebrated in the first of these odes, it seems from the erasure of both addresses from the text that the ode itself might now be both "ancient and out-of-date," no longer an ideal conduit for lyric exaltation, address, or tribute. However, to first find entry into the world of this country house, Woolf approached by way of praise and playful gravitas. In the odes themselves, she does not use line breaks, yet her semi-colons seem to serve a similar function. She returns again to the quotidian, to the sense of the irregular and incongruous, keeping away from the frozen realm of beauty. The lamp, like the beams from a lighthouse, offers security and stability while civilized life drops its vestments; the daylight bird chuckles about life rather than singing of death. These lines are replaced in the published version with: "It was a summer's night and they were talking, in the big room with the windows open to the garden, about the cesspool. The county council had promised to bring water to the village, but they hadn't" (*BTA* 5).

John Whittier-Ferguson astutely argues that the revisions to this novel, "when read in the order of their composition, reveal a text in the process of forgetting itself: a novel that grows more elliptical, less discursive, less explanatory with each revision; a novel in which conversations unravel and characters become more opaque as Woolf reworks them" (301-302). The process of "unwriting" that one can track in these drafts points to "an audience's failures to recall fully or with adequate understanding its culture's foundational texts." We see evidence of a kind of "cultural amnesia," a forgetting of the English literary tradition (303-305).[26] As references to writers such as Chaucer and to generations of readers who take up his books in the Pointz Hall library are cut from later iterations of the novel, this tradition "falls silent," and what is underscored in the final work is the sense that "To be modern is to forget, to be forgotten" (308, 309). Woolf's eventual deletion of her discursive and lofty odes can thus be read as part of a larger process of forgetting that exposes the shallowness of the modern moment.[27] Rather than continuity, what we get in *Between the Acts* is a clash between different tones, registers, modes, voices, and styles that becomes the very fabric of the novel, and particularly of the pageant within it.

After Miss LaTrobe's choppy historical pageant, which begins with Queen Elizabeth and ends in the present day—a summer's afternoon on the brink of the Second World War—the playwright deems the performance a failure. But then her thoughts are interrupted:

> Then suddenly the starlings attacked the tree behind which she had hidden. In one flock they pelted it like so many winged stones. The whole tree hummed with the whizz they made, as if each bird plucked a wire. A whizz, a buzz rose from the bird-buzzing, bird-vibrant, bird-blackened tree. The tree became a rhapsody, a quivering cacophony, a whizz and vibrant rapture,

---

[26] Pamela Caughie also discusses "An Unwritten Novel" as a text that is being literally *unwritten* (92-93).

[27] As Whittier-Ferguson notes, Woolf was "re-moulding" English literary tradition before she conceived of *Reading at Random* (later titled *Turning the Page*). According to Brenda Silver, "...Woolf's diary records side by side with the progress of *Pointz Hall* ... a steady stream of reading for the book she now described as threading a necklace through English life and literature. Much of her reading was linked to her plan to begin her history as she had begun the pageant in her novel—with the early forms of English literature and society, and with the anonymous men and women who created them" (357). We see English literature become fragmented in *Between the Acts* while it is taken up more directly and fully in her last, uncompleted, critical works, "Anon" and "The Reader." In all of these texts, a classical literary heritage is excised, or banished, to a remote past.

branches, leaves, birds syllabling discordantly life, life, life, without measure, without stop devouring the tree. Then up! Then off! (124)

We can see an echoing here of the passage discussed above from "An Unwritten Novel," describing individuals as moths or butterflies, flying up, then off at the slightest movement of the hand. Yet this passage is also electric with sound and motion as the tree hums with whizzing birds, pelting it, creating a "vibrant rapture," "syllabling discordantly, life, life, life, without measure." This discordant speech encapsulates a different odic register from what we have seen in Woolf's previous works, one rooted in the kind of disjunctions of her "Ode" to Cutbush while also moving beyond it. The violence of the rhapsody, which "devour[s] the tree" and then ends, marking the change from day to night, civilized society to a more primal state without individual identity, also signals a new beginning. After this rhapsody, La Trobe sits in the dimness of a pub, raises a glass to her lips, and listens: "Words of one syllable sank down into the mud. She drowsed; she nodded. The mud became fertile. Words rose above the intolerably laden dumb oxen ploughing through the mud. Words without meaning—wonderful words" (125). *Between the Acts* fleetingly offers and envisions a different register for the encomiastic, one that celebrates the discordant and the dissonant, the clash of poetry and prose, and that relishes in its minor key. We are given a fragmented reality from which a new "play" might be written:

> Then down beneath a force was born in opposition; then another. On different levels they diverged. On different levels ourselves went forward; flower gathering some on the surface; others descending to wrestle with the meaning; but all comprehending; all enlisted. The whole population of the mind's immeasurable profundity came flocking; from the unprotected, the unskinned; and dawn rose; and azure; from chaos and cacophony measure; but not the melody of surface sound alone controlled it; but also the warring battle-plumed warriors straining asunder: To part? No. Compelled from the ends of the horizon; recalled from the edge of appalling crevasses; they crashed; solved; united. (112)

This passage seems to have a remnant within it of the original opening to *Pointz Hall*, with the lamp unifying "the discordant [in unity; God or Goddess]." The elation and high spirits of Woolf's earlier odes here somehow plays like a tune "with its feet always on the same spot," becoming "sugared, insipid," boring "a hole with its perpetual invocation to perpetual adoration" (72). What Woolf leaves us with in her final novel is something sublime and potentially dangerous: a brief rhapsody that sings achingly in the moment, without past or future.

Although Whittier-Ferguson does not explicitly suggest that Woolf's revisions to the novel can be linked to the pressing realities of the Second World War, we might deduce this given the fact that the first major revisions to the draft occurred after the start of the war. Between the composition of the early and later typescript drafts, Woolf recorded in her diary, "This war has begun in cold blood. One merely feels that the killing machine has to be set in action. ... It seems entirely meaningless—a perfunctory slaughter, like taking a jar in one hand, a hammer in another. Why must this be smashed? Nobody knows. This feeling is different from any before" (*D5* 235). In his biography of his aunt, Quentin Bell cites a passage from the last volume of Leonard Woolf's autobiography, exemplifying as it does "the image that stared Leonard and Virginia in the face in July 1940"—the "quality of the enemy who now had victory almost within his grasp and who, having achieved it, would be released from all restraints" (216). Woolf and others had long anticipated the outbreak of another war, yet perhaps in response to its actual devastations and threats, and the absurdity of what MacKay deems this war's "sheer secondness" (*Modernism* 5), Woolf could only imagine a form of praise that merged violence with renewal, a merging that is suggested in the final lines of the novel, with its references to enmity and love, fighting and embracing, "from which another life might be born" (129).

The odes of Virginia Woolf, composed throughout her career, are experiments with a classical form that can productively be read alongside her elegies. They express reverence while overturning traditional hierarchies of gender and class; celebrate artistry without insisting upon mastery; and express an adoration for all that remains elusive, unknowable, and irrecoverable in any attempt to grasp at life and meaning. Ultimately, Woolf's work shifts registers and gestures towards further experiments with the encomiastic and with forms of praise that lay, for Woolf at least, beyond the ends of the horizon. Yet her work is a testament to the power of prose to not only chant the elegy but to also hymn the love and beauty that makes loss meaningful.

I would like to take this opportunity to express my deep gratitude to Maria DiBattista, who commented on a previous draft of this essay, and who has fostered my adoration of Woolf for years with her marvelous teaching and writing. The idea for this article first developed in a seminar on the ode led by Susan Stewart, and I am thankful for her inspiration and guidance. My sincere thanks goes as well to the anonymous readers who offered such insightful feedback on the essay. Lawrence Lipking kindly sent me the collection of Woolf books belonging to his late wife, Joanna Lipking: I am grateful for their generosity, and for the chance to make use of books so lovingly and well read.

Works Cited

Abrams, M.H., and Geoffrey Galt Harpham. "Ode." *A Glossary of Literary Terms*, Eleventh Edition. Cengage Learning, 2015, pp. 262-63.

Beer, Gillian. "Hume, Stephen, and Elegy in *To the Lighthouse*." *Virginia Woolf: The Common Ground*, U of Michigan P, 1996, pp. 29-47.

Bell, Quentin. *Virginia Woolf: A Biography*. Quality Paperback Book Club, 1972, 1992.

Caughie, Pamela. *Virginia Woolf & Postmodernism: Literature in Quest & Question of Itself.* U of Illinois P, 1991.

Cavitch, Max. *The American Elegy: The Poetry of Mourning from the Puritans to Whitman.* U of Minnesota P, 1984.

Cook, David A. "The Content and Meaning of Swinburne's 'Anactoria.'" *Victorian Poetry*, vol. 9, no. 1/2, 1971, pp. 77-93.

DiBattista, Maria. "Virginia Woolf's Winter's Tale." *Virginia Woolf's Major Novels: The Fables of Anon,* Yale UP, 1980, pp. 64-110.

Dillard, Annie. *Pilgrim at Tinker Creek.* Harper Perennial Modern Classics, 2013.

Forster, E. M. "The Novels of Virginia Woolf." *Virginia Woolf: The Critical Heritage*, edited by Robin Majumdar and Allen McLaurin, Routledge, 1975, pp. 171-176.

Froula, Christine. "Mrs. Dalloway's Postwar Elegy: Women, War, and the Art of Mourning." *Virginia Woolf and the Bloomsbury Avant-garde: War, Civilization, Modernity,* Columbia UP, 2005, pp. 87-128.

Fry, Paul H. *The Poet's Calling in the English Ode.* Yale UP, 1980.

Fuss, Diana. *Dying Modern: A Meditation on Elegy.* Duke UP, 2013.

Gay, Ross. *A Catalog of Unabashed Gratitude.* U of Pittsburgh P, 2015.

Goldman, Jane. "From *Mrs. Dalloway* to *The Waves*: New elegy and lyric experimentalism." *The Cambridge Companion to Virginia Woolf,* Second edition, edited by Susan Sellers, Cambridge UP, 2010, pp. 49-69.

Heath-Stubbs, John. *The Ode.* Oxford UP, 1969.

Hopkins, Gerard Manley. "Pied Beauty." Poetry Foundation https://www.poetryfoundation.org/poems-and-poets/poems/detail/44399.

Hussey, Mark. Preface. Virginia Woolf. *Between the Acts*, annotated with an introduction by Melba Cuddy-Keane. Harcourt, Inc., 2005.

Kennedy, David. *Elegy*. Routledge, 2007.

Knox-Shaw. "*To the Lighthouse:* The Novel as Elegy." *English Studies in Africa*, vol. 29, no. 1, 1986, pp. 31-52.

Latham, Sean. "Elegy for the Snob: Virginia Woolf and the Victorians." *"Am I a Snob?": Modernism and the Novel,* Cornell UP, 2003, pp. 59-89.

Lee, Hermione. *Virginia Woolf.* Alfred A. Knopf, 1997.

Lewis, Pericles. *Religious Experience and the Modernist Novel,* Cambridge UP, 2010.

MacKay, Marina. "Going Nowhere in Modernist London." *PMLA,* vol. 124, no. 5, 2009, pp. 1600-1613.

——. *Modernism and World War II.* Cambridge UP, 2007.

Maddisson, Carol. *Apollo and the Nine: A History of the Ode.* Johns Hopkins UP, 1960

Martini, Arturo, "Sculpture Dead Language." *The Modern Sculpture Reader,* edited by Jon Wood, David Hulks, Alex Potts, Henry Moore Foundation, 2007, pp. 165-179.

McGavran, James Holt Jr. "Shelley, Virginia Woolf, and *The Waves*: A Balcony of One's Own." *South Atlantic Review,*Vol. 48, No. 4, 1983, pp. 58-73.

Oxner, Alex. "Characterizing Absence: Virginia Woolf's New Elegy in *Jacob's Room.*" *The Explicator,* vol. 72, no.3, 2014, pp. 210-214.

Penner, Erin Kay. "The Order of a Smashed Window-Pane: Novel Elegy in Woolf's *The Waves.*" *Twentieth-Century Literature,* vol. 61, no. 1, 2015, pp. 63-91.

Pindar. *The Complete Odes.* Edited by Stephen Instone, translated by Anthony Verity, Oxford UP, 2007.

Ramazani, Jahan. *Poetry of Mourning: The Modern Elegy from Hardy to Heaney.* U of Chicago P, 1994.

Rothman, Roger. "On Beauty," blog post for Aesthetic Turns, 2 July 2016, *Modernism/modernity* Print Plus <https://modernismmodernity.org/forums/posts/beauty-again>.

Scarry, Elaine. *On Beauty and Being Just.* Princeton UP, 2001.

Shafer, Robert. *The English Ode to 1660: An Essay in Literary History.* Haskell House, 1966.

Shuster, G.N. *The English Ode from Milton to Keats.* Columbia UP, 1940.

Smythe, Karen. "Virginia Woolf's Elegiac Enterprise." *NOVEL,* vol. 26, no. 1, 1992, pp. 64-79.

Stevenson, Randall, and Jane Goldman. "'But what? Elegy?': Modernist Reading and the Death of Mrs. Ramsay." *The Yearbook of English Studies,* vol. 26, 1996, pp. 173-186.

Swinburne, Charles Algernon. *Poems and Ballads & Atlanta in Calydon.* Edited by Kenneth Haynes, Penguin, 2000.

——. "Sapphics." Poetry Foundation < https://www.poetryfoundation.org/poems-and- poets/poems/detail/45302>

Vickery, John B. *The Prose Elegy: An Exploration of Modern American and British Fiction.*Louisiana State UP, 2009.

Whitman, Walt. *The Complete Poems.* Edited by Francis Murphy, Penguin, 2004.

Whittier-Ferguson. "The Burden of Drafts: Woolf's Revisions of *Between the Acts.*" *Text,* vol. 10, 1997, pp. 297-319.

Woolf, Virginia. *A Room of One's Own* and *Three Guineas*. Edited by Morag Shiach, Oxford UP, 1998.
———. "An Unwritten Novel." *A Haunted House and Other Short Stories,* Harcourt, Brace & World, 1972, pp. 8-21.
———. *Between the Acts*. Introduction and Notes by Gillian Beer, edited by Stella McNichol, Penguin, 1992.
———. *Diary of Virginia Woolf.* Vol 3, 1925-1930. Ed. Anne Olivier Bell, Assisted by Andrew McNeillie. Harcourt, 1980.
———. *Jacob's Room*. Edited by Kate Flint. Oxford UP, 2008.
———. "A Sketch of the Past." *In Moments of Being: A Collection of Autobiographical Writings.* Edited with an introduction and notes by Jeanne Schulkind. Second Edition. Harcourt, Inc., 1985.
———. "Mr. Bennett and Mrs. Brown." *The Essays of Virginia Woolf,* Vol. 3, 1919-1924, edited by Andrew McNeillie, Harcourt Brace Jovanovich, 1988, pp. 384-389.
———. *Mrs. Dalloway*. Harcourt Inc., 1981.
———. "Ode Written Partly in Prose on seeing the name of Cutbush above a butcher's shop in Pentonville." *The Complete Shorter Fiction of Virginia Woolf,* edited by Susan Dick. Harcourt Brace Jovanovich, 1985, pp. 231-235.
———. "Poetry, Fiction, and the Future." *Virginia Woolf Selected Essays*, edited with introduction and notes by David Bradshaw. Oxford UP, 2008, pp. 74-84.
———. *Pointz Hall: The Earlier and Later Typescripts of Between the Acts*. Edited with Introduction, Annotations and Afterword by Mitchell A. Leaska, University Publications, 1983.
———. "Street Haunting: A London Adventure." *The Death of the Moth and Other Essays,* Harcourt Brace Jovanovich, 1970, pp. 20-36.
———. *The Voyage Out.* Harcourt, Inc., 1948.
———. *To the Lighthouse.* Harcourt, Inc., 1981.
———. *To the Lighthouse: The Original Holograph Draft.* Edited by Susan Dick. Hogarth, 1983.
Zonana, Joyce. "Swinburne's Sappho: The Muse as Sister-Goddess." *Victorian Poetry*, vol. 28, no. 1, 1990, pp. 39-50.
Zwerdling, Alex. "*Jacob's Room:* Woolf's Satiric Elegy." *ELH,* vol. 48, no. 4, 1981, pp. 894-913.

Guide to Library Special Collections

This list reflects updates or changes received in 2016. Readers are advised to check an institution's website for the most current information. Suggestions for additions to this list are welcome.

Name of Collection: The Beinecke Rare Book and Manuscript Library

Contact: Kevin Repp, Curator of Modern Books and Manuscripts
Nancy Kuhl, Curator of American Literature

Address: Yale University Library
P.O. Box 208240
New Haven, CT 06520-8240

URL: http://beinecke.library.yale.edu/

Access Requirements: Registration required at first visit.

Holdings Relevant To Woolf: General Collection includes autograph manuscript of "Notes on Oliver Goldsmith." Comments on Edward Gibbon, William Beckford Collection. Letters from Virginia Woolf in the Bryher Papers, the Louise Morgan and Otto Theis Papers, and the Rebecca West Papers. Related material: 41 letters from Vita Sackville-West to Violet Trefusis; files relating to Robert Manson Myers's *From Beowulf to Virginia Woolf* in the Edmond Pauker Papers.

Yale Collection of American Literature includes typewritten manuscripts of "The Art of Walter Sickert," "Augustine Birrell," "Aurora Leigh," "How Should One Read a Book?" "Letter to a Young Poet," "The Novels of Turgenev," "Street Haunting." Dial/Scofield Thayer Papers: manuscripts of "The Lives of the Obscure," "Miss Ormerod," and "Mrs. Dalloway in Bond Street." Letters from Virginia Woolf in the William Rose Benet Papers, the Benet Family Correspondence, Henry Seidel Canby Papers, the Seward Collins Papers, the Dial/Scofield Thayer Papers, and the *Yale Review* archive. Material relating to translations of Woolf in the Thornton Wilder papers.

Related material: Clive Bell, "Virginia Woolf" (Dial/Scofield Thayer Papers); 43 letters from Leonard Woolf to Helen McAfee (*Yale Review*); 11 letters from Leonard Woolf to Gertrude Stein.

Name of Collection: The Henry W. and Albert A. Berg Collection of English and American Literature

Contact: berg@nypl.org for access procedures
Isaac Gewirtz, Curator
isaacgewirtz@nypl.org

Address: New York Public Library, Room 320
Fifth Avenue & 42nd Street
New York, NY 10018

Telephone: 212-930-0802
Fax: 212-930-0079
Email: isaacgewirtz@nypl.org

Hours: Tue.–Wed. 11 am–6:45 pm
Thu.–Sat. 10 am–5:45 pm
Closed Sun., Mon. and legal holidays

Access Requirements: After acquiring Library card in room 315, check outerwear and all containers (briefcases, computer cases, handbags, folders, etc.) in Ground Floor cloakroom, and proceed to the Berg Collection. Traceable and photo identification required. Undergraduates working on honors theses need letter from faculty advisor to be sent to the Berg's Curator and to receive an affirmative response prior to scheduling an appointment with the Berg librarians. No books may be brought to the reading tables, including notebooks.

Restrictions: Virginia Woolf's bound MSS, because of their fragile condition, are made available on microfilm and CD. URL for Berg finding aid: http://www.nypl.org/research/manuscripts/berg/ brgwoolf.xml. N.B. All the Berg's Woolf MSS are on microfilm and 90 percent of them are on CD, published by Research Publications and available at many research libraries.

GUIDE TO LIBRARY SPECIAL COLLECTIONS 143

Holdings Relevant To Woolf: Manuscripts/typescripts of all of the novels except *Orlando*, including: *Between the Acts, Flush, Jacob's Room, Mrs. Dalloway* (notes and fragments), *Night and Day, To the Lighthouse, The Voyage Out, The Waves, The Years*; 12 notebooks of articles, essays, fiction and reviews, 1924–1940; 36 volumes of diaries; 26 volumes of reading notes; correspondence with Vanessa Bell, Ethel Smyth, Vita Sackville-West and others. Su Hua Ling Chen's Bloomsbury correspondence; proof copy of *A Room of One's Own* (July 1929); ALS Vanessa Bell to Vita Sackville-West, April 29, 1941 [in Marler, *Selected Letters* 478-80]; Frank Dean, *Strike While the Iron's Hot: Frank Dean's Life as a Blacksmith and Farrier in Rodmell*, ed. Susan Rowland (S. Rowland, 1994) [includes map, accounts of search for VW's body and of her funeral]; Vita Sackville-West, *Marian Stranways*, autograph manuscript, [1913].

Name of Collection: The British Library Manuscript Collections

Contact: Manuscripts and Maps Reference Team

Address: 96 Euston Road
London NW1 2DB
England

Telephone: 0207-412-7513
Fax: 0207-412-7745
Email: mss@bl.uk

Hours: Mon. 10 am–5 pm; Tues.–Sat.: 9:30 am–5 pm

Access Requirements: British Library Reader Pass (signed I.D. required and usually proof of post-graduate academic status, or other demonstrable need to use the collections—see www.bl.uk). In addition, access to most literary autograph material only available with letter of recommendation.

Restrictions: Paper Copies, Microfilms, and Photography of selected items available upon receipt of written authorization for photo duplication from the copyright holder.

Holdings Relevant To Woolf:	Diaries 1930–1931 (microfilm); *Mrs. Dalloway* and other writings (1923–1925) three volumes (Add MS 51044-51046); letter from Leonard Woolf to H. G. Wells (1941) (Add MS 52553); two letters from Virginia Woolf and three letters from Leonard Woolf to John Lehmann (1941) (Add MS 56234); letters from Virginia Woolf (1923-1927) and one written on behalf of Leonard Woolf to S. S. Koteliansky (1946) (Add MS 48974); notebook of Virginia Stephen (1906–1909) (Add MS 61837); Stephen family papers (Add MS 88954); travel and literary notebook of Virginia Woolf (Add MS 61837); A sketch of the past revised ts (1940) (Add MS 61973); letters from Virginia Woolf in the correspondence files of Lytton and James Strachey (Add MS 60655-60734); letter from Virginia Woolf to Mildred Massingberd (Add MS 61891); letter from Virginia Woolf to Harriet Shaw Weaver(1917) (Add MS 57353); (in the same volume as the letter on behalf of Leonard); letter from Virginia Woolf to Frances Cornford (1929) (Add MS 58422); letter from Virginia Woolf to Ernest Rhys (1930) (Egerton MS 3248); correspondence of Virginia Woolf in the Society of Authors archive (1934–1937) (Add MS 63206-63463); letter and postcard from Virginia Woolf to Bernard Shaw (1940) (Add MS 50522); three letters (suicide notes) from Virginia Woolf (1941) (Add MS 57947). "Hyde Park Gate News" 1891–1892, 1895 (Add. MSS 70725, 70726). Letters of Virginia and Leonard Woolf to Lady Aberconway, 1927–1941 (Add MS 70775). Letters from Virginia Woolf to Macmillan Co. 1903, 1908 (Add MS 54786-56035). Collection of RPs ("reserved photocopies"– copies of manuscripts exported, some subject to restrictions).
Name of Collection:	Harry Ransom Center
Contact:	Head, Research Services
Address:	Harry Ransom Center The University of Texas at Austin P.O. Box 7219 Austin, TX 78713-7219

Telephone:	512-471-9119
Fax:	512-471-2899
Email:	reference@hrc.utexas.edu
Hours:	See web site for most current information: www.hrc.utexas.edu
Access Requirements:	Completed online research application; current photo identification.
Holdings Relevant To Woolf:	The manuscript collection includes the typed manuscript with autograph revisions of *Kew Gardens,* and the typed manuscript and autograph revisions of "Thoughts on Peace in an Air Raid." The Center holds 571 of Woolf's letters, including correspondence to Elizabeth Bowen, Lady Ottoline Morrell, Mary Hutchinson, William Plomer, Hugh Walpole and others. Further mss. relating to Virginia Woolf include letters to her from T. S. Eliot and reviews of her work. A substantial collection of the first British and American editions of Woolf's published works, as well as 130 volumes from Leonard and Virginia Woolf's library and a collection of books published by the Hogarth Press, is also housed. An art collection holds a landscape painting of Virginia's garden and a series of Cockney cartoons in a sketch book, signed "V.W." The center also has extensive holdings of materials related to Leonard Woolf, Ottoline Morrell, Mary Hutchinson, Lytton Strachey, Dora Carrington, E. M. Forster, Clive Bell, Roger Fry, Vanessa Bell, Bertrand Russell, Elizabeth Bowen, William Plomer, Stephen Spender and Hugh Walpole.
Name of Collection:	Houghton Library (Monk's House Photograph Albums)
Contact:	Houghton Public Services
Address:	Harvard Yard Cambridge, MA 02138 United States

Telephone: 617-495-2440
Fax: 617-495-1376
Email: houghton_library@harvard.edu

URL: http://hcl.harvard.edu/libraries/houghton/
Hours: Mon, Fri, Sat 9-5
Tue-Thu 9-7

Restrictions: http://hcl.harvard.edu/info/special_collections/index.cfm

The Monk's House photographs are restricted due to fragility. Users should consult the digital surrogates linked from the finding aids below. Access to originals requires permission from the curator of the Harvard Theatre Collection.

Holdings Relevant To Woolf: Virginia Woolf Monk's House photograph album, MH-1
Virginia Woolf Monk's House photograph album, MH-2
Virginia Woolf Monk's House photograph album, MH-3
Virginia Woolf Monk's House photograph album, MH-4
Virginia Woolf Monk's House photograph album, MH-5
Virginia Woolf Monk's House photograph album, MH-6
Virginia Woolf Monk's House photographs

User can also page through the albums by following the links on our website (http://press.pace.edu/woolf-studies-annual-wsa/)

Name of Collection: The Lilly Library

Contact: Joel Silver, Director
Cherry Williams, Curator of Manuscripts

Address: The Lilly Library, Indiana University
1200 East Seventh Street
Bloomington, IN 47405-5500

Telephone:	812-855-2452
Fax:	812-855-3143
Email:	liblilly@indiana.edu, silverj@indiana.edu, chedwill@indiana.edu
Hours:	Mon.–Fri. 9 am–6 pm; Sat. 9 am–1 pm; *Closed Sundays and Major Holidays*
Restrictions:	Closed stacks; material use confined to reading room; wheelchair-accessible reading room and exhibitions (but no wheelchair-accessible restroom).
Holdings Relevant To Woolf:	Corrected page proofs for the American edition of *Mrs. Dalloway*; letters to Woolf from Desmond and Mary (Molly) MacCarthy; 77 letters (published in *Letters*) from Woolf to correspondents including Donald Clifford Brace, Robert Gathorne-Hardy, Barbara (Strachey) Halpern, Richard Arthur Warren Hughes, Desmond MacCarthy and Molly MacCarthy; "Preliminary Scheme for the formation of a Partnership between Mr Leonard Sidney Woolf and Mr John Lehmann to take over The Hogarth Press" (includes contract signed by Lehmann, Leonard Woolf, and Virginia Woolf and receipt for Lehmann's payment to Virginia Woolf to purchase Virginia Woolf's share in the Hogarth Press); photographs of Virginia Woolf, Leonard Woolf, Lytton Strachey, Strachey family, Roger Fry, and Vanessa Bell (Hannah Whitall Smith mss.); (Richard) Kennedy mss. (four hand-colored lithographs of Virginia Woolf: artist's proofs for RK's portfolio, VIRGINIA WOOLF: "AS I KNEW HER"; Sackville-West, V. mss. (10,529 items: includes the correspondence of Vita Sackville-West, and Harold Nicolson); MacCarthy mss. (ca. 10,000 items: papers of Desmond and Molly MacCarthy); correspondence between LW and Mary Gaither regarding publication of *A Checklist of the Hogarth Press* (1976, repr. 1986); Todd Avery, *Close and Affectionate Friends: Desmond and Molly MacCarthy and the Bloomsbury Group* (The Lilly Library/Indiana University Libraries, 1999).

Name of Collection: 1. Katherine Mansfield Papers
2. Arts Club of Chicago Papers

Contact: Martha Briggs, Lloyd Lewis Curator of Modern Manuscripts
Liesl Olson, Director, Scholl Center for American History and Culture

Address: The Newberry Library, 60 West Walton Street, Chicago, IL, 60610

Telephone: 312-255-3554 (Briggs)
312-255-3665 (Olson)

Email: briggsm@newberry.org
olsonl@newberry.org

Hours: Tuesday-Friday: 9-5
Saturday: 9-1

Access Requirements: The Newberry's reading rooms are open to researchers who are at least 16 years old or juniors in high school. Before using the collections, all researchers must apply for and receive a reader's card. Issued in the Reference Center on the third floor, cards require a valid photo ID, proof of current home address, and a research interest that is supported by the Newberry's collections.

Holdings Relevant To Woolf: The papers of the Arts Club of Chicago—since 1916, a private club and preeminent exhibitor of international art—contain material related to Bloomsbury artists and how they were received in Chicago. The papers of Katherine Mansfield contain manuscript copies of some of Mansfield's most important work, and outgoing correspondence—the bulk to artist Dorothy Brett and Lady Ottoline Morrell. There are a few incoming miscellaneous letters, printed works, photographs and memorabilia.

Name of Collection: Jane Marcus Collection

Contact: Mount Holyoke College Archives and Special Collections

GUIDE TO LIBRARY SPECIAL COLLECTIONS 149

Address: Mount Holyoke College
50 College Street
8 Dwight Hall
South Hadley MA 01075

Telephone: 413-538-3079
Fax: 413-538-3029
Email: archives@mtholyoke.edu

Hours: Monday through Friday; 9:30am to noon and 1 to 4:30pm

Access Requirements: Please contact the staff to make an appointment for your visit. Researchers complete a registration form upon arrival.

Restrictions: The Jane Marcus Collection was received in December 2016 and is currently being reviewed. Please contact the Archives and Special Collections staff for updated access information.

Holdings Relevant To Woolf: Jane Marcus, who died in May 2015, laid the groundwork for feminist studies to become a mode of inquiry within the academy and her work established Virginia Woolf as a major canonical writer. The collection includes several of Marcus's unpublished manuscripts, as well as her research files and correspondence.

Name of Collection: Literature & Rare Books, Special Collections, University of Maryland Libraries

Contact: Doug McElrath, Acting Head of Special Collections and University Archives (SCUA)

Address: University of Maryland
2208 Hornbake Library
College Park, MD 20742

Telephone: 310-405-9212
Fax: 301-314-2709
Email: askhornbake@umd.edu

Hours: Dates and hours of operation subject to change.

Regular hours are Monday-Friday, 10 am to 5 pm. Extended hours are available on select days during the academic school year.
Email askhornbake@umd.edu before planning a research visit.

Access Requirements: Photo ID.

Holdings Relevant To Woolf: Papers of Hope Mirrlees contain five autograph letters and postcards (1919–1928) from Virginia Woolf to Mirrlees. Also in the collection are 113 letters from T. S. Eliot to Mirrlees, and three letters from Lady Ottoline Morrell to Mirrlees. A finding aid is available at http://hdl.handle.net/1903.1/1536.

Name of Collection: Monks House Papers/Leonard Woolf Papers/Charleston Papers/Nicolson Papers

Contact: University of Sussex, Special Collections

Address: The Keep
Woollards Way
Brighton & Hove
BN1 9PB

Telephone: 01273 482349
Email: library.specialcoll@sussex.ac.uk
URL: http://www.thekeep.info

Access Requirements By appointment. Identification to be presented on arrival. Registration and material requests can be made through our website.

Restrictions: Photocopying strictly controlled.

Holdings Relevant To Woolf: The University of Sussex holds two large archives relating to Leonard and Virginia Woolf: The Monks House Papers, primarily correspondence and MSS of Virginia Woolf, including the three scrapbooks relating to *Three Guineas*, and Virginia Woolf's engagement diaries from 1930 to her death in 1941; and The Leonard Woolf Papers, primarily correspondence and other papers of Leonard Woolf. Monks House Papers are available on microfilm

GUIDE TO LIBRARY SPECIAL COLLECTIONS 151

in many research libraries. The Charleston Papers consist in the main of letters written to or by Clive and Vanessa Bell and Duncan Grant which had accumulated in their home; the library houses Quentin Bell's photocopied set; letters from Roger Fry, Maynard Keynes, Lytton Strachey, Virginia Woolf, Vita Sackville-West, E. M. Forster, T. S. Eliot, Frances Partridge and others. The Maria Jackson letters comprise some 900 letters from Maria Jackson to Julia and Leslie Stephen. The Nicolson Papers complement these three Sussex archives relating to the Bloomsbury Group, and consist of Nigel Nicolson's correspondence relating to his editorial work as principal editor of the six-volume *Letters of Virginia Woolf*, published between 1975 and 1980.

The Bell Papers. A. O. Bell's correspondence relating to her editorial work on Virginia Woolf's diaries, a parallel collection to the Nicolson Papers. Collection level description may be accessed at www.archiveshub.ac.uk

Name of Collection: The Morgan Library & Museum

Contact: Reading Room

Address: 225 Madison Avenue
New York, NY 10016

Telephone: 212-590-0315
Fax: readingroom@themorgan.org
URL: www.themorgan.org

Access Requirements: Admission to the Reading Room is by application and by appointment.
See www.themorgan.org/research/reading.asp for application form.

Holdings Relevant To Woolf: Virginia Woolf. Autograph manuscript notebook, 1931 Sept. 24. 1 item (52 p.) ; 265 x 208 mm. Contains drafts of "A Letter to a Young Poet," a brief letter to the press entitled "The Villa Jones" [ff. 3–5] and a monologue by a working-class woman [ff. 44–46]. MA 3333. Purchased on the Fellows Fund with the special assistance of Anne S. Dayton, Enid A. Haupt, Mrs. James H. Ripley, Mr. and Mrs. August H. Schilling, and John S. Thacher, 1979.

Virginia Woolf. Autograph letters signed (2) and typed letter signed, dated London [etc.], to E. McKnight Kauffer, 1931 Apr. 4–23, and undated. 3 items (4 p.). Concerning a drawing of her and a bibliography of her works. MA 1679. Purchased in 1959.

Vanessa Bell. 84 autograph letters, 3 typed letters, 7 postcards, and 3 telegrams. Most, but not all, are written by Vanessa Bell to John Maynard Keynes. Concerning Duncan Grant, Roger Fry, Clive Bell, the Bell children, Leonard and Virginia Woolf, Lytton Strachey, John Maynard and Lydia Lopokova Keynes, David Garnett, Ottoline Morrell, and others. MA 3448. Items in this collection are described in 97 individual records (MA 3448.1-97). Purchased on the Fellows Fund, special gift of the Gramercy Park Foundation (Mrs. Michael Tucker), 1980.

Name of Collection: University of Reading Special Collections

Contact: Special Collections Service

Address: Special Collections Service
University of Reading
Redlands Road
Reading RG1 5EX

Telephone: 0118-378-8660
Fax: 0118-378-5632
Email: specialcollections@reading.ac.uk
URL: http://www.reading.ac.uk/special-collections/

Access Requirements: Prior appointment suggested to consult material. Permission required to consult or copy material in the Hogarth Press, Jonathan Cape, and Chatto & Windus collections from Random House:

GUIDE TO LIBRARY SPECIAL COLLECTIONS 153

Random House Group Archive & Library
1 Cole Street
Crown Park
Rushden
Northants. NN10 6RZ
rushdenqueries@randomhouse.co.uk

Holdings Relevant To Woolf: Hogarth Press (MS 2750): editorial and production correspondence relating to publications of the Press including Woolf's own titles. Production ledgers 1920s–1950s. Correspondence between Leonard Woolf and Stanley Unwin about progress with his collected edition of the works of Freud. Order books – e.g. lists of booksellers, book clubs and how many books they have ordered for a particular title. Newscuttings—press clippings of advertisements for Hogarth Press books including Virginia Woolf publications.

Chatto & Windus (CW): small number of letters 1915–1925; 1929–1931. Various letters and notes by Leonard Woolf; outgoing letters to Leonard Woolf: 22 November 1927 (CW A/119); outgoing letters to Virginia Woolf: 29 January 1936 (CW A/172), 22 December 1931 (CW A/135), 31 December 1931 (CW A/135), 15 December 1920 (CW A/100), 20 December 1920 (CW A/100).

George Bell & Sons (MS 1640): 5 letters from Leonard Woolf 1930–1966.

Routledge (RKP): Reader's report by Leonard Woolf on George Padmore's "Britannia rules the blacks" (1935); "How Britain rules Africa." 1 letter from Leonard Woolf (June 1941) from Miscellaneous publishing correspondence 1941-1942 Wi-Wy RKP 174/15. Draft introduction by Leonard Woolf to *Letters on India* by Mulk Raj (1942) and 1 letter to Leonard Woolf from Mulk Raj Anand 1942-1943 RKP 178/3. Correspondence concerning the publication of *The War for Peace* by Leonard Woolf, 1939-1940 RKP 160/5. 1 letter from Virginia Woolf declining an invitation from Routledge to write a biography of Margaret

Bondfield, 25 May 1940 RKP 160/5.
Megroz (MS 1979/68): 2 letters from Leonard Woolf, 1926.

Allen & Unwin (MS 3282): Correspondence with Leonard Woolf c.1914-1918 (re. his book *International Government*), 1923-1924; 1939-1940; 1943; 1946; 1950-1951; 1953; 1965 (concerning ill-founded rumors about the Hogarth Press); 1967 (concerning a reprint of *Empire and Commerce in Africa*).

Jonathan Cape (MS 2446): All correspondence from file JC A43. Correspondence between Jonathan Cape and Virginia Woolf and Cape and A. C. Gissing concerning Virginia Woolf's introduction to George Gissing's *Ionian Sea* to which A. C. Gissing objects. 1 postcard (1935), 1 letter (1933), 2 letters (1932) from Virginia Woolf. 1 letter (1932) from Virginia Woolf declining to write an introduction to Jane Austen's *Northanger Abbey*. 4 letters (1931) from Virginia Woolf declining to write an introduction to one of Miss Thackeray's books.

Letters from Vanessa Bell: 1 letter from Bell CW 152/2; 1 letter from Bell CW 171/10; 2 letters from Bell CW 578/1; 1 letter from Bell CW 59/9; 1 letter from Bell (1936) CW 61/10. Artwork by Vanessa Bell for various Virginia Woolf titles.

Artwork by Angelica Garnett, Philippa Bramson and others for various books in the Chatto & Windus archive.

Name of Collection: Frances Hooper Collection of Virginia Woolf Books and Manuscripts.
Elizabeth Power Richardson Bloomsbury Iconography Collection.

Contact: Karen V. Kukil, Associate Curator of Special Collections

Address: Mortimer Rare Book Collection
Young Library

GUIDE TO LIBRARY SPECIAL COLLECTIONS

Smith College
7 Neilson Drive
Northampton, MA 01063

Telephone: 413-585-2908
Email: kkukil@smith.edu
URL: www.smith.edu/libraries/libs/specialcollections

Hours: Mon.–Fri. 9 am–5 pm
Please note: The Mortimer Rare Book Collection will be closed June – August 2017

Access Restrictions: Appointment to be made with the Curator.

Holdings Relevant To Woolf: The Hooper Collection emphasizes Woolf as an essayist but also includes many Hogarth Press first editions, limited editions of Woolf's works, and translations. The collection includes page proofs of *Orlando, To the Lighthouse*, and *The Common Reader*, corrected by Woolf for the first American editions, a proof copy of *The Waves* that Woolf inscribed to Hugh Walpole, and the proof copies of *The Years* and of *Flush*. The Collection also has one of the deluxe editions of *Orlando* that was printed on green paper. Other items include twenty-two pages of reading notes from 1926, three pages of notes on D. H. Lawrence's *Sons and Lovers,* thirty- three pages of notes for *Roger Fry,* a six-page ms. "As to criticism," a five-page ms. of "The Searchlight," and a fourteen-page ms. of "The Patron and The Crocus." The Hooper Collection also owns 140 letters between Woolf and Lytton Strachey as well as other correspondence, including a 13 February [1921] letter to Katherine Mansfield and ten letters to Mela and Robert Spira.

The Richardson Collection is a working collection of books and materials used by Richardson in preparing her *Bloomsbury Iconography*. It includes Leslie Stephen's photograph album, ninety-eight original exhibition catalogs dating back to 1929, clippings and photocopies of such items as reviews of early Woolf works, and Bloomsbury material from British *Vogue* of the 1920s. The Collection also has three preliminary pencil drawings by Vanessa Bell for *Flush*.

The Mortimer Rare Book Room also owns Woolf's 1916 Italian ms. notebook and her corrected typescripts of "Reviewing" and "The Searchlight." In addition, there is a 1923 photograph of Woolf at Garsington. Original cover designs for Hogarth Press publications include *The Common Reader, On Being Ill*, and *Duncan Grant*. The Mortimer Rare Book Room also has a Sylvia Plath collection that includes eight of Woolf's books from Plath's library, several of which are underlined and annotated, as well as Plath's notes from her undergraduate English 211 class at Smith (1951–1952) in which she studied *To the Lighthouse*. The collection also includes Woolf's 26 February 1939 letter to Vita Sackville-West, a 1931 bronze bust of Virginia Woolf by Stephen Tomlin, a 1923 Hogarth Press edition of T. S. Eliot's *The Waste Land*, a 1919 Hogarth Press edition of *Paris* by Hope Mirrlees and first editions of Vita Sackville-West and Katherine Mansfield publications. Additional Bloomsbury items include *Original Woodcuts* (Omega Workshops, 1918), Vanessa Bell's original woodcut for the cover of *Monday or Tuesday* (1921), and exhibition catalogs for *Manet and the Post-Impressionists* (Grafton Galleries, 1911), Friday Club Members (Mansard Gallery, 1921) Paintings and Drawings by Vanessa Bell (Independent Gallery, 1922). Additional photographs include the Mary L. S. Bennett (née Fisher) Family Photographs. Online exhibitions are available on the Mortimer Rare Book Room's website.

Name of Collection: Woolf/Hogarth Press/Bloomsbury

Contact: Lisa J. Sherlock

Address: Victoria University Library
71 Queens Park Crescent E.
Toronto M5S 1K7
Ontario Canada

GUIDE TO LIBRARY SPECIAL COLLECTIONS 157

Email: victoria.library@utoronto.ca
URL: http://library.vicu.utoronto.ca/special/bloomsbury.htm

Hours: Mon.–Fri. 9 am–5 pm

Access Requirements: Prior notification; identification.

Restrictions: Limited photocopying.

Holdings Relevant To Woolf: This collection, the most comprehensive of its kind with nearly 5,700 items, contains all the work of Virginia and Leonard Woolf in various editions, issues, variants and translations; all the books hand-printed by Leonard and Virginia Woolf at the Hogarth Press, including many variant issues and bindings, association copies and page proofs; a nearly comprehensive collection of Hogarth Press machine printed books to 1946 (the year Leonard Woolf and the Press joined Chatto & Windus) including presentation copies, signed limited editions, page proofs, variants as well as substantial amounts of ephemera, such as the *Catalogue of Publications to 1939* with annotations by Leonard Woolf. The collection is also very strong in Bloomsbury Art and Artists, especially the decorative arts, including important examples of Omega Workshops publications and exhibition catalogues. Materials include the catalogue of the second post-impressionist exhibition, 1912; catalogues relating to Vanessa Bell and Duncan Grant exhibitions; bronze medal of Virginia Woolf by Marta Firlet; oil on canvas portrait of Amaryllis Garnett by Vanessa Bell (c.1958); Portrait sketch of Leonard Woolf by Vanessa Bell; Duncan Grant and Vanessa Bell designed Clarice Cliff dinner plates; original Vanessa Bell and Duncan Grant sketches and designs for dust jackets, novels, and other special projects; Duncan Grant charcoal portrait of Virginia Woolf (1968); Quentin Bell set of five pottery plates based on the novels of Virginia Woolf (ca. 1979); Quentin Bell pottery figurine in aid of Charleston (ca. 1980); bronze busts of Lytton Strachey and Virginia Woolf by Stephen

Tomlin (1901–1937); as well as the Marcel Gimond bust of Vanessa Bell and the Tomlin bust of Henrietta Bingham. Book hand bound by Virginia Woolf. Wooden plaque from the Hogarth Press at 24 Tavistock. Examples of programmes, posters, and handbills relating to productions of plays, movies, and dance productions with content relating to Bloomsbury group members. Original correspondence and mss. material includes that by Vanessa Bell; Leonard Woolf; Ritchie family re: Anne Thackeray Ritchie/Stephen family; Duncan Grant; Quentin Bell; S. P. Rosenbaum mss. Letters from E. M. Forster, Bertrand Russell, James Strachey, Raymond Mortimer, David Garnett, Nigel Nicolson and others in the Bloomsbury Circle; as well as biographers, scholars and bibliographers such as Joanne Trautmann, Carolyn Heilbrun, J. Howard Woolmer, Leon Edel, Leila Luedeking, P. N. Furbank, Noel Annan and others. Large Ephemera Collection includes items revealing Virginia Woolf's effect on popular culture.

Name of Collection: Library of Leonard and Virginia Woolf (Washington State University)

Contact: Trevor James Bond
Head, Manuscripts, Archives, and Special Collections

Address: Washington State University Libraries
Pullman, WA 99164-5610

Email: tjbond@wsu.edu
URL: www.wsulibs.wsu.edu/holland/masc/masc.htm

Hours: Mon.–Fri. 8:30 am–4:30 pm

Access Requirements: Letter stating nature of research preferred; student or other identification.

Restrictions: Materials must be used in the MASC area under supervision. Photocopying or photographing is permitted only when it will not harm the materials and is permitted by copyright.

GUIDE TO LIBRARY SPECIAL COLLECTIONS

Recent Aquisitions: Correspondence to Clive and Vanessa Bell (approximately 30 items), with most items addressed to Clive. Correspondents include Stephen Tallant, Eric MacLagan, John Pollock, H. J. Norton, Lyn Irvine (including one letter mentioning Mrs. Raven Hill), Sir George Grahame, Karen Costelloe, John Alford, Ivor Churchill, the Earl of Sandwich, George Lansbury, Clifford Sharp, F. H. S. Shepherd, Gilbert Seldes, Lord Evan Tredegar, C. E. Stuart, Max Eastman, E. Hilton Young, Col. Heward Bell.

Holdings Relevant To Woolf: WSU has the Woolfs' basic working library including many works which belonged to Woolf's father, Sir Leslie Stephen, and other family members. Over 800 titles came from their Sussex home, Monks House, including some works bought at auction soon after Leonard Woolf died in 1969. Later additions include: 1,875 titles from his house in Victoria Square, London; 400 titles from his nephew Cecil Woolf; and over 60 titles from Quentin and Anne Olivier Bell. WSU has been actively collecting: all works in all editions by Virginia Woolf; all titles by Leonard Woolf; dust jackets; works published by the Woolfs at the Hogarth Press through 1946; books by their friends and associates, especially those by Bloomsbury authors and about Bloomsbury artists; relevant correspondence and original works of art. Original artwork by Vanessa Bell; scattered letters by Vanessa Bell, E. M. Forster, Roger Fry, Leslie Stephen, Lytton Strachey, and Leonard Woolf. Original artwork by Richard Kennedy for illustrations in his book *A Boy at the Hogarth Press;* scattered letters by Roger Fry, Leslie Stephen, Ethel Smyth, and Leonard Woolf. Virginia Woolf's initialed copy of *Cornishiana*; Leonard Woolf's annotated copy of *An Anatomy of Poetry* by A. Williams-Ellis; Leslie Stephen's copy of *Lapsus Calami and Other Verses,* inscribed by James Kenneth Stephen. Several letters from Virginia Woolf, including two written in 1939 to Ronald Heffer, and a letter to Edward McKnight Kauffer. New in the Hogarth Press Collection are a copy of E. M. Forster's *Anonymity, an Enquiry,* bound in cream paper boards, and what Woolmer calls the third label state of Forster's *The Story of the Siren.* The Library of Leonard and Virginia Woolf is once again shelved separately so that scholars visiting Pullman may see the collection apart from the other rare book collections.

Name of Collection: Yale Center for British Art

Contact: Elisabeth Fairman, Senior Curator of Rare Books and Manuscripts

Address: 1080 Chapel Street
P.O. Box 208280
New Haven, CT 06520-8280

Telephone: elisabeth.fairman@yale.edu
Fax: 203-432-2814
Email: 203-432-2814

Hours: Tue.-Fri. 10 am-4:30 pm

Access Requirements: Permission needed in order to reproduce.

Holdings Relevant To Woolf: Rare Books & Mss Department: 94 letters from Vanessa Bell and Duncan Grant to Sir Kenneth Clark; Prints & Drawings Department: 4 drawings by Vanessa Bell; 4 drawings by Duncan Grant; 6 drawings by Wyndham Lewis; 1 drawing by Frederick Etchells; Paintings Department: 1 painting by Vanessa Bell, 4 paintings by Duncan Grant (including portrait of Vanessa Bell); 3 paintings by Roger Fry. 6 letters from Lytton Strachey (to Clive Bell, Siegfried Sassoon, et al.).

Reviews

Queer Bloomsbury. Brenda Helt and Madelyn Detloff, eds. (Edinburgh: Edinburgh UP, 2016) xiv + 288 pp.

"The very phrase 'queer Bloomsbury' is in its way redundant," the editors of *Queer Bloomsbury* readily admit, "implying that there could somehow be a neutral or 'unqueer' Bloomsbury" (5). Yet ever since *A Writer's Diary* (1953), Leonard Woolf's highly selective edition of his wife's diaries, edited "to protect the feelings or reputations of the living" (*AWD* vii), there is a history of earnestly protective (comedic and/or damaging) cultural and critical attempts to prevent or diminish common understanding of Bloomsbury as a byword for queer, as well as a history of homophobic Bloomsbury bashing (alarmingly consonant with queer bashing), by mainstream media and academic specialists alike. It took Michael Holroyd's *Lytton Strachey: A Critical Biography* (1967-1968) and Nigel Nicolson's frank account of his parents' polyamorous bisexuality, *Portrait of a Marriage* (1973)—both books only publishable following the decriminalization of homosexuality by the watershed Sexual Offences Act of 1967—to begin to spell out what Edward Albee's notorious play, *Who's Afraid of Virginia Woolf?* (1962), not to mention Bloomsbury in the first instance, had already quite heavily hinted at: Bloomsbury's revolutionary assault on the absolute charade that was hegemonic patriarchal heteronormativity.

Yet "queer Bloomsbury" is not so much a pleonasm as an anachronism to those who wish strictly to date the term "queer" to many decades after first wave Bloomsbury, when it was taken up in the 1990s as an "identity marker (synonymous with Lesbian, Gay, Bisexual, and, to a lesser extent, Trans identity categories)" (5), and who object to retrospectively stuffing the likes of Lytton Strachey, Virginia Woolf, and Duncan Grant into the famous Outrage "Queer as Fuck" T-shirt that Alan Sinfield has Oscar Wilde wear on the cover of his book, T*he Wilde Century: Oscar Wilde, Effeminacy and the Queer Moment* (1994). Yet this "apparent paradox" does indeed dissolve "if we turn the equation round and derive 'queer' from Bloomsbury," as Brenda Helt and Madelyn Detloff rightly suggest. They invoke queer theorist Eve Sedgwick's "potent theorization of the power of contiguity" (2) to derive the term from the:

> "wide range of desiring, identifying, representing, repelling, paralleling, differentiating, rivaling, leaning, twisting, mimicking, withdrawing, attracting, aggressing, [and] warping" ... that Bloomsbury made possible. That is, Bloomsbury's habits of intimate, sensual, artistic and philosophical conviviality intentionally resist the heteronormative "logic of cultural intelligibility" that underpins western neoliberal ideals for social and familial organization. (5)

Here the active, transformative aspect of queer as a verb (doing and becoming) is emphasized rather than its static categorical qualities as noun and adjective (being). Bloomsbury was queer *avant la lettre*, or queer before its modern positive usage or inflection at least, given that queer was fast becoming a "chiefly derogatory" term designating homosexuality at the time of early Bloomsbury and was turned to advantage as a neutral then positive term of militant public self-avowal in the late 1980s.

The editors wisely refrain from serving up set definitions of "queer" or of "Bloomsbury" in advance of the two clusters of essays they have collected in *Queer Bloomsbury*, although they do name around a dozen of the personally, erotically and artistically entangled personnel of "a core set of Bloomsberries": Thoby Stephen, Adrian Stephen, Virginia Woolf, Vanessa Bell, Duncan Grant, Roger Fry, Leonard Woolf, Strachey, Desmond MacCarthy, Clive Bell, Maynard Keynes, E. M. Forster, and Saxon Sydney-Turner (1). The first part of the collection comprises five republished "Ground-Breaking Essays" from 1968 to 2010, a most welcome resource allowing readers (and essayists) to take stock of important previously dispersed landmarks in queer Bloomsbury scholarship, already required reading in any course on Bloomsbury (with or without the redundant "queer" tag). The five essayists whose work is made productively contiguous in the first part of *Queer Bloomsbury* are Carolyn Heilbrun (introduced by Brenda Silver), Christopher Reed, George Piggford, Bill Maurer, and Brenda Helt. The second part of *Queer Bloomsbury* has nine "New Essays" also judiciously placed in productive conviviality, offering significant reflections and truly scintillating departures for the twenty-first century, by Regina Marler, Darren Clarke, Todd Avery, Gretchen Holbrook Gerzina, Gaile Pohlhaus, Jr., and Madelyn Detloff, Elyse Blankley, Mark Hussey, Jodie Medd, and Kimberly Engdahl Coates. *Queer Bloomsbury* will, I have no doubt, shortly become indispensable reading for any serious aficionado or scholar. Here is a wealth of new arguments and material on the work and lives of core Bloomsberries such as Grant, Vanessa, Virginia, Leonard, Clive Bell, and Forster, but also of outliers to the group, or at least those not on Helt's and Detloff's opening list, such as Dora Carrington, Ludwig Wittgenstein, and T. E. Lawrence.

To neatly define either queer or Bloomsbury would be an injustice to both of these most slippery of sliding signifiers, but it is nevertheless instructive to turn (as I did after reading *Queer Bloomsbury*) to the *Oxford English Dictionary* to discover Arnold Bennett, no less, famed pantomime rival of Bloomsbury, cited as the earliest source in Britain of queer's modern "chiefly derogatory" usage, in a diary entry of 26 March 1915 (published in 1932) —although it is difficult to assess how derogatory, if at all, Bennett's usage in fact is: "An immense reunion of art students, painters, and queer people. Girls in fancy male costume, queer dancing, etc." (*OED*; Bennett 550). How splendid, furthermore, on turning to the source to discover that the evening in question was a thoroughly Bloomsbury affair, involving a visit to an exhibition of radical art by the London Group ("some nice things but all imitative"), and thence to dinner with Lady Ottoline Morrell, where Bennett finds "Lowes Dickinson, Bertrand Russell, Whitehouse. All these very much upset by the war, convinced that the war and government both wrong, etc." (Bennett 550). Having witnessed the Bloomsbury related art and pacifism that inform many of the contributions to *Queer Bloomsbury*, Bennett's account of his evening with the Morrells concludes with a glimpse of Bloomsbury masquerade, orientalism, and queer sexualities too:

> Afterwards, an immense reunion of Art Students, painters, and queer people. Girls in fancy male costume, queer dancing etc. A Japanese dancer. We left at 12.15. Pianola. Fine pictures. Glorious drawings by Picasso. Excellent impression of host and hostess. (Bennett 550)

The "queer people" on this occasion did not include Virginia Woolf, whose debut novel, *The Voyage Out,* was published the day after this party (i.e. 26 March 1915), and who was convalescing in a nursing home following a bout of mental illness, but it seems likely that her sister and other Bloomsbury members were present. Woolf's novel, which incidentally Vanessa Bell on its publication described as "a queer business" (Spalding 137), "appeared amid a season of unparalleled gaiety," according to Bloomsbury biographer Frances Spalding, when "[a]s if in defiance of the war, Lady Ottoline Morrell was holding parties every Thursday" (137). Spalding cites a letter from Vanessa in April 1915 describing to Hilton Young what such evenings entailed:

> you might see Bertie Russell dancing a hornpipe with Titi (Hawtrey's young woman), Lytton and Oliver and Marjorie Strachey cutting capers to each other, Duncan [Grant] dancing in much the same way that he paints, [Augustus] John and Arnold Bennett and all the celebrities of the day looking as beautiful as they could in clothes seized from Ottoline's drawers—and Ottoline herself at the head of the troup of short-haired young ladies from the Slade prancing about ... one can't describe the queer effect all these people had on each other. (137)

Clearly, then, the dictionary definition of "queer" rests on a record of what Helt and Detloff, invoking Sedgwick, call Bloomsbury's "conviviality" and "*becoming together*," a concept that "captures both the contingency and the generativity of inhabiting space *beside* one another" (Helt and Detloff 2). This certainly supports the stance that Bloomsbury and queer are synonymous. On the other hand, while it is satisfying to find these two contemporary accounts of the same Bloomsbury event and constellation of Bloomsbury people both employing the term "queer," it is worth attending to Vanessa Bell's enigmatic, but certainly not derogatory, summary of the "queer" scene she has described as indescribable. In saying "one can't describe the queer effect all these people had on each other," she perhaps alerts us to the very real dangers and legal consequences at the time of making too plain what "queer" might mean, as well as demonstrating how deploying the word as she does here both signals and erases (queers) the queerness it seeks to (mis)represent. In a sense, the present collection *Queer Bloomsbury*, mindful of queer's in-built resistance to describability, is testimony to the multiplicitous explorations made in the last century toward understanding and inhabiting the proliferating and complex "queer effect all these people had on each other" and on the queer generations that have followed.

Queer Bloomsbury, furthermore, points to its own particular timeliness too since it is published in a world where "'queer' may have lost its practical usefulness" (5). Helt and Detloff cite Dennis Allen's response to the pressing question, "How Queer is Now?," to identify the present historical moment when "the LGBT community itself has largely abandoned both this [queer] identity and this practice, focusing instead on recognition by the dominant culture, including, pre-eminently, an insistence on the right to 'marriage equality,' a concept that would have been anathema to any self-respecting 1990s queer" (5; Allen 106). In this regard, *Queer Bloomsbury* may be understood as a rallying cry, urging us to acknowledge a queer Bloomsbury in danger now of going straight in previously unforeseen ways. In the light of recent developments in public and legal sanction of gay marriage under conservative governments such as David Cameron's in the UK, we must re-examine Bloomsbury's notorious contiguities of dissident sexualities with dissident politics such as pacifism, anti-fascism, and socialism. The proximity of homosocial to homosexual was already being tested by the undergraduate Strachey's own "queer effect" on Cambridge, which was "corrupted" by his radical shift from the esteemed establishment "Higher Sodomy" toward "open sodomy," according to the bemused Leonard Woolf. Not least, Bloomsbury economics as pioneered by Maynard Keynes are under urgent new scrutiny following the financial crash of 2008. In the wilderness for thirty years, it is no surprise to find Keynes is suddenly back in fashion. And it is heartening to find him so prominently featured in *Queer Bloomsbury*.

Bloomsbury's (relative) openness of behavior and equally of *verbal acknowledgment* of that behavior are what make it radical and queer. Strachey's notorious utterance, at the drawing room threshold on or around Spring 1910, pointing "at a stain on Vanessa's white dress," of the single word question "Semen?" is Woolf's "best illustration" of how Bloomsbury moved from its early "monastic" phase to its second, utterly queer one:

> Can one really say it? I thought and we burst out laughing. With that one word all barriers of reticence and reserve went down. A flood of the sacred fluid seemed to overwhelm us. Sex permeated our conversation. The word bugger was never far from our lips. We discussed copulation with the same excitement and openness that we had discussed the nature of good. (*MOyB* 213)

The origin of the legendary semen is of course never disclosed by Woolf in her memoir ("I do not know if I invented it or not"), but she teasingly closes it with Logan Pearsall Smith's hearsay "fact that Maynard had copulated with Vanessa on a sofa in the middle of the drawing room" (*MB* 218). But to reduce the power of this free-floating utterance about free-floating semen to mere frankness about a chance and specifically heterosexual coupling between two of Bloomsbury's triangulating lovers would be, of course, to overlook its enabling Bloomsbury context of open homosexuality, bisexuality and polyamory, and the ramifications thereof, as Woolf's deliciously camp memoir surely teaches.

Little wonder that Strachey's "Semen?" is a running trope through the pages of *Queer Bloomsbury*. Avery rightly terms the moment "semengate" (175), and it is interesting to follow the discussions on it that punctuate both sections of *Queer Bloomsbury*. For Piggford (in 1997) it signals the "birth of Bloomsbury as an enclave in which sexual possibilities might be discussed and explored" (66-67), and further it "arguably marks the conception" of the Bloomsbury Group's "systematic, if playful and parodic, dismantling of the moral and aesthetic underpinning of the class system that provided" the very privileges they themselves enjoyed (84); for Helt (in 2010) it is "the advent of modernism," noting "Bloomsbury's fascination with sexuality was consistent with that of other avant-garde groups now considered modernist" (115); and for Avery (in 2016) it has become a moment to be "gloss[ed]" by Robert Caserio's "description of the ideological force exerted during the early twentieth century by same-sex challenges to dominant assumptions about human sexuality… For, much like Strachey in a doorway of the hotbed of cultural and sexual unconventionality that was Bloomsbury, 'Homosexuality as we know it arrives at the centre of modernism's revolutionary challenge to cultural repertories'" (175; Caserio 203). Avery deploys "semengate" as endorsement of Caserio's contention that "the arrival of homosexuality and of 'queer' sexualities in general on the threshold of modernism as representing a 'challenge … so comprehensive that modernism seeks to break with religion, nationality, and the state'" (176; Caserio 203). Gerzina (2016), meanwhile, reminding us that "'homosexuality' was not a word that anyone in Bloomsbury used" (194), underscores Reed's salutary prompt (in a recent essay published elsewhere) to twenty-first century readers, some of whom may be lucky enough to take as axiomatic openly "queer" mainstream cultures, that "the criminalization of 'gross indecency' between men in Britain precluded open acknowledgement of homosexuality and exposed even subtle expressions of homoerotic feelings to threats of blackmail—as Bloomsbury men knew from experience" (194; Reed 71-2). Bloomsbury's queer subculture persisted in a time of horrific, violent, and mortal persecution. Gerzina, in her fantastic essay on Carrington, notes the "imaginative field for humour" made possible by the "subjection of language to this political and social reality," a point lost to "many in their earnest scholarly evaluations." Semengate is then Bloomsbury's "moment when language was released and everything changed" (194).

The reader is served well indeed by having in its entirety Reed's truly important essay, "Bloomsbury Bashing: Homophobia and the Politics of Criticism in the Eighties" (1991), which I for one consider essential reading for anyone hoping to make sense of the political contexts and critical stakes for that key period in the explosive expansion of Bloomsbury and modernist scholarship across several disciplines, along with Mark Hussey's "Mrs. Thatcher and Mrs. Woolf" (2004), which would not go amiss either reprinted in the present collection. Reed, Piggford, and Maurer all revisit their essays with helpful prefatory reflections.

Heilbrun's foundational and pioneering essay, "The Bloomsbury Group" (1968), rightly opens the collection, and Brenda Silver's introduction to it is testimony from "one of those of us who lived through the days when Bloomsbury was not considered serious or seriously" to the importance of Heilbrun's admirably risk-taking work on Bloomsbury androgyny, achieved as that rare thing for the time—a feminist in the highly patriarchal academy of the 1960s and 1970s. Silver's is an important reminder of the embodied lives lived by fellow scholars and the costs and consequences to previous generations in endurance of very real intellectual hostility to what now we might be tempted to take for granted. Heilbrun's essay is published in its entirety and, as it was originally, "without source information for quoted material" (25), which may preserve its sense as a period piece, but is nevertheless a minor frustration for readers coming to this topic for the first time. The editors might have offered supplementary source notes and bibliography.

Piggford has taken the opportunity to "slightly" revise (64) his important essay (1997) on Forster and queer Bloomsbury's pioneering camp biography. His close attention to various forms of camp is richly instructive in comparing textual strategies of irony, parody, and allusion, shared by Strachey, Woolf, and Forster in their revolutionary work on queer(ing) biography. In my mind, his work sits adjacent to and, in some senses, makes possible later scholarship such as Georgia Johnston's monograph on queer autobiography (2007), which investigates Bloomsbury members Woolf and Vita Sackville-West, along with H. D. and Gertrude Stein, but which alas does not directly cite Piggford. His contribution to the present volume, if space permitted, might have been an opportunity to reflect on this and a selection of other such works where queer biography and queer autobiography intersect.

Likewise, in a lengthier form this volume might have solicited a longer reflection from Maurer on his fascinating (and after 2008, even more so) essay, "Redecorating the International Economy: Keynes, Grant and the Queering of Bretton Woods" (2002), and on subsequent scholarship. It would have allowed for this truly important essay's reproduction without the abridgements here, some of which make for unfortunate jolts in the argument. It is difficult to make sense of the assertion, for example, that Keynes was led by the pull of "the dominant modernity" at one point "to consider gazing down the 'alternative' modern paths of National Socialism" (110) without recourse to the original essay for the missing material. The latter, by the way, is in itself not convincing but it is nevertheless necessary if Maurer wishes to retain that particular assertion and have it make any sense at all. And without editorial ellipsis the reader is not made aware of where precisely such cuts have been made. I also regret the elision of Maurer's discussion of the somatic, drawing on the work of Elizabeth Grosz—and not least a citation of Keynes himself from 1908: "[Disembodied] spirits will be cold creatures and we must hope for the resurrection of the body." (Maurer, "Redecorating" 126) This is a missed opportunity for the present collection as a whole. But Maurer's essay, even in abridgement, remains an important pioneering intervention in its careful wrangling of Keynesian economics and Postimpressionist aesthetics into the morphologies and discursive folds of queer Bloomsbury.

Helt's stimulating essay (2010) on bisexuality and Woolf's "Opposition," as the refreshingly challenging subtitle has it, "to Theories of Androgyny and Sexual Identity," is more smoothly abridged, and without a preface (presumably on the grounds of its relatively recent publication), but again, if space permitted, the unabridged version with even a short preface would be preferable. Nevertheless, this is an important and appropriate essay with which to close the section of *Queer Bloomsbury* that opens with Heilbrun's. Helt offers nuanced and sensitive close readings of *Orlando* and *A Room of One's Own* to explore Woolf's tracing of polymorphous and bisexual desires as they are trapped by and/or released from specific lived realities of social strictures (124). Closely attending to Woolf's subtle opening up of the metaphors she deploys to readerly deconstruction, Helt argues persuasively against received and often unexamined readings of the much cited passages on androgyny in *A Room of One's Own*. Woolf is "engaged in encouraging women to write history, psychology, even science from a woman's perspective, not an androgynous one" (125).

Marler ushers in the second set of *Queer Bloomsbury* essays with her splendidly performative contribution, a breezy, gossipy, and camp exposition on "The Bloomsbury Love Triangle" where even the endnotes are all a-chatter with choice campy asides. Did you know (or need to know)—that "Clive Bell got his leg over Molly MacCarthy, which Desmond felt freed him," or that Virginia's mother's first cousin "discovered her husband's infatuation with a young man and sued him for custody of their son" (149)? Marler certainly makes the case for knowing such things: Bloomsbury's "embrace of unconventional amours is as much a part of their modernist project as Vanessa Bell's radical abstract paintings or the stories collected in Virginia Woolf's *Monday or Tuesday*" (148). Hers is followed by Darren Clarke's excellent essay, "Duncan Grant and Charleston's Queer Arcadia," written by a relatively new kind of scholar-cum-curator. Having completed an AHRC-sponsored PhD in collaboration with the University of Sussex and the Charleston Trust, and as Curator at Charleston, Clarke brings a powerful sense of contiguity with the art and the habitus he examines, offering sensitive and informative readings of the house and garden, a tenancy "rooted in queerness" and "home for pacifism and conscientious objection," a unique Bloomsbury heritage site which has "achieved a kind of queer permanence as a museum" (156). He reads with equal sensitivity a number of the "secret erotic" drawings and gouaches that were only made public in 1989, over a decade after Grant's death in 1978. Clarke offers a poignant reminder that this remarkable artist and dissident "lived to see the decriminalization of male homosexuality in 1967—a partial reversal of the Criminal Law Amendment Act ... introduced in 1885, six months before [he] was born" (169).

Avery's essay on Strachey's recorded experiments in the erotics of crucifixion, as recounted in his letters to his lover Roger Senhouse, is a compelling account of Strachey's "queer aestheticism" and "queer ethics," exploding received critical wisdom that Strachey should be regarded "either as a simple scourge of religion or as someone who was fundamentally 'indifferent' to it" (186). What emerges is an astonishingly ambitious and complex project to turn to queer advantage, so to speak, the key tropes and symbolism of orthodox Christian religious moralism which, as Avery shows, he recognized to have "poisoned modern lives" (186). Strachey's detoxification of "conventional religiosity" (187), as so eloquently outlined by Avery here, may also be at work in other Bloomsbury texts, not least in the much cited messianic trope engaged by Woolf in *A Room of One's Own* where she posits the resurrection of Judith Shakespeare, but also in more obscure examples such as the remark by Keynes unfortunately elided in the abridgement of Maurer's essay.

Strachey's "queer epistolary performances" (195; Reed 75) feature again, unsurprisingly, in Gerzina's essay, reflecting on "The Queer Potential of Carrington's Art" thirty years after the publication of her unsurpassed biography, *Carrington: A Life* (1989). But it is the bisexual Carrington's beautifully illustrated letters (two are reproduced in the collection) to her lover Popett John, daughter of Augustus John, that stand out among the queer epistolary riches in this compressed but detailed account of Carrington's life, art, and loves. Reed's recent essay, "Bloomsbury as Queer Subculture" (2014) is productively mined by Gerzina to revisit the short but packed life of this most non-normative member of Bloomsbury.

Hussey's excellent essay on Clive Bell, on the other hand, comes ahead of the biography he is currently working on. On this evidence, it promises to be richly rewarding, both clarifying and revisionary, restoring the radical libertarian that was Bell in his youth, heroic conscientious objector in the Great War, and Wildean voluptuary, his incendiary force as champion of queer dissidence lately more often lost to a received stale caricature of Bloomsbury's comedically straight, reactionary, male chauvinist squire. This essay on Bell is adjacent to Elyse Blankley's similarly revisionary essay, "Deviant Desires and the Queering of Leonard Woolf," in which the capaciousness of the term "queer" is helpfully scrutinized before the compelling argument is made to consider the "queer straightness" (224) of Leonard Woolf in his life and his writings, including his still relatively neglected novel, *The Wise Virgins* (1914). This work is shown to contend with the discourses of homophobia and anti-Semitism converging in the wake of "two infamous miscarriages of justice: the trials and imprisonment of Alfred Dreyfus and of Oscar Wilde" (229). The collection as a whole makes frequent reference to Wilde's ordeal, and how dangerously proximate it felt to Bloomsbury. Timing is everything for *Queer Bloomsbury*. The fictitious queer novel, *Life's Adventure*, in which "Chloe liked Olivia," exists nowhere yet, except in its staged citations in *A Room of One's Own*. Likewise, Medd's wonderful essay on Forster and T. E. Lawrence speculates on how the correspondence between one who "had never written a novel" and one who "planned never to publish another" may be understood to compose "an inventive collaborative epistolary novel of and about aesthetic intimacy" (273), a work that exists nowhere yet, except in the citations of these melancholy letters so delicately sutured in this essay.

The capacious umbrella terms "Bloomsbury" and "queer" are admirably tested to lend shelter to the "perplexing and thus often neglected" (211) figure of Ludwig Wittgenstein in the enjoyably provocative "Making Sense of Wittgenstein's Bloomsbury and Bloomsbury's Wittgenstein" by Pohlhaus and Detloff. They make short work of demonstrating his right to a place under Bloomsbury's shelter, and a most witty and perceptive lengthier case for the queer Wittgenstein, at the expense of his entrusted translator and disciple, Elizabeth (G. E. M.) Anscombe. Anscombe's blustering letter of November 1973 to the *Times Literary Supplement* angrily taking to task his biographer for claiming the great philosopher's penchant for "the company of tough boys in London pubs," it is shown, "bears a remarkable generic similarity to the catalogue of excuses that Eve Sedgwick identified for ignoring evidence of same-sex erotic attachments" (212-213). Wittgenstein's logic is most convincingly and entertainingly applied here:

> The real question provoked by Anscombe's "nine questions" is not whether we can be absolutely sure that Wittgenstein went cruising in Prater Park or London pubs, or even whether he and David Pinsent actually got naked together on their romantic holiday to Iceland in between their steamy

conversations about logic, but rather, to quote Wittgenstein, "whether it can make any sense to doubt it" (*On Certainty* §2). (214)

A crucial point of this excursus into the heated debate on the queerness or otherwise of Wittgenstein's erotic life is to return us to the vexed history of the usage of the term "queer" itself. For Pohlhaus and Detloff point up "moments" in Wittgenstein's work where he "gives voice to experiences and feelings previously translated by Anscombe herself as 'queer'" that they find to have "distinct resonances to queer theory as we understand it today" (216), and to queer Bloomsbury too. Yet, can we be sure, when Anscombe's (1953) translation was revised and updated and the word "queer" entirely eradicated (in 2009) as translation of both *seltsame* and *merwurkdig*, that this "merely corrects the use of a dated word, replacing it with one that does not carry a sexual connotation" (216)? Likewise, I would add, when Woolf recalls in her unpublished memoir of Bloomsbury "buggers," read to the Memoir Club in 1922, how "one began to meet a queer faun-like figure" who turns out to be Duncan Grant in the loving portrait that ensues (MB 215), and given Bennett's deployment of the term in 1915 to denote queer sexuality, can we be entirely sure that "queer" here is merely a dated word and better read more strictly as "odd, peculiar, perhaps even uncanny," words nevertheless freely available to Woolf, "but not as recognizably homosexual" (216)?

Coates's essay on "Virginia Woolf's Queer Time and Place: Wartime London and a World Aslant" aptly closes the collection. Productively drawing on Sedgwick's "queer moments" and Sara Ahmed's "queer phenomenology," it looks for moments of queering the straight and straightening the queer, and begins to trace Woolf's deployment of the word "queer" in a sampling of letters and her "war novels" (277), which are here specified as *Jacob's Room*, *Mrs. Dalloway*, *The Waves*, and *The Years*, strangely ignoring *To the Lighthouse* and *Between the Acts*. Coates certainly makes us aware of how very often and how very queerly Woolf repeats the word "queer." Her focus is on the city of London's logic of normative verticality and Woolf's tilting against it. The essay is particularly stimulating in its close attention to Woolf's complex textual representation of Jacob's struggles in the context of that city and Septimus's failed efforts to "straighten up" (279). Yet locking the reader's sights on the narrative's middle distance of the London scenes in *Jacob's Room* seems to distract Coates from considering just how radically queer is the epistolary double opening of the novel. Forcing the reader to look aslant from Betty Flanders's letter, Woolf shifts the narrative cross-hairs to train the reader to look aslant at the text itself and its troubling representation of that hilarious primal Cornish beach scene so lewdly depicting and enacting queered verticality: "The entire bay quivered; the lighthouse wobbled; and she had the illusion that the mast of Mr. Connor's little yacht was bending like a wax candle in the sun. She winked quickly. Accidents were awful things. She winked again" (*JR* 3). Queer Bloomsbury is hidden here in plain sight!

—Jane Goldman, *University of Glasgow*

Works Cited

Allen, Dennis, Judith Roof and Alanna Beroiza, "The Queer Debt Crisis," *Journal of the Midwest Modern Language Association*, vol. 46, no, 2, 2013, pp. 99-110.
Bennett, Arnold, *The Journals*. Cassell, 1932-1933.
Caserio, Robert, "Queer Modernism." *Oxford Handbook of Modernisms*, edited by Peter Brooker, Andrzej Gasiorek, Deborah Longworth and Andrew Thacker, Oxford UP, 2010, pp. 199-217.
Maurer, Bill. "Redecorating the International Economy: Keynes, Grant, and the Queering of Bretton Woods." *Queer Globalizations: Citizenship and the Afterlife of Colonialism,* edited by Arnaldo Cruz-Malave and Martin F. Manalanson, New York UP, 2002, pp. 100-33.
Reed, Christopher. "Bloomsbury as Queer Subculture." *The Cambridge Companion to the Bloomsbury Group,* edited by Victoria Rosner, Cambridge UP, 2014, pp. 71-89.
Spalding, Frances, *Vanessa Bell,* Weidenfeld & Nicolson, 1983.

The Value of Virginia Woolf. Madelyn Detloff
(New York: Cambridge UP, 2016) viii + 135pp.

According to the Cambridge University Press online catalogue, the series The Value of "aims to combine the accessibility and commercial success of such similar series as A Very Short Introduction to and Why X Matters." Despite sharing qualities like accessibility, brevity, and affordability, however, there is one notable difference between the Cambridge series and those respectively published by Oxford and Yale University Presses; while the latter two series cover topics across the arts, humanities, and sciences, the former focuses exclusively on literature. This disciplinary focus is suggestive; in a financialized climate inimical to critical thinking and feeling, perhaps literary study is still worth something.

Indeed, Madelyn Detloff's *The Value of Virginia Woolf* explicitly situates the question of why "Woolf still matters in an age of tweets and apps and Instagrams" within "a more fundamental conversation about why and how the life of the mind still matters" (10). While there is no dearth of Woolf sightings in the CUP catalogue—with its many companions, introductions, and editions—Detloff takes a unique approach to the "guide" genre, investigating four concepts: eudemonia, incandescence, interdependence, and civilization. These terms suggest that this is not just a book about why Woolf still matters but an argument about why that which mattered *to Woolf* should matter to us. While its theoretical framework occasionally falters and its exegeses do not necessarily pay homage to "the deep attentive[ness] . . . of New Critical close reading" (12), Detloff's book is a powerful challenge to teachers, researchers, administrators, and students to value language, literary studies, the humanities, and thus the life of the mind.

Chapter One, "Eudemonia: The Necessary Art of Living," offers a rich meditation on Woolf's consistent promotion of happiness—understood here as "a way of . . . thriving," as "something one live[s] as a continual practice" (15). Detloff swiftly sketches a number of coordinates for studying happiness in Woolf's writings—her interest in the ancient Greeks, her reading of G.E. Moore, the influence of Walter Pater, the agnosticism of Leslie Stephen, and the devastation of World War I—all of which elegantly frame the hypothesis that Woolfian eudemonia consists of a disciplined, if ultimately limited, resistance to "the fragility and brevity of life" (19). The readings of *The Voyage Out* (1915) and *To the Lighthouse* (1927) that close this chapter show how happiness might also transform the coercive "effects of cultural roles that declare," for instance, "women are for *this* . . . men are for *that*" (22). Here, Evelyn Murgatroyd's thoughts and actions after the death of Rachel Vinrace—refusing "the consoling platitudes of her fellow travelers" (24), refusing Mr. Perrott's marriage proposal, encouraging him to forge another kind of happiness—take on a philosophical robustness. Likewise, Lily Briscoe's concluding vision evinces a compassionate and aesthetically-minded brilliance capable of keeping "nihilism and despair at bay"; happiness here becomes "an end in itself and a means of connecting [oneself] to others who share a disposition to cultivate it" (28).

Chapter Two, "Incandesence: Attention and Illumination," takes its central term from Woolf's judgment of William Shakespeare in *A Room of One's Own* (1929) and attempts to recuperate it as "*situated incandescence*" (31). While it seems a bit hasty to claim, as Detloff does, that Woolf's account of Shakespeare in *A Room* is epistemically arrogant (40), her later accounts of epistemic humility in *Three Guineas* (1938) and *Orlando* (1928) persuasively sketch "a contextual [rather than egocentric] way of knowing" attuned and attentive to the particularity of the relation among others and oneself (34). Woolf retools the very limitations imposed on women in these texts into perspectives that *illuminate* "networks of power" and *incandescently* "[burn] away . . . impediments of self-interest" (44), fostering "a form of radical openness to the world" that enables eudemonia (45).

Chapter Three, "Interdependence: Pattern and Precarity," explores the philosophical warrant for why one should value openness, humility, and happiness: namely, the social and ontological dependence of human beings on one another. "Woolf invites us," Detloff argues, "to perceive the particle and the wave, the node and the circuitry, the atom and the organism as mutually constitutive components of an interconnected ecology, or 'pattern' of living" (47). Though *The Waves* (1931) dramatizes the metaphysical interdependence of six "complex adaptive systems" (52), Detloff's analysis of *The Years* investigates social interdependence, establishing Woolf as a keen observer and critic of biopower. Detloff agrees that several chapters deploy ableist language but also points out that mental and physical atypicalities do not signify monologically in this novel. Colonel Pargiter's missing fingers might exhibit "his masculine value" (63), and Sara, Crosby, and Nicholas may be "depicted as unfit and extraneous to the generational throughline of the story" (64), but Woolf complicates this binary division in her final chapter. When North and Peggy call for living differently, they challenge others to recognize lives made precarious by heteronormative ideologies and to sense a vital pattern across generations, sexualities, and classes.

This affirmation of Woolf's critique transitions nicely into Chapter Four, "Civilization and Barbarism: A Reparative Exegesis," which takes up the challenge of Woolf's "ethically indigestible references to marginalized others" (71). Inspired by the writings of Eve Kosofsky Sedgwick, Detloff aims not to defend Woolf from criticism but, rather, to remain open to her indictments of civilization's violence (76). From the "withering gaze" (82) *The Voyage Out* casts on the British leisure class (82) to the Conradian allusion at the end of *Between the Acts* (1941), Woolf's oeuvre suggests, despite its representational limits, that one must remain open and alert to how the context of a life's "potential making [may be] rife with images of savagery ... of the human 'civilized' kind that Conrad exposed" (92). Though this survey of Woolf's fiction is compelling, the theoretical deployment of Sedgwick seems underdeveloped. Detloff's openness to limitations and surprises no doubt resonates with reparative reading, but a few moments in the chapter seem out of sync with Sedgwick. The conflation of the orts and fragments of *Between the Acts,* for instance, with Kleinian "part-objects" confuses shards of a broken whole—that is, "the veneer of civilization" (91)—with the plenitude a child (or a scholar) confers on cultural (partial) objects never known in full (Sedgwick 146-51).

The book's frequent quotation of Barbara Herrnstein Smith is also somewhat underdeveloped. *Contingencies of Value* (1988), after all, is not just a meditation on the double discourse of aesthetics and economics (Detloff 3). Additionally, it is a critique of efforts to fix truth value, to deny use value, and to overvalue objectivism. Indeed, the radicalness of Smith's apology for relativism, which is largely the aim of her work, seems blunted in *The Value of Virginia Woolf*. Though it makes sense to cite Smith as a warrant for attending to community and context in the process of evaluation, for Smith all texts *are* contexts, and the history of one's own rereading of a single text is always already riddled with varying and competing contingencies. With Smith, we might conclude that Woolf has remained valuable not just because "she lived the life of a thinker who was not afraid to inquire into the meaning of life" (Detloff 102), but also because "texts that survive will tend to be those that appear to reflect and reinforce establishment ideologies" (Smith 51). It should not surprise us, then, that Woolf has survived when those of us who favor deconstruction, formalism, history, ideological critique, and/or continental philosophy find justification for our methods in the writings of Woolf herself—who seems to have become, among other things, a deconstructivist, a political theorist, a historicist, and a philosopher over the last several decades. This is to say that Smith's sobering challenge to interpretive and evaluative projects occasionally seems at odds with Detloff's arguments (and to The Value of series itself).

Yet the pedagogic value of *The Value of Virginia Woolf* is undeniable. The chapters' treatment of multiple texts from across Woolf's life show students how to select key passages, to differentiate multiple works, and thus to attend to the consistency and mutability of an author. Moreover, the introduction and conclusion operate as teacherly bookends, the former moving readers through theoretical challenges, personal reflections attentive to diverse reading groups, and the importance of critical evaluation, while the latter reflects on Woolf's theories of reading and language and re-poses questions that should continue to preoccupy us in our readings of Woolf and in our learning and teaching. "How is one to live? What makes a good life? A free life? What is my responsibility to others? What is love and how ought I practice it? How do I intervene in cultural practices, customs, and institutions that appear brutal, unfair, and unjust if I am only one voice, and a small voice at that?" (101). Detloff teaches us that one of the values of continuing to tarry with Woolf is her courage to face such questions and improvise answers. Such is the work of a life that practiced happiness, attentiveness, openness, and humility.

—Benjamin D. Hagen, *University of South Dakota*

Works Cited

Sedgwick, Eve Kosofsky. *Touching Feeling: Affect, Pedagogy, Performativity.* Durham, 2003.

Smith, Barbara Herrnstein. *Contingencies of Value: Alternative Perspectives for Critical Theory.* Harvard UP, 1988.

"The Value of." *Cambridge University Press,* 2016. www.cambridge.org/re/academic/subjects/ literature series/value.

Virginia Woolf: Ambivalent Activist. Clara Jones
(Edinburgh: Edinburgh UP, 2016) vi + 246pp.

Clara Jones's *Virginia Woolf: Ambivalent Activist* takes up a familiar topic: Woolf's abstruse and conflicting politics. Yet, this monograph proves to do more than rehearse frustrating contradictions found within Woolf's life and work. Grounded in extensive archival research, *Virginia Woolf: Ambivalent Activist* provides a nuanced look into Woolf's involvement with four early twentieth-century institutions: Morley College, the People's Suffrage Federation, the Women's Co-operative Guild, and the Rodmell Women's Institute. Each chapter focuses on a different institution and demonstrates how the political ideology of that group influenced Woolf's writing.

By foregrounding class rather than gender, Jones invites readers to see a slightly different side of Woolf's politics, albeit one marked by ambivalence. The monograph shows that many of Woolf's feminist ideals are informed by her concerns regarding labor, enfranchisement, and solidarity between social classes, but it also demonstrates Woolf's struggle to put these democratic ideals into practice. The individual chapters illustrate the ways in which ambivalence marks Woolf's commitment to each of these organizations and their political agendas.

Jones's introduction clarifies that although Morley College and the Women's Institute are not activist groups, these purportedly apolitical organizations nevertheless responded to important social and political questions of Woolf's time (5). After providing a brief overview of the field and the title's key terms, Jones extensively recounts a clash from the late seventies and early eighties between Jane Marcus and Quentin Bell regarding Woolf's political legacy. This discussion points to contradictory readings of the author and allows Jones to situate her work as an inheritor of and respondent to that dispute: "This book, with its emphasis on the subtleties and ambivalences of Woolf's political practice, responds directly to these arguments and retrieves Woolf's activism from a debate in which 'Marxism' comes to stand in for politics" (13). Jones achieves this objective, but by framing her monograph in this way, she misses an opportunity to position her work in relationship to more recent scholarship on Woolf's political engagement, including but not limited to papers presented at the 2011 Annual Conference on Virginia Woolf, "Contradictory Woolf," held at Glasgow University (Ryan and Bolaki).

Chapter One, "Virginia Stephen and Morley College, 1905-7," considers the impact of Stephen's volunteer teaching at Morley College upon her early fiction. The chapter interrogates the legacy of the nineteenth-century reform movement in the foundation of various schools, including Morley College, and highlights the College's unique status as a coeducational institution. Jones provides evidence of Stephen's concurrent devotion to and unease with her working-class students.

Sustained close readings of gender and class in the "Morley Sketch" and "The Journal of Mistress Joan Martyn" appear at the center of this chapter. Jones provides a recuperative analysis of Stephen's "Morley Sketch," a text that first appeared in Bell's 1972 biography of Woolf under the name "Report on Teaching at Morley College." Jones argues that this is not, in fact, a report, but rather an experimental work of fiction; by retitling the text, Jones emphasizes this crucial distinction. A copy of the manuscript and Jones's transcription of it appear in the appendix to *Virginia Woolf: Ambivalent Activist*. Through these archival readings, Jones reinforces what we already know of Woolf—including her subversive treatment of history and emphasis upon women's life-writing—but notably locates these values and aesthetic considerations in Stephen's pedagogy and her early short fiction (1905-1906). The chapter concludes by examining the imagery of passageways in *The Voyage Out* through the critical lens of the "Morley Sketch."

Chapter Two, "Virginia Stephen and the People's Suffrage Federation, 1910," makes valuable distinctions between the various suffrage platforms of the early twentieth century and clarifies Stephen's position as an "Adult Suffragist" who advocated for the enfranchisement of all adult men and women regardless of property ownership. Using "only scattered references to [Stephen's] voluntary work for the suffrage" (65), Jones challenges scholarly assumptions regarding Stephen's political affiliation, and provides evidence of her work within the People's Suffrage Federation, which, she contends, maintained an "uncompromising adultist agenda" (72).

The final two-thirds of this chapter focuses primarily on Woolf's complicated portrayal of suffrage campaigners in *Night and Day*. Jones writes, "I would argue that the criticisms levelled against suffrage campaigners in the novel can be read as expressions of Woolf's adultist sympathies" (79). Her historicist approach produces a persuasive interpretation of Mrs. Seal and her suffrage society as inheritors of late Victorian conservative values and supporters of a platform contingent upon property ownership. According to Jones, Woolf's depiction of Mrs. Seal and Miss Markham "encourages us to see the suffrage society in *Night and Day* as not only based on the [Women's Social and Political Union], but also as sending up the Pankhursts in particular" (82). Jones concludes the chapter by considering the political merit of self-questioning through an examination of Mary Datchet from *Night and Day* and North and Eleanor Pargiter from *The Years*.

Chapter Three, "Virginia Woolf and the Women's Co-operative Guild, 1913-31," provides the most stark and striking examples of Woolf's "ambivalent activism." The chapter begins with an overview of the Women's Co-operative Guild (WCG) and Woolf's somewhat contentious relationship with its president, Margaret Llewelyn Davies. Although initially formed as a traditional women's group that espoused the maintenance of separate spheres, the WCG, under the leadership of Llewelyn Davies, expanded its social and political agenda to include progressive, working-class issues (110-111). Llewelyn Davies invited the Woolfs to attend a Guild conference in 1913, and when the Richmond branch formed in 1916, Woolf became an active participant.

Jones suggests that in spite of Woolf's long-term commitment to the Guild, her socio-economic class often frustrated her efforts to establish solidarity with the working-class women. Woolf's insensitivity and lack of class-consciousness come through in quoted letters that express her annoyance with the Guildswomen's lack of interest in issues beyond food during a noted food shortage in 1917 (112-115). Jones contrasts Woolf's callousness with her more sympathetic portrayal of working-class concerns in the "Cook Sketch."

The remainder of the chapter offers a bold reading of Woolf's "Introductory Letter" to a 1931 collection of Guildswomen's autobiographical writing entitled *Life As We Have Known It*. Jones carefully considers the letter's experimental narrator, its meditation on memory, and its purported audience (116-123). The first half of the letter reflects upon the 1913 conference Woolf attended, and the second half "stages the present-day narrator's receipt and reading" of the Guildswomen's writing and offers a newfound understanding of the 1913 convention (117). Given that Woolf drafted this introduction in the same summer that she prepared the Hogarth Press edition of *On Being Ill*, and considering that Woolf suffered a breakdown just weeks after attending the conference, Jones contends that the "Introductory Letter" indirectly reflects upon and conflates elements of Woolf's breakdown and recovery with the conference itself. According to Jones, this accounts for Woolf's undue emphasis upon the physicality of the Guildswomen, but it also allows her to imaginatively connect with them. Jones's argument is most convincing in her reading of the letter's paralysis motif: "Woolf's grotesquely amputated version of the traditional body politic metaphor not only illustrates the Guildswomen's stunted political agency without the power of the suffrage, but also encodes the frustration and helplessness she experienced as a result of the enforced inactivity of her rest-cure" (124-5).

Chapter Four, "Virginia Woolf and the Rodmell Women's Institute, 1940-1," is the most compelling and cohesive section of the book. Jones commences with an overview of Woolf's service to the Rodmell Women's Institute (WI), which, she argues, has been critically ignored (154). The chapter then persuasively connects Woolf's ambivalent involvement with the WI's drama group in 1940 to her complicated portrayal of the village pageant at the center of *Between the Acts*.

Jones integrates impressive research on the history of the WI and the village drama movement to ground her discussion of the (real and fictional) village plays in contemporary debates concerning history, collective identity, authenticity, and class. The chapter reveals how both World Wars shaped the WI's political agenda, including its "emphasis on rural women as almost spiritual custodians of a particular and authentic kind of Englishness" (158). Close readings of *Between the Acts* expose allusions to the WI's agenda and underscore its fraught attempts at cross-class identification and solidarity. Jones argues that the novel registers Woolf's "uneasiness about assuming too substantial a role in the WI, which she believed should be run 'by the village women themselves'" (189).

The chapter's other major contribution is its insightful discussion of Woolf's 1940 talk for the WI. Jones shows that Woolf, by delivering a speech on her 1910 involvement with the Dreadnought Hoax, subverted the WI's agenda—she was invited to speak at "a Book tea" (164)—and used her narrative to subtly critique patriarchy, imperialism, and war. Jones's thorough study of Woolf's letters, the *East Sussex News*, and the WI's papers reveals that while Woolf seems to have won over her working-class audience with humor, her challenge to the WI's right-leaning ideology did not go unnoticed by its middle-class leaders (170-176).

The monograph ends with a very brief conclusion. Jones's later chapters provided some connections to earlier claims, but a more comprehensive synthesis of her argument would have been helpful to readers. Nevertheless, *Virginia Woolf: Ambivalent Activist* is a welcome addition to the existing scholarship on Woolf's politics. Jones's historical and archival research merits high praise. Woolf scholars will appreciate the book's meticulous efforts to ground Woolf's politics in the particularities of the organizations with which she took part.

—Meghan C. Fox, *LaGuardia Community College, CUNY*

Work Cited

Ryan, Derek, and Stella Bolaki, editors. *Contradictory Woolf: Selected Papers from the Twenty-First Annual International Conference on Virginia Woolf.* Clemson Digital P, 2012.

A Companion to Virginia Woolf. Ed. Jessica Berman
(Chichester, UK: John Wiley and Sons, 2016) xii + 501 pp.

Long gone is the ethereal, introverted, and insulated Virginia Woolf — a figment of new critics' gendered imaginations. Today's Woolf, as reflected in Jessica Berman's *Companion to Virginia Woolf*, is made of flesh and bone, with Hogarth Press ink-stains on her fingers. Yet Woolf the feminist heroine has also been redrawn, as critics tackle her racist and classist diary entries and assess the British chauvinism complicating her anti-imperialist, feminist imagination. Woolf scholars are still working through this latter dimension. Because earlier charges of elitism were often implicit sexist and homophobic efforts to discredit Woolf and the Bloomsbury circle (as Mark Hussey has noted [2004]), Woolfians have moved cautiously, and sometimes defensively, in this terrain of critique. Yet Berman's collection gives signs that a more seasoned balance is in the making.

First it's helpful to appreciate the range and richness of *A Companion to Virginia Woolf*. Expertly edited by Berman, this collection strikes a fine balance of scholarly and teacherly. Each essay deftly describes the lay of the land for newer readers while also developing fresh lines of analysis that will stimulate further dialogue among long-time scholars of Woolf. The essays are thus cutting-edge in thought and classroom-friendly in orientation.

The *Companion*'s thirty-three essays are organized into three sections. The first includes individual studies of each of Woolf's novels and her other writings: her essays and diaries, her biographical writing, her short fiction, and one each on *A Room of One's Own* and *Three Guineas*. The second section features an array of approaches to Woolf—Ecocritical, Crip, Digital, Queer, and Feminist Woolf, as well as on Woolf and the law, the sciences, the visual, war and peace, and the politics of class. The final section opens up more angles on "Woolf in the World" with several essays on space, geography, and geopolitics; and others on Woolf in translation, the Bloomsbury Group's intimately lived public lives, and the international publishing networks of the Hogarth Press. One limit within this spread is worth noting. Several essays draw rather selectively from the deep archive of Woolf criticism on their subjects, so readers should not depend on them for knowledge of the longer scholarly dialogue about subjects such as time, bodies, and empire.

Meanwhile, however, the collection weaves rich patterns of analysis from essay to essay, which Berman encourages us to explore in her list of suggested "cross references" at the close of each essay. One could follow the weave even further. For instance, scholars of animal studies will not only find philosophically inflected interpretations of animals in *Orlando* (Derek Ryan) and of course in *Flush* (Jane Goldman); they can also situate these readings within the coordinates drawn in Christina Alt's piece on Woolf's scientific interests, in Bonnie Kime

Scott's analysis of Woolf's ecological imagination, and in Madelyn Detloff's Crip reading of Woolf. And because Goldman and Ryan also highlight the erotic and queer currents feeding into Woolf's animal attunements, readers might likewise consider these together with Melanie Micir's reading of queer temporality in Woolf and with Susan Stanford Friedman's tracing of queer rewrites of Woolf by contemporary authors and artists.

These discussions also resonate with the several essays on Woolf and the senses, including Maggie Humm's on Woolf's visual aesthetics, Alison Booth's on Woolf's houses, and Emma Sutton's, Marina McKay's, and Kime Scott's discussions of the "sonic" in Woolf. McKay and Scott link the aural and sonic elements to the technologies of the wireless, the gramophone, and the radio, while Sutton highlights Woolf's braiding of sound, silence, and the unsaid—a familiar scholarly theme in Woolf studies also taken up here by Vincent Sherry. This branching path of considerations is just one of many offered by the collection. And as Pamela Caughie, Anne Fernald, and Laura Marcus remind us by tracking Woolf's voluminous reading and its threading into her many texts, these interweaving readerly patterns partly mirror Woolf's writerly ones. Meanwhile, as Mark Hussey points out here, although new digital resources promise even deeper mining of Woolf's allusive webs, these methods also require a new "vigilance" if we are to stay in touch with Woolf's undigitizable legacies (272).

Woolf the philosopher—existential, political, and literary—emerges clearly in this collection. Happily, Woolf criticism now regularly analyzes the existential level at which Woolf's political and aesthetic mediations operate. Speaking as a critic who has approached Woolf's intertwining of objects, bodies, history, and politics at this level, I think this is a salutary trend. In addition to essays about bodies and materiality already mentioned, we could add Anna Snaith's on the mixing of time scales in *The Years* and Jessica Berman's on the temporal politics encoded in the interruptive mode of *Three Guineas*. Especially welcome are the essays that reveal Woolf's interest in historicity, *per se*, an angle that has deserved more attention. For instance, as Elizabeth Outka sees it, Woolf's *Night and Day* is not merely an early novel halfway-arrived at modernism; instead, it builds a "Vicmod" mode of imagination (56), purposefully encompassing historical and narrative continuity as well as rupture, so as to convey the disavowals (of WWI, for instance) lurking within dailiness. Vincent Sherry interprets *Jacob's Room* as a book whose historicity resides in narrative slippages, which not only harbor the missing persons of war but also mirror the historic "failure of rationalist language in English liberalism" as antidote to war (76). Here I would put in a bid for building on these studies through more attention to Woolf's long-historical imagination, for my sense is that there is also a philosophy of history embedded in Woolf's evocations of earlier periods, from primeval to Renaissance—with implications for how we think about "modernity" as well as geomodernisms.

Several essays nicely think through the workings of time and space together. Some tend toward the psychoanalytical, like Maud Ellmann's essay on Woolf's spatial passageways as meditations on temporal passageways, ultimately into death. Others are more sociological, such as Tamar Katz's exploration of the ways that Woolf's aesthetic "rides on the back of rhythm," especially urban rhythms (407). Paul Saint-Amour's reading of *Mrs. Dalloway* highlights the way that certain temporal moments, such as dusk, create spatio-temporal vertigo for characters: as spatial boundaries dissolve in the liminal light, deep time floods in, and objects—such as "orienting" imperial monuments—become "molten," undercutting the grounds of social belonging or position (86). Andrew Thacker focuses on space as the locus for Woolf's "thematics of power" (412), and his concluding remark could also describe Woolf's dynamic sense of time: for if, "[l]ike Lefebvre, Woolf believed that space is alive and speaks to us," she would have said the same of history as it lives in spaces and things (423).

Nels Pearson's essay might be read in dialogue with Saint-Amour's, as a more pointed postcolonial reading of moments of spatio-temporal collapse. Like Jane Garrity and Supriya Chaudhuri, Pearson thoughtfully assesses the ambiguous political force of Woolf's aesthetics, especially in the context of British empire. Pearson notes that in *To the Lighthouse* Woolf's rendering of the "history-engulfing space" of night's darkness calls out a roving consciousness "diverted from linear time" which "counteract[s] the control of . . . the political state" (432). Yet he also traces how Woolf's scenes of ruptured belonging sometimes portray a specifically Anglo-European experience of rupture, linked to imperial demise. Thus, problematically, Woolf imagines "the loss of one historical belonging as an erasure of all belonging" (431). That is, British political-existential crisis sometimes gets cast as a universalized, individual crisis. There's room for further dialogue on these points (and one could wish that Pearson cited more of the Woolf criticism that intersects with his), but his reading of Woolf's narration at this level is well-balanced and thought-provoking.

Jane Garrity's essay on "global objects" in *The Waves* (that "eyeless" book) similarly finds a certain imperializing perspective in the novel's cosmic reach. Her punning title refers not only to the novel's global themes but also to its imagery of spheres, circles, and rounded shapes. Linking this imagery to the book's all-encompassing perspectives, especially in the interludes, Garrity interprets these as Woolf's grappling with British global hegemony and related questions of totality—involving both her identifications with globalized Britishness and her political self-consciousness about these identifications. Although Garrity does not extend her analysis to global time, one could likewise explore its complementary presence and ambivalence in the novel.

Undertaking a further postcolonial widening of the frame, Supriya Chaudhuri's essay positions us outside and before Woolf. She begins with Rasasundari Dasi (1809-1900), who surreptitiously stole time from domestic duties to produce her autobiography, now a classic; and Saroj Nalini (1887-1925), who founded the feminist *mahila samiti* movement which built women's centers or "institutes" for Indian women. Chaudhuri establishes how close, yet far, these women were to Woolf. For the Hogarth Press published Gurusaday Dutt's biography of Saroj Nalini while Woolf was writing *A Room of One's Own;* and Dasi's life epitomized those "sisters" about whom Woolf was writing. In further counter-balancing moves, Chaudhuri juxtaposes Woolf's racist remarks about "darkies" against her anti-imperial critiques in her fiction; and she establishes the kinship between Woolf's political aesthetics and those of her Indian contemporaries, Rashid Jahan, Ismat Chughtai, and Qurratulain Hyder. Chaudhuri invites us to read these authors as (absent*ed*) presences in Woolf's writing—who deserve, in turn, more visibility in geomodernist scholarship.

Other essays similarly open wider horizons around Woolf. Susan Stanford Friedman also creates a "sisterly" counterpoint, noting analogies between Woolf's relation to her educated brothers and the contemporaneous author Swarnakumari Devi's relation to her brother, Rabindranath Tagore. In this context she tracks the "afterlives" of Woolf in postcolonial "sister" artists, such as Pamela Mordecai and Kabe Wilson, who "write back" to Woolf, in both dialogue and critique. Although not directly concerned with imperialism, Battershill and Southworth's co-authored piece on the international networks of the Hogarth Press also supplement this widening of the frame around Woolf, as do Brassard's and Lojo-Rodríguez's essays on translations of Woolf, including the global ripple effects of her feminism and her aesthetics. And Jean Mills offers a fresh vocabulary for understanding Woolf's class politics.

Reading these many essays together, we see both the worldly and the provincial Woolf, the visionary author and the self-circumscribed Englishwoman. We see that to overlook one Woolf is to miss the import of the other. Placing Woolf back into the larger world from which she sprung, this *Companion* thus brings us to that most productive place: the place of co-forming relations, even across hemispheres. That is, it situates Woolf within the dynamics of relationality—including disavowed relationality.

In her essay on Woolf and the law, Ravit Reichman discusses Woolf's sense of "justice" over "law" as the proper "sphere of care" (242). Woolf herself did not always honor this kind of relational justice. But in her luminous, dynamic visions of its importance, she crafts a legacy for us to emulate, emend, and expand.

—Laura Doyle, *University of Massachusetts-Amherst*

Work Cited

Hussey, Mark. "Mrs. Thatcher and Mrs. Woolf." *Modern Fiction Studies* 50.1 (Spring 2004): 8-30.

REVIEWS

Woolf: A Guide for the Perplexed. Kathryn Simpson (London: Bloomsbury, 2016) 203pp.

It's a bit of a truism that modernist texts both call for mastery and frustrate its exercise. T. S. Eliot's footnotes to *The Waste Land* are snide little reminders of this fact; and though James Joyce's *Ulysses* can be read through Harry Blamires's *The New Bloomsday Book* or Djuna Barnes's *Nightwood* through the OED, for either text, it is nigh impossible to "come to an appreciation of its meaning as a whole" (Eliot xi). Of Hope Mirrlees's *Paris: A Poem* one might say "What a lark! What a plunge!" (MD 3), but what a soundscape to place into a metalanguage, which would calm these symptoms of modernity by turning text into object, fixed by the critic's pen.

The Bloomsbury series *A Guide for the Perplexed* works less to fix than to illuminate, and it has provided guides to topics historical, religious, philosophical, and literary. In the category of modernist literature, Kathryn Simpson's *Woolf* joins Steve Ellis's guide to *T.S. Eliot* (2009) and Peter Mahon's *Joyce* (2009) in a familiar constellation of the canon. However, rather than using chronology to proceed Mr. Ramsay fashion through her modernist's corpus, as these do, and rather than grouping the author's texts according to genre, as in *Kafka* by Clayton Koelb (2010) and *Beckett* by Jonathan Boulter (2013), Simpson takes a more fluid approach to Woolf as "an inherently complex and contradictory figure, as much the subject of controversies as a promoter of them" (1). The six chapters of *Woolf: A Guide for the Perplexed* focus on issues that transcend specific times or texts. While not quite fifty pairs of eyes, these interrelated lenses—Woolf's Modernism; Formal Innovation; Narrative Technique; Characterization; Gender, Sexuality and Class; and Empire and Jewishness—allow Simpson to engage generatively with Woolf's life and writings, suggesting that "acceptance of diversity, plurality, contradiction and an on-going fluidity of interpretation is what we need to aim for as readers of her work" (2).

The book's structure is appropriately wave-like, as the discussions move backwards and forwards through Woolf's modernist style and preoccupations. There are overlaps, since texts and theories are covered more than once, but the organization finds its rationale in Simpson's reading of the spiralling, shell-like narrative of "A Mark on the Wall." In both texts, it seems, form "is used as a structuring device but is simultaneously radically revised or even undermined," and like the story, by the end of Simpson's guide, "the many issues and themes raised are still on-going and open for discussion" (61).

Given the complexity of this approach, the introduction provides a valuable overview of Woolf's social and artistic contexts, where short (1-2 page) sketches of biography, history, and culture provide a backdrop to Woolf's writings. Addressing the influence of her family and Bloomsbury, of Bergson and Freud, of suffrage and education, of the British empire and monarchy, it is an efficient presentation of Woolf's modern moment, and Simpson signals the later points in the guide at which these issues are again addressed or applied in more detail. Each of the six chapters also begins with a short overview, indicating the key points and the texts that will be examined, and providing orientation for the short readings that follow and that are clearly marked by subheadings.

Simpson's deft handling of Woolf's literature, politics, and cultural position is grounded in her comprehensive understanding of both modernity and modernism. For example, in the first chapter, she introduces Woolf's critique of H. G. Wells, John Galsworthy, and Arnold Bennett through the figure of Henry James (39), before shifting into detailed readings of Woolf's essays on "modern fiction" (42), and then demonstrating Woolf's precepts in an analysis of "The Lady in the Looking-Glass: A Reflection" (48-54). Simpson expands upon Woolf's experimental techniques in "Formal Innovation," where the subjective experience of time becomes a base for an analysis of "A Mark on the Wall" in terms of what is fact and fiction. While Henri Bergson is addressed in the introduction (14-16), Simpson refers back to his influence in a subsection on "Time and Narrative Form" (57), and then moves to short analyses of *Jacob's Room, Orlando*, and *The Waves* to illustrate Woolf's deviation from conventions informing biography and life writing. Simpson addresses *Three Guineas* to further exemplify Woolf's sense that "The process of engaging with the topic and exploring possible ways of understanding it are as important, if not more important, than simply reaching a secure conclusion" (71), and the chapter ends with *A Room of One's Own* as it "blurs the generic boundaries between essay and fiction" (74). The next chapter, "Narrative Technique," engages with *Jacob's Room, Mrs. Dalloway*, and *Between the Acts* according to Woolf's play with point of view, language and image patterns, and syntactic structures. Simpson's work with Woolf's "polyphonic" narrative in her final novel is typical of the efficiently persuasive analyses that emerge, as an explanation of centre of consciousness is illustrated using the shifts in perspective between Mrs. Sands and Lucy Swithin (97). The chapter "Characterization" returns to the essays in which Woolf presents theories of the new realism, but also to the cultural and ideological forces that influence her engagement with the "palimpsestic" nature of identity, especially in the short story "In the Orchard" (111). These sections lead into very fine treatments of interconnected experience through *Jacob's Room, Mrs. Dalloway*, and *The Waves*.

The identity politics that inform Woolf's presentation of characters are addressed overtly in the chapter "Gender, Sexuality and Class," where Simpson integrates a range of critical perspectives and close readings to explore the issues Woolf was herself exploring. Simpson's work with androgyny in *A Room of One's Own* is typical of the layered treatment of debates arising from and surrounding Woolf.

Glossed by references to Elaine Showalter, Pamela L. Caughie, and Simone de Beauvoir, as well as by readings of Mary Carmichael, Orlando, and Lily Briscoe, Simpson contextualizes "the highly sexualized language" that seems at odds with Woolf's linguistic "challenge" to "binary modes of thought and meaning" (132, 133). Equally nuanced is Simpson's approach to gender in *To the Lighthouse* through the imagery of eyes, as the limiting effects of the male gaze, symbolized by Mrs. Ramsay's "myopia" (142), are met by Lily's artistic "vision" (143). The same novel introduces a discussion of Woolf's representations of class, especially through the figures of Mrs. McNab and Mrs. Bast, where Woolf's layered style both draws attention to and challenges "the authority of the middle-class narrator" (153). The final chapter, "Empire and Jewishness," engages with colonial and racist attitudes in Woolf's work, as well as the ways in which texts such as *The Voyage Out* and "The Duchess and the Jeweller" complicate imperial and patriarchal norms. Simpson acknowledges Woolf's use of stereotypes, and she places those references in relation to Woolf's anxiety surrounding her own social position (168). What emerges is not just critique, then, but also a sense of the writer read through modernism according to the logic of her own situation. Thus, just as the anti-Semitism of *The Years* is interpreted as, in part, Sara's "attempt to fend off unsettling feelings of her own status as a social outsider" (180), so Simpson's emphasis on Woolf's own "unexpected parallels" with "racial others" (183), moves less to judgement and more to a consideration of the aims of the authorial project: "to think through these complex and entangled issues and to provoke her readers to do the same—however difficult that might be" (184). While landing less often on the pointed side of criticism, Simpson addresses Woolf's cultural and social biases through considered analyses, and she presents a range of possible interpretations through informed, detailed, and theoretically inflected work.

Given the insights and the framework, which result in focused and easily located perspectives, the guide is of value not just for an academic audience but also for the common reader. That said, it does not include a chronology of Woolf's works or life, (though publication dates are included at the beginning of chapters), and there are moments at which literary and theoretical vocabulary is used with some expectation of existing familiarity. I'm thinking of terms such as "Angel in the House" (136) or "focalization" (89), which are invoked without initial explanation and seem at odds with the otherwise careful presentation of concepts that may be discipline- or theory-specific, such as ideology (105) or "the other" (158). On a perhaps related note, citations of Woolf's essays often direct the reader to the six volumes of *The Essays of Virginia Woolf* rather than to the titles of the essays themselves, which suggests an audience that has access to university or college library holdings. Simpson's is, indeed, a text I would assign for a Woolf honors or a graduate seminar, not just for the historical contextualization and analyses, but also for its bibliographical material and suggestions for further reading.

There are some typographical errors, and I found myself distracted by a bit of repeated word usage, but these are minor glitches. It is a guide in the truest sense, sharing a scholar's insight and vision, following a clear and informed philosophy, and providing some illuminating views of an author and her decades-long body of writing.

—Ann Martin, *University of Saskatchewan*

Work Cited

Eliot, T. S. Introduction. Djuna Barnes. *Nightwood*. 1937. New York: Penguin, 1961, pp. xi-xvi.

Virginia Woolf and the Professions. Evelyn Tsz Yan Chan (New York: Cambridge UP, 2014) x + 219pp.

Anyone who has read widely in Virginia Woolf's writing has encountered her fraught and sometimes contradictory attitudes towards professionalism. The doctors Bradshaw and Holmes in *Mrs. Dalloway*—their perceptions blinkered by their specialized training, their compassion thwarted by their drive for honors and distinction—are only the most obvious of Woolf's many egregious professional characters. A critique of the traditional professions of medicine, law, and divinity lies at the heart of *Three Guineas*, which trenchantly asserts that professionalism depends upon and nurtures the compulsive, male drives towards wealth, property, and status that were about to plunge Europe into world war again. And yet, simultaneously, Woolf looked at the radically popularized print culture of her time and reached out, ambivalently and intermittently, to professionalism as a way of safeguarding quality and staving off chaos. To cite just one instance, a *Three Guineas* footnote—later expanded and revised into the Hogarth Press pamphlet "Reviewing"—suggests reforming book reviewing along professional lines, with an expert panel "who would practice like doctors and in the strictest privacy" (*TG* 175-6).

While a number of fine, book-length studies of professionalism and modernism exist, and several Woolf critics have published shorter explorations of her engagements with the topic, Evelyn Tsz Yan Chan's book is the first to focus exclusively on Woolf's vigorous, career-long critique of professionalism. The book is an impressive work of synthesis, lucidly explaining the contested status of professionalism in the early twentieth century and constructing a detailed and accessible account of Woolf's evolving ideas on the issue. Chan draws on an impressive amount of material, ranging widely among the novels, letters, diaries, and manuscripts and pulling in useful contextual material, such as A. M. Carr's important and seldom-cited *The Professions* (1933). Chan's readings of primary texts sometimes rest on thin textual evidence, and at other times lean too much on the work of previous critics. On balance, though, the book offers a thorough and coherent account of Woolf's struggle with the ideologies and practices of professionalism and the place of the serious writer within them.

Woolf, Chan argues, took a skeptical view of professionalism from an early age, recognizing the promises and the dangers entailed by the opening of the professions to women with the 1919 Sex Disqualification Removal Act. It was crucial to Woolf, Chan asserts, that women have access to the professions, so they could do meaningful work and make their livings, thereby gaining freedom from the need to serve and flatter fathers, brothers, and husbands. Yet in the actual functioning of the professions, Woolf saw excessive specialization and bald drives for power and wealth painted over with a veneer of ritual and civilization. "Professions, which were established to address 'human needs' and render their services accordingly, had in Woolf's eyes become so 'privileged' that they had paradoxically become detached from those needs," Chan writes (7). Would the entry of women reform the professions, making them more socially conscious? More collaborative? More humane? Or would professional women adapt by developing the competitiveness, aggression, and ego inflation evident in such figures as Dr. Bradshaw or *A Room of One's Own*'s Professor Von X? Woolf's "attempts to disparage and escape the professions were tempered by a sense of inextricability: The professions were too important—especially for women who had been denied access to the public sphere in previous centuries—to dismiss entirely" (17). Woolf, faced with these difficulties, conducted a life-long critique of professionalism in an effort to "shape the professions so that they could become individually and personally, not just materially and socially, more rewarding pursuits" (8).

Chan begins with an efficient overview of where the professions stood when Woolf's career began. The gradual and contested professionalization of law and, more crucially, medicine in the nineteenth century, was firmly in place—if not universally celebrated—by the early twentieth century. Chan reminds us that the development of the British Medical Association, while officially devoted to standardizing training and improving practices, was also a means of ensuring adequate pay for credentialed doctors by muscling out non-credentialed ones. While credentialing may create minimum standards of training and practice, it also creates scarcity: limiting the number of practitioners raises prices, while credentialing justifies high rates of pay. Even by the 1920s, Chan shows, there was a suspicion that the BMA's "monopoly" over medical credentialing was less about standards than it was about money. Nonetheless, by this time the professions were institutionalized and an ideology of professionalism was in place: it posited the practitioner as answering to a vocation or calling of unquestioned social value, and thus existing above or outside the commercial economy, and it undergirded regimes of training and credentialing that entitled him or her to social respect and "autonomy from financial concerns" (5). Indeed, the rhetoric of professionalism was so successful by this time that many other workers, from builders to journalists, were aspiring to professional status—forming societies and articulating standards.

Woolf's response to all this, as Chan's synthesis makes clear, circled around two difficult, speculative problems: whether, how, and to what extent literature and the creative arts should be seen and practiced as professions, and whether women's difference could reform and reinvigorate the professions. For Chan, Lily Briscoe in *To the Lighthouse* and Miss LaTrobe in *Between the Acts* represent Woolf's attempts to distill the positive aspects of professionalism (a sense of vocational commitment and satisfaction combined with serious self-training and careful practice) while purging the negative (self-promotion driven by ego, greed, and a desire for power). Both characters achieve a sort of outsider's professionalism—pursing their vocations with total commitment while remaining outside the commercial sphere— but at the cost of relative poverty and social isolation. Miss LaTrobe expresses her dramatic vision, but much of her meaning goes unrecognized, and she is left on the margins of the village society she addresses. Lily completes her painting with a robust flourish, seemingly accepting the fact that it will earn her no money and be stowed under someone's bed. Much to Chan's credit, here and elsewhere she does not ignore the irresolvable tensions in Woolf's theories of professionalism. The creative lives of Lily and LaTrobe, Chan writes, embody "the type of 'professionalism' which Woolf sought to create, while at the same time showing the problems in her vision that remained unresolved" (115).

This problem of the creative "professions" animates the first half of the book, which includes chapters on Woolf's critique of medicine, her fraught but indecisive grappling with literature's status as a profession, and the figures of Lily and LaTrobe. Chan's strongest arguments center on this issue, as she carefully traces Woolf's attractions to a vision of artistic labor as private and amateur. Woolf's "struggle with anxieties about public recognition and opinion" and her resentment of "the influences of commercialism and professionalism in writing" led her toward idealized visions of untroubled amateurism (80). Yet this lure of creativity freed from social and institutional constraints competed with Woolf's powerful desire for literature to influence society and a broad cultural sense that amateurism might denote lack of skill, commitment, and expertise. Writing novels, of course, fit inexactly into the regimes of professionalism: there were no exams or credentials for novelists; and, as Chan reminds us, Woolf cast a jaundiced eye on the growing professionalization of literary criticism in universities. Yet "[a]mong existing professions, writing seemed particularly subversive of the professional-amateur dichotomy, and Woolf made use of this to envision it as an activity which should have attributes of both positions" (84).

The second issue at the core of Chan's account is the great question of feminine difference. Were women fundamentally different from men? (Woolf thought so, it seems.) And could this difference be marshalled to reform the professions and society more generally? Or would the inertia of the professions require that women conform, losing their salutary differences ("disinterestedness" for Woolf, to which Chan adds sympathy and compassion). If the latter, the threat is that women entering the professions would merely lend new energy to the ongoing circuit "round and round the mulberry tree, the sacred tree, of property" (TG 74). Introduced in Chan's first section, this problem takes center stage in the second half of the book, which consists of two chapters: the first contextualizes and fleshes out a critique of the professions that is largely implied in *The Years*, with reference to *Three Guineas* and *The Pargiters*; the second finds, in *Between the Acts*, a critique of excessive specialization in modern societies. Here I do not find Chan's textual readings consistently fresh and convincing, which is why I say that *Virginia Woolf and the Professions* succeeds more as a work of synthesis and exposition than as a bold new reading of Woolf.

Indeed, Chan's interpretations frequently fall somewhere between the self-evident and the familiar. She tends to build out from well-known or consensus readings, layering issues of professionalization on top of them, with mixed success. Her reading of *Between the Acts*, for instance, begins by reiterating consensus readings: the novel "contains a regressive yearning for the prehistoric and protectionist nostalgia for past national culture and Englishness" but also "does not accept these as final states"; it "broods over the shattered state of modernity" (174). This interpretation relies heavily on Gillian Beer's much-cited "The Island and the Aeroplane," which argued that the novel's references to pre-history suggest a commonality in contrast to the political and personal divisions of the dangerous present. Atop this base, Chan layers a discussion of modern specialization as a divisive force. She quotes Aldous Huxley, whose *Beyond the Mexique Bay* (1934) had posited specialization as an early force towards civilization, but one which had grown, with modern science, to threaten humanity with oblivion. Now, there is no doubt that specialization was a fundamental force of both professionalism and modernity, or that belief in specialization as a social good was imperiled in the 1930s. But finding explicit reference to it in *Between the Acts* is another matter, sending Chan deep into the *Pointz Hall* manuscript and to a strained reading in which Giles's status as a stock broker makes him emblematic of specialization writ large. "[S]pecialization," Chan asserts, is "the historical bridge for the two extremes of unspecialized prehistory on the one hand and overspecialized professional society on the other" (154). She argues that "in expressing 'the simultaneity of the prehistoric in our present moment' Woolf found solace not only in the continuity of the prehistoric in the here and now, but also enacted the retreat from overspecialization necessary to reach a balance in modern life" (154). (The partial quotation is from Beer's essay.) Effectively, Chan is pursuing her own critique of modern specialization by synthesizing Huxley and Woolf. There's nothing wrong with that, but as a reading of Woolf's intentions it feels strained to me.

This dynamic recurs a bit in *Virginia Woolf and the Professions*. Chan at times finishes arguments only suggested in Woolf's work, or attributes to Woolf a chain of logic that is actually Chan's own. In this vein she finds, by reading across *Mrs. Dalloway* and *Three Guineas*, not merely a critique of medical professionalism but Woolf's "advice on how to improve the professional system underpinning medicine" (49). True, *Three Guineas* shows Woolf more strident and programmatic than her early novels. But a critical practice of distilling specific "advice" by reading across Woolf's texts reduces their suggestive power, I think; it verges on turning Woolf into the kind of "political writer" she explicitly rejected in "Mr. Bennett and Mrs. Brown," the kind that wants the reader "to join a society or, more desperately, to write a cheque" (326). Thankfully, Chan is usually better attuned to the incompletions and tensions in Woolf's work, recognizing her tendency to approach issues "from a broader and less restrictive political perspective" (46).

What my quibbles show, of course, is that Chan's work will stimulate disagreement and discussion on Woolf's novels, on her ideas about the professions, and on the important, and far from exhausted, topic of modernism's relations with professionalism. Scholars taking up this question will benefit from Chan's wide-ranging and well-researched account.

—Patrick Collier, *Ball State University*

Work Cited

Woolf, Virginia. "Mr. Bennett and Mrs. Brown." *Collected Essays Vol. 3*. Harcourt, 1967, pp. 319-37.

Natural Connections: Virginia Woolf and Katherine Mansfield.
Bonnie Kime Scott. Bloomsbury Heritage Series 71.
(London: Cecil Woolf, 2015) 48 pp.

"Eternally in yr Debt": The Personal and Professional Relationship Between Virginia Woolf & Elizabeth Robins.
Hilary Newman. Bloomsbury Heritage Series 72.
(London: Cecil Woolf, 2015) 28 pp.

Saxon Sydney-Turner: The Ghost of Bloomsbury.
Todd Avery. Bloomsbury Heritage Series 73.
(London: Cecil Woolf, 2015) 32 pp.

Virginia Woolf as Memoirist: "I am made and remade continually."
Alice Lowe. Bloomsbury Heritage Series 72.
(London: Cecil Woolf, 2015) 32 pp.

Mistress of the Brush and Madonna of Bloomsbury, The Art and Life of Vanessa Bell: A Biographical Sketch and Comprehensive Annotated Bibliography of Writings on Vanessa Bell. Suellen Cox. Bloomsbury Heritage Series 75.
(London: Cecil Woolf, 2015) 79 pp.

Septimus Smith: Modernist and War Poet: A Closer Reading.
Vara S. Neverow. Bloomsbury Heritage Series 76.
(London: Cecil Woolf, 2015) 32 pp.

The wit and vigor evident in the exuberant decoration of Charleston Farmhouse, the home in Sussex to which Vanessa Bell and Duncan Grant moved in 1916, find an echo in the appearance of the Bloomsbury Heritage monographs. Their unattributed cover design resembles Vanessa Bell's dust jackets for Virginia Woolf's books. In an outline drawing, the head, shoulders and arms of a naked woman with downcast eyes lean over a loop of symmetrically draped fabric pinned up by roses like the one the woman holds in one hand. The card wrappers make the little books inviting. The inclusive impetus for the series is to provide "concise, original and authoritative introduction" to a wide range of topics "for the general reader as well as for the academic reader." The publisher, Cecil Woolf, Leonard and Virginia Woolf's nephew, and his wife, the general editor Jean Moorcroft Wilson, allow their writers to wander down byways, emerging with surprising information or celebrating a life that usually appears as a footnote in accounts of the most significant members of the Bloomsbury Group.

The strength of the form is that its brevity can encapsulate an idea which might suggest a new area for research, such as Bonnie Kime Scott's *Natural Connections;* its danger is expressed by Woolf herself and quoted in *Virginia Woolf as Memoirist* when Woolf notes, of an excess of essays, that "too many were written about things the authors didn't know much about and were little more than expressions of likes and dislikes" (19). An extra hazard is the level of misinformation in the pamphlets; they are carelessly proofread, with errors in spelling and punctuation in all of them, and two pages in *Natural Connections* are duplicated. The date of Virginia Woolf's death is mistakenly given as 1942 in the *Annotated Bibliography of Writings on Vanessa Bell.* Much more significant mistakes occur, distorting the argument and unnerving the reader, as when Hilary Newman in *"Eternally in yr Debt,"* writes that women with distinguished male relations such as Dorothy Wordsworth and Mary Shelley "have remained mostly in obscurity, putting in an appearance only in the biographies of the famous male relatives they assisted" (19). A dramatised version of Shelley's *Frankenstein* was staged at the English Opera House in 1823, initial evidence of what became overwhelming and continuing public fascination with Shelley's Frankenstein and his creature; after a selection from Dorothy Wordsworth's journals was published in 1897, edited by William Knight, interest in her writing has grown consistently.

The six pamphlets reviewed here fall into distinct categories. One is an annotated bibliography, two are biographical and three engage in literary analysis. The title of Suellen Cox's *Mistress of the Brush and Madonna of Bloomsbury, The Art and Life of Vanessa Bell* suggests that it may take a somewhat hagiographic approach but its focus is on information. This pamphlet justifies the series' claim that these are authoritative introductions; it is evidently painstakingly researched. After a brief preface and a biographical sketch, the section called "Monographs" is efficiently separated into parts, dividing books by Bell from books about her, books that mention her, and books about Charleston Farmhouse. "Exhibition Catalogues" is comprehensive and covers exhibitions in Italy, the USA, South Africa, and Australia. It goes back to a catalogue from 1908 and includes information about the specific paintings exhibited, from the early twentieth century up to 2011. Cox's analysis of the preoccupations and approaches of the contributors to the various catalogues is useful, as are her incisive summaries in "Exhibition Notices and Reviews," "Periodicals," "Dissertations and Theses," "Bibliographies," and "Reference Sources." The coverage creates a powerful impetus in this reader to see the paintings again, and the admirable "Museum and Gallery Holdings" tells us where to find them. Oddly, Berwick Church is not included here, though it is mentioned elsewhere, and the rather laconic "Towner" needs to be located in Eastbourne, but these are quibbles about a monograph that admirably fulfils the aim of interesting an academic or a common reader.

Of the two biographical monographs, Hilary Newman's *"Eternally in yr debt": The Personal and Professional Relationship Between Virginia Woolf & Elizabeth Robins* is the least securely researched. The relationship between the American actor, writer, and supporter of women's rights Elizabeth Robins and Virginia Woolf was not a close one but Woolf was eager for accounts of her parents whom Robins had met. Leonard Woolf commented briskly that Robins's anecdote about Julia Stephen enabled him to see her "for the first time a living woman, a very different figure from the saintly dying duck of her husband's memories" (4). Robins and Woolf kept in touch intermittently; there is a comparison between the feminist ideology articulated in novels and essays by both writers. In a footnote about Robins's companion, a self-contradictory statement is characteristic of the problematic nature of Newman's writing: "Virginia Woolf did not speculate on the nature of the relationship between Elizabeth Robins and Octavia Wilberforce. I do not intend to do so either, apart from stating that it appears to have been a platonic friendship" (27). The footnote continues with Wilberforce's account of her own ignorance as a student of homoerotic desire, though she was a mature woman when she lived with Robins. The nature of their relationship is not relevant to the theme of the pamphlet but the lengthy footnote appears to be a defense of platonic friendship, after an opening disclaimer. In a comparison of Woolf's and Robins's fiction we read that in "Woolf's novels, the destructive side of war is shown" (15). This kind of banality is damaging to the series, as is the attempt to define *The Years* as a "Condition of England" novel: "Thomas Carlyle first used the phrase 'the Condition of England Question' in 1939 in his 'Chartism'" (24). The essay appeared in 1839, and was specifically a response to the Industrial Revolution which was then developed in the fiction of Disraeli, Dickens, Kingsley, Gaskell, and Charlotte Brontë; if the term is to be applied in a totally different context it needs a cogent argument to support it. Similarly, it is not acceptable to flick through a work that is used to support an opinion: "Even skimming Light's book gives an impression that Woolf's relationships with her servants were difficult and unsatisfactory" (24).

Todd Avery, in his brief biography, *Saxon Sydney-Turner: The Ghost of Bloomsbury*, cannot be accused of inadequate research. He located and read hundreds of pages of manuscript letters, some of them in the Strachey Papers in the British Library. As Avery says, rather poignantly, we only know of Sydney-Turner from casual references in Bloomsbury letters, memoirs, and diaries "as if we were watching a documentary of his life from which he himself is curiously absent, in which the only voice unheard is his" (7). Having been one of the Apostles in Cambridge, where he became a friend of Leonard Woolf and Lytton Strachey, he was offered a post in the Treasury and stayed there for his working life. Avery's task must have been laborious as he remarks that his subject's "letters seldom rise beyond even the lowest pitch of interest" (11). He tries to make a case for Sydney-Turner's poems, misquoting W. B. Yeats's "Among School Children" in the process, but Leonard Woolf's stinging comment on them seems apt: "it's all about as pale as he is himself: it's like the ghost of a ghost" (12). The revelation that Sydney-Turner wrote stories involving necrophilia, incest, and pedophilia startlingly distinguishes him from his Bloomsbury contemporaries though the stories' perversity is derivative. One of them, "Eidolon," is quoted in full as Avery reads it as an insight into gender as performance.

In one of the three pamphlets focusing on literary criticism, Vara S. Neverow has a quirky and interesting idea. In *Septimus Smith: Modernist and War Poet: A Closer Reading*, she assumes that Smith can be aligned with the artists whose work caused uproar in 1910 in Roger Fry's exhibition, "Manet and the Post-Impressionists." Neverow justifies the inclusion of Smith in this category by reference to his diagrams and designs, though they sound more like doodles than sketches as they are circles traced round coins and caricatural stick figures. Linking Smith to the War Poets is more persuasive. As Neverow says, the reader has no access to any of his poems, but the state of mind communicated in his sections of the novel chimes with poems by Wilfred Owen, and Neverow draws parallels with passages from Ezra Pound and T. S. Eliot. Though Smith's experience of the trenches resembles Siegfried Sassoon's, the affinity here is overstated, as Sassoon's demotic and sardonic register differs significantly from the heightened apocalyptic prose of Smith's delusions in the park. The overblown conclusion does a disservice to the vitality of the essay: "If Septimus rightfully envisions himself as 'the poet of the immortal ode,' granting himself the authority to speak poetically for all those who fought in, died in[,] or survived the war, including those who chose to take their own lives in the aftermath, then he becomes the quintessence not only of all the war poets but of all the victims of war and all the survivors" (25). It is surely the specificity of Smith's plight and his medical treatment that is moving, and his creativity shows most clearly in his ability to design a hat as according to his wife "he had a wonderful eye."

Alice Lowe's *Virginia Woolf as Memoirist: "I am made and remade continually"* opens with a lucid distinction between the terms "autobiography" and "memoir," using as a pivot Woolf's description of her method in "A Sketch of the Past": "I think I have discovered a possible form for these notes. That is, to make them include the present – at least enough of the present to serve as platform to stand upon. It would be interesting to make the two people, I now, I then, come out in contrast" (4). As the daughter of a biographer and a biographer herself, Woolf continually meditated on life writing, and played with it in *Orlando*. Woolf's fascination with memory in her fiction as well as her memoir was one of her strongest bonds with Katherine Mansfield, though the reference to Mansfield in the essay is misleadingly dependent on John Middleton Murry's erratic edition of her journals rather than on the much more recent scholarly version edited by Gerri Kimber and Claire Davison (Edinburgh UP, 2016). Lowe places Woolf's life writing in the context of her experiments with memoir by her contemporaries such as Elizabeth Bowen, H. G. Wells, and Rebecca West. The final section, "Woolf's Legacy," is a slightly random list, but returns to a sharp focus on Woolf with the observation that Woolf's diaries and letters can be read as an extended memoir.

Natural Connections by Bonnie Kime Scott is the most ambitious of the monographs discussed here as it proposes that Woolf's and Mansfield's representations of the natural world "along with their challenge to the traditional divisions between nature and culture" make the work of these two writers "highly suitable for eco-feminist analysis" (5). After lengthy biographical ground-clearing, to use an eco-metaphor, Scott reaches her theme, that eco-feminist analysis rejects the essentialism implied by the term "mother nature" and encourages "contextual and relational thinking" (20), in some instances decentring human experience and focusing on animals, other creatures, and plants. There are sections on "Where Writing Meets Nature"; "Children's Encounters with Nature"; "Collaborations with Animals"; "Floral Cultivation"; "Towards a Politics of Flowers"; and "Final Lessons." These sections juxtapose passages in which Woolf and Mansfield address the topic of the section providing introductory raw material for a potential researcher but they do not demonstrate a methodology of eco-criticism – how it engages with the texture of a work.

There are several errors in spelling and detail. D. H. Lawrence did not contribute a story to *Rhythm* (8) but to the *Blue Review*; Mansfield reported that "Prelude" was piping away in the cage provided by Leonard and Virginia Woolf, not that they themselves were in it (14). The passage about Bertha's fruits in "Bliss" is misquoted (36) as is "a numeral" (27), which should read "nemeral." The aloe in "Prelude" is a plant not a great tree; Kezia is bemused by its thorny leaves, and Linda by its fleshy stem (37). It may seem a niggling response to comment on careless proofreading, editing, and recording of detail, but one wants this enterprising series to succeed. Imagination and lateral thinking need to be combined with careful scholarship if they are to make the impact that they should.

—Angela Smith, *University of Stirling*

Moving Modernisms: Motion, Technology, and Modernity.
David Bradshaw, Laura Marcus, and Rebecca Roach, eds.
(Oxford: Oxford UP, 2016) xii + 315pp.

Virginia Woolf moves. Her work depicts and interrogates mobility through time and space, as felt by different bodies and at different scales. Because motion is so central to her corpus, Woolf scholars should be especially interested in Bradshaw, Marcus, and Roach's edited collection *Moving Modernisms*. Though Woolf is not the main focus of any one chapter, her work comes up in several as an example, counterpoint, or precursor. More important than specific readings of Woolf though, this volume provides new ways of getting at one of the central questions of modernism, the relationship between thought's movement through the mind and matter's movement through the world.

Mobility studies is a relatively new critical framework in our field, one that first came to prominence in work such as Andrew Thacker's *Moving Through Modernity*. In *Moving Modernisms,* this approach complements a wide variety of other critical lenses. The book cycles through different ways of thinking about movement with a restless curiosity. While some chapters deal with literal instances of motion such as transportation and travel, others consider literary movements, shifts in the temporal and spatial boundaries of the field, the dialectical movement of thought, and the transformation of ideas across genres and media. The analysis of movement becomes a central strategy in comparative and counterfactual arguments alike. And it helps illuminate the dazzling cultural histories that the New Modernist Studies does so well.

The book's first section, "Times and Places," includes three essays that consider issues of scale and circulation among different parts of the world. They work to unsettle some of the major concepts in global modernist studies, transnationalism, and planetarity. Andrew Thacker reconsiders the older model of modernist "internationalism" (12), and shows how transnationalism's global focus can elide important differences within nations and between regions. Tim Armstrong reads what he calls a "trajectories" of "micromodernisms," charting the paths of writers from New Zealand and Australia who interacted in modernist London. David Ayers moves from the micro to the macro with a more philosophical approach, proposing ways to resolve the ever vexed relationship between modernism and modernity through a new narrative of modernity that decouples it from capitalism.

The second section, "Horizons," reverses the relation between center and periphery, showing how two ostensibly exotic locales are central to modernist thought. Wai Chee Dimock writes about Gibraltar and the multitude of purposes it serves in the work of James Joyce, Ezra Pound, and Paul Bowles. Robert J. C. Young focuses on D. H. Lawrence's writings on Sardinia, asking "What if Sardinia were to look at Lawrence and translate him instead?" (70). Young's essay sardonically juxtaposes Lawrence's privileged reading of Sardinia as a primitive space with the desperate poverty of Sardinian native and Marxist theorist Antonio Gramsci. Both of these essays offer productive reconsiderations of the primitivist and utopian impulses modernists bring to travel writing.

"Energies and Quantities" scales movement down from the geographical to the physiological. Enda Duffy (he of *The Speed Handbook*) makes a compelling argument that affect is a central concern of modernist narration: "modernist literature," he says, "is a somatic literature" (84). We can see how the minute descriptions of physical and mental feelings fit into a larger social consideration of emotional labor in the early twentieth century. This historicizing of perception continues in Steven Connor's "Numbers It Is," which examines competing ideas about continuity and discontinuity in the period. (Woolf's diaries serve as an important example in this essay.) Olga Taxidou argues that we should understand Isadora Duncan's dancing body at the intersection of embodiment and signification. Modern movement blurs the lines between performance, poetry, athletics, and theater, making Duncan a founding figure for understanding interdisciplinary modernism itself.

The "Avant-Gardes" section presents two fascinating meditations on the ways that ideas transform between media and genres. Marjorie Perloff's "'A Cessation of Resemblances'" acknowledges the most common transmedia pairing in modernism—Pablo Picasso and Gertrude Stein—before asking us to think about the reverse, "the influence, if any, of Stein's verbal composition on the visual artwork of her contemporaries" (128). She mines a productive vein of commonality between Stein's work and that of Marcel Duchamp, particularly as his female alter ego Rrose Sélavy. Jean-Michel Rabaté brings Joyce's epiphanies into dialogue with Franz Kafka's aphoristic fragments in order to compare the ways that these discursive moments "move us" (143).

"Discourses/Voices" returns to the public sphere with a focus on how the circulation of language defines local and universal ideals, in-groups and out-groups. Rachel Potter's chapter considers the work of the PEN International, an association of writers who imagined how to foster international dialogue and universal conceptions of artistic freedom erasing cultural difference. Here, Woolf's political writing—both in novels and in nonfiction—plays an important part in the argument. Potter's work is very much in line with Greg Barnhisel's *Cold War Modernists* and the burgeoning critical interest in the relation between modernist art and modern diplomacy. Ken Hirschkop examines how public opinion creates a community and how modernist thinkers imagine myth as a concept that can do this work. Patricia Waugh discusses a group without a unifying myth, writers of "British fiction of the middle years of the twentieth century" (191). Waugh's chapter proposes a new mode of midcentury novel, the neo-expressionist; *Mrs. Dalloway,* she argues, is an early model for this epoch's blurring of the boundaries between interior and exterior as well as between self and other. She suggests that it is not the external history of the period, but their shared feeling of instability, that unites them and makes their work seem so resonant today.

For scholars interested in mobility studies in the most literal and technological forms, the section on "Motion Studies" offers the most salient critical material. The section gives two critical takes on motion and stillness in media, followed by two on the relation between transportation and modernist writing. Paul K. Saint-Amour gives an illuminating reading of René Clair's *Paris qui dort*, one that shows how the modern film anticipates the union of speed, stasis, and capital in the postmodern era. Like Garrett Stewart's "Frame-Advance Modernism," Saint-Amour's chapter highlights the ways that film enters into dialogue with the photographic image. Stewart brilliantly argues for the intertextual prominence of German visual art in Fritz Lang's film *M*. He shows how *M*'s "surveillance ethos" implicates the viewer in the broader culture of observation (254). Deborah Longworth does a great service to modernism and mobility studies alike by bringing the history of bicycling out of the gay nineties and into the speedy, spectacular era of six-day bicycle races. She shows how avant-gardists including Alfred Jarry and F.T. Marinetti were influenced by this incredibly popular sport, suggesting that two-wheeled dynamism may in fact be more modern that the four-wheeled variety. Julian Murphet concludes the collection with an essay that places the streetcar not within modernism but naturalism; "modernism seized hold of the streetcar image as precisely 'dated' and cognitively depleted" (284). The networked infrastructure and focus on cognition are signifiers of an earlier period, one that evokes a deep nostalgia in modernist writers.

This volume expands on a four-day "agenda-setting conference" that took place in Oxford in 2012.[1] Most of its agenda was fairly prescient: while the recent Modernist Studies Association conference in Pasadena had more media and archival studies, it was deeply absorbed in questions of scale, transnational movement, and the relationship between politics and aesthetics on display in this volume. I was hoping for more of the direct engagement with vehicular modernity displayed in Longworth and Murphet. Nevertheless, *Moving Modernisms* is a worthwhile snapshot of a field in (and on and through) motion.

—Sunny Stalter-Pace, *Auburn University*

---

[1] Jessica Palmieri, "'Moving Modernisms' Conference in Oxford," http://www.italianfuturism.org/moving-modernisms-conference-in-oxford/

Edward Upward: Art and Life. Peter Stansky
(London: Enitharmon, 2016) 368pp.

Edward Upward (1903-2009) is one of the most unduly neglected British writers of the twentieth century, his work having been relegated to an especially dark corner of literary history due to his lifelong (albeit ideologically complex) allegiance to Marxism-Leninism. Following Upward's death in 2009, there has been a significant revival of critical interest in his oeuvre—including new work by Stuart Christie, Valentine Cunningham, Nick Hubble, Rod Mengham, Glyn Salton-Cox, Helen Small, and others. This body of work—along with the (re)publication of Upward's writings by the English publisher Enitharmon—has done much to establish Upward's place as one of the foremost figures of his generation, as a chronicler of twentieth-century left-wing culture, as an uneasy Surrealist-cum-Marxist modernist, and as a poet of "late life." Peter Stansky's superb biography is a much needed addition to this body of scholarship. Importantly, by opening up new angles on Upward's "art and life," Stansky manages to show how much Upward has to offer to literary scholars and intellectual historians interested in twentieth-century writing and the history of left-wing thought in Britain. As the publication of Upward's 1930s classic *Journey to the Border* by the Hogarth Press in 1938 indicates, Upward's early work should also be of special interest to Woolf scholars.

Until recently, Upward's claim to literary fame seemed limited to his affiliation with the group of poets that surrounded W. H. Auden in the 1930s. According to Stephen Spender's recollection of Upward in his autobiography *World within World* (1951): "just as Auden seemed to us the highest peak within the range of our humble vision, for Auden there was another peak, namely Isherwood, whilst for Isherwood there was a still further peak, [Upward]" (Spender 112). Spender's metaphor achieves a paradoxical double effect: it places Upward at the heart of the 1930s while also relegating him to its extreme periphery. Partly as a result of Spender's faint praise, Upward's own voice has often only been heard obliquely through the literary works of Isherwood and, at a second remove, of Auden—a situation which has led at least one critic to wonder: "Did Upward himself really exist?" (Arblaster 179). Stansky's biography remedies this neglect, and it makes Edward Upward visible as an intellectual and artistic presence in his own right.

Building on substantial new archival research, including Upward's seventy-six unpublished diaries, as well as on interviews with Upward's friends and family, Stansky is a sympathetic narrator of Upward's life—from Upward's early upbringing in Romford and his school days at Repton to his formative years at Cambridge (where he collaborated with Christopher Isherwood on the quasi-surrealistic Mortmere stories), his work as a teacher at Alleyn's School in South London, and his later years (notably his involvement in the Campaign for

Nuclear Disarmament and his painful struggles to come to terms with the ideological commitments of his younger years). Stansky's biography puts literary critics in a position to understand the rich biographical, historical, and intellectual contexts from which Upward's works emerged and in relation to which they need to be understood. To be sure, Stansky never engages in a biographical reductionism which suggests that Upward's works are insignificant beyond their autobiographical or anecdotal content—an assumption that guided much earlier scholarship and that has led critics to mistake Upward's deliberately plain prose for an indication of its "artlessness." Instead of reducing Upward's fiction to its autobiographical content, the central merit of Stansky's biography is that it points to the troubled and unresolved relationship between Upward's "art and life" as the central theme of Upward's fictional, critical, and journalistic work.

Stansky presents Upward as an individual who tried to think of himself both as an English "gentleman" and as an anti-establishment "rebel." Upward considered himself a "'natural' rebel [...] having a profound conviction that the entire system, as represented by Repton and Cambridge, was thoroughly corrupt"—but at the same time, as Stansky accurately notes, "it is a little unclear why he hated his world so" (88), given that he found lifelong employment at a prestigious private school. Arguing along similar lines, Stansky unpacks the complexities of Upward's commitment to Marxism-Leninism: being a communist meant that Upward had to demonstrate full ideological conformity to the party line (a degree of conformism which he was increasingly reluctant to grant), while also making him persona non grata amongst the literary establishment, thus imperiling his place in the twentieth-century literary canon.

Stansky's biography offers a much needed corrective to the conventional literary-historical account of Upward's career. According to this account, the exuberant creativity of Upward's early work of the 1920s (the Mortmere stories) and 1930s (*Journey to the Border* as well as the stories "The Colleagues," "Sunday," and "The Island") dried up when he decided to encase himself in what John Lehmann called Upward's "Iron Maiden" of communist dogma (Lehmann 244). Most significant in this respect is the second half of Stansky's book which focuses on decades that have been gaps in accounts of Upward's life—the "silent years" between 1945 and 1962 (the year that finally saw the publication of "In the Thirties," the first volume of Upward's *Spiral Ascent* trilogy) as well as the years of his retirement and old age (when, after a hiatus of several decades, and now well into his eighties, he resumed writing). This book offers important new insight into Upward's friendships, literary influences, and intellectual interests during these periods, and Stansky's account contributes much to a more complete account of Upward's career as a writer.

The chapters of Stansky's biography which deal with the 1920s and 1930s cover more familiar terrain, but they succeed in shedding important new light on this comparatively well-known period of Upward's life. Stansky's discussion of Upward's fascinating and fraught relationship to Bloomsbury modernism will likely stimulate debate among Woolf scholars. Upward admired Woolf as a writer even as he was wary of her class position. Stansky points out that Upward's close friend Isherwood was instrumental in "persuad[ing] the Woolfs to publish the novel [*Journey to the Border*]" (211), but it is also possible that Woolf decided to publish the book because she sympathized with the its incisive depiction of mental illness. Stansky complicates Upward's relationship to younger affiliates of the Bloomsbury group such as John Lehmann, whose much-cited "Iron Maiden" comment has cast a long shadow on Upward scholarship. As Stansky suggests, Lehmann's early encouragement (and subsequent dismissal) of Upward might be symptomatic of a wider literary-historical constellation—the modernist establishment's alternately "confrontational and cooperative relationship" to the young political writers of the 1930s (209). While in the 1930s the Woolfs had been willing to boost talent among the younger generation of politicised poets (through publications that included the poetry collection *New Signatures*, an urtext of 1930s literature), Leonard Woolf's decision to turn down *In the Thirties* in a letter to Upward ("The pace is much too slow and there is, I feel, much too much internal questioning about Communist principles"; qtd. on 246) indicates a momentous shift in post-war literary-political sensibilities.

Stansky's biography is impressively researched. It is as comprehensive and illuminating an account of Upward's life as we are ever likely to have. However, *Edward Upward: Art and Life* is unlikely to be the last word on Upward as a writer: because it has more to say about Upward's "life" than about his "art." Stansky's biography demonstrates how much work remains to be done by literary critics. This will include the unpicking of individual literary influences (by earlier authors such as John Bunyan, Emily Brontë, Mark Rutherford, and William Morris as well as on later writers such as Peter Carey, whose 1974 collection *The Fat Man in History* includes prominent Upwardian echoes); but such work will also include debates about the place of politicized writing in the twentieth-century literary canon. Finally, it is to be hoped that a selection of passages from Upward's seventy-six unpublished diaries (now held by the British Library) will be published in the near future. As Stansky's magisterial biography shows, these diaries—which Upward kept between the 1920s and the early 2000s—offer a crucial insight into the life and works of one of Britain's central left-wing authors.

—Benjamin Kohlmann, *University of Freiburg*

Works Cited

Arblaster, Anthony. "Edward Upward and the Novel of Politics." *1936: The Sociology of Literature,* edited by Francis Barker. University of Essex, 1979, pp. 179-96.

Lehmann, John. *Autobiography,* 3 vols. Eyre and Spottiswoode, 1955-66, III (1966).

Spender, Stephen. *World within World* (1951). The Modern Library, 2001.

International Notes

Il Faro in una stanza: The First Italian Woolf Festival, 2016

From November 25 to 27 the beautiful town of Monza (close to Milan) hosted *Il Faro in una stanza* (*The Lighthouse in a Room*), the first Italian Literary Festival dedicated to Virginia Woolf. The Festival was organized by Elisa Bolchi, post-doc researcher at Università Cattolica of Milano, Liliana Rampello, literary critic and essayist, and by bookseller Raffaella Musicò, who has recently opened 'Virginia e co.', a bookshop dedicated to Virginia Woolf in the heart of Monza, in the premises that used to host another literary bookshop, 'Hemingway & co.'

The Festival opened on Friday the 25th with a dinner, followed by the first Italian performance of the comedy *Freshwater*, interpreted by amateur actors and introduced by Mara Barbuni, independent scholar and author of *Sui passi di Elizabeth Gaskell* (*In the Steps of Elizabeth Gaskell*) who led the public on a virtual tour through the places where Freshwater is set. On Saturday morning Raffaella Musicò spoke about bookshops and libraries as places of democracy, supported by readings from *A Room of One's Own* and *To the Lighthouse*. Writer Sandra Petrignani, author of *La scrittrice abita qui* (*The Writer Lives Here*, Neri Pozza 2002), gave an entertaining talk about Woolf's house in Rodmell.

In the afternoon, at the beautiful theater at Villa Reale, Elisa Bolchi discussed with Sara Sullam, researcher at Milan State University and author of the book *Tra i generi: Virginia Woolf e il romanzo* (*In Between Genres: Virginia Woolf and the Novel*, Mimesis 2016), trying to map the territory of Woolf's writing to make it more accessible to "common readers." The day closed with the presentation of the first complete translation of Woolf's short stories, published last November by Racconti Edizioni with the title *Oggetti solidi* (*Solid Objects*), edited by Liliana Rampello, also the editor of a rich anthology from Woolf's essays, *Voltando Pagina* (Saggiatore 2011) and the author of *Il canto del mondo reale* (Saggiatore 2006).

On Sunday morning, Liliana Rampello conversed with Bianca Tarozzi, scholar, poet and translator of Anglo-American literature and of Woolf's diaries for Rizzoli, and entertained the public with an inspirational speech on Woolf's diaries. Elisa Bolchi closed the Festival with a focus on Woolf's reception in Italy, on which she has written two books, *Il paese della bellezza. Virginia Woolf nelle riviste italiane tra le due guerre* (T*he Land of Beauty: Virginia Woolf in Italian literary magazines during the interwar period*, EDUCatt 2007) and *L'indimenticabile artista. Lettere e appunti sulla storia editoriale di Virginia Woolf in Mondadori* (*The Unforgettable Artist. Letters and Notes on Virginia Woolf's publishing history with Mondadori*, Vita e Pensiero 2015).

The Festival enjoyed great success, and media coverage proved beyond the organizers' expectations, with articles both in the main Italian newspapers (*Il Corriere della Sera and La Repubblica*) and online. But above all the Festival saw an enthusiastic participation of the public, with crowded venues and a Sunday morning attendance of more than 100 people! This enthusiastic response, together with the numerous requests of the participants, has led the organizing committee to plan a second edition of the Festival, to be held in November 2017, in Monza. The aim of the organizing committee, which from next year will include also Sara Sullam, is to make the Festival an annual appointment and, hopefully, to reach beyond Italian borders and turn it into an International Annual Festival in the future.

—Elisa Bolchi

Please send news of Woolf-related events to woolfstudiesannual@gmail.com
before January 5th

Notes on Contributors

Candis E. Bond is an Assistant Professor of English at Augusta University, where she also serves as director of the Writing Center. Her research interests include British modernism, 19th- and 20th-century British literature, and the politics of space in literature, cities, and Writing Centers. She has articles forthcoming in The *D.H. Lawrence Review* and *Clio: A Journal of Literature, History, and the Philosophy of History* and is currently working on a book project investigating the significance of alleys in modernist fiction by E. M. Forster, Virginia Woolf, and Joseph Conrad. She has presented on Woolf and other modernist writers at several international conferences.

Claire Davison is Professor of Modernist Studies at the Université Sorbonne Nouvelle, Paris, where her teaching and research focus on intermedial borders and boundaries of modernism: translation and reception of Russian literature in the 1910s-20s; literary and musical modernism; modernist soundscapes and broadcasting. She was the Chair of the French Virginia Woolf Society (SEW) from 2008 until 2016. She is the author of *Translation as Collaboration – Virginia Woolf, Katherine Mansfield and S. S. Koteliansky* (2014) published by Edinburgh University Press, and the co-editor (with Gerri Kimber) of a number of recent volumes on literary modernism, including the fourth volume of *The Edinburgh Edition of the Collected Works of Katherine Mansfield, in Four Volumes* (Edinburgh 2012-6);*The Collected Poetry of Katherine Mansfield* (Edinburgh, 2016) and *Katherine Mansfield's French Lives*, (Brill-Rodopi, 2016). She also coedited volume 16 (2016) of *International Ford Madox Ford Studies: Cosmopolis: Ford Madox Ford and the Cultures of Paris* (Rodopi, 2016).

Amanda Golden is Assistant Professor of English at the New York Institute of Technology. She previously held a Marion L. Brittain Postdoctoral Fellowship at the Georgia Institute of Technology and the Post-Doctoral Fellowship in Poetics at Emory University's Fox Center for Humanistic Inquiry. She is the author of *Annotating Modernism: Marginalia and Pedagogy from Virginia Woolf to the Confessional Poets* (Routledge, forthcoming), editor of *This Business of Words: Reassessing Anne Sexton* (UP of Florida, 2016), and has published in *Modernism/modernity, The Ted Hughes Society Journal*, and *Woolf Studies Annual*.

Patricia Novillo-Corvalán is Senior Lecturer in Comparative Literature at the University of Kent, UK. She is the author of *Borges and Joyce: An Infinite Conversation* (2011) and the editor of the collection of essays, *Latin American and Iberian Perspectives on Literature and Medicine* (2015). Her second monograph,

Modernism and Latin America: Transnational Networks of Literary Exchange, is forthcoming with Routledge in 2017.

Jacqueline Shin is an assistant professor of English at Towson University. She specializes in twentieth-century British literature, particularly the intersections between late modernist fiction and the visual arts. Her essays on Sylvia Townsend Warner's *Lolly Willowes* and the "arts of dispossession" as well as the role of statuary in the film *The Third Man* have been published in *Modernism/modernity*. She has also written about Elizabeth Bowen and photography, unsettled vision in Woolf's *Between the Acts*, and is currently working on a monograph that explores modernism's varied forms of praise.

Submission Guidelines

*W*oolf
*S*tudies
*A*nnual invites articles on the work and life of Virginia Woolf and her milieu. The *Annual* intends to represent the breadth and eclecticism of critical approaches to Woolf and particularly welcomes new perspectives and contexts of inquiry. Articles discussing relations between Woolf and other writers and artists are also welcome.

Articles are sent for review anonymously to a member of the Editorial Board and at least one other reader. Manuscripts should not be under consideration elsewhere or have been previously published. It is strongly advised that those submitting work to *WSA* be familiar with the journal's content. Among criteria on which evaluation of submissions depends are whether an article demonstrates familiarity with scholarship already published in the field, whether the article is written clearly and effectively, and whether it makes a genuine contribution to Woolf studies.

Preparation of Copy

1. Articles are typically between 25 and 30 pages, and do not exceed 8,000 words. This is a guide rather than a stipulation, and inquiries about significantly shorter or longer submissions should be sent to the Editor at woolfstudiesannual@gmail.com.

2. A separate file should include the article's title, author's name, address, phone number, and email address. The author's name and any other identifying references should not appear on the manuscript to preserve anonymity for our readers.

3. All submissions must include an abstract of no more than 250 words.

4. Manuscripts should conform to the most recent MLA style.

5. Submissions should be sent as Word files by email to woolfstudiesannual@gmail.com.

6. Authors of accepted manuscripts are responsible for any necessary permissions fees and for securing any necessary permissions.

All editorial inquiries should be addressed to woolfstudiesannual@gmail.com.

Inquiries concerning orders, advertising, reviews, etc. should be addressed to PaceUP@pace.edu.

Other Woolf titles available:

Virginia Woolf and Communities: Selected Papers from the Eighth Annual Conference on Virginia Woolf, edited by Jeanette McVicker and Laura Davis

Virginia Woolf and Trauma: Embodied Texts Ed. Suzette Henke & David Eberly (2007)

Virginia Woolf Out of Bounds: Selected Papers from the Tenth Annual Conference on Virginia Woolf, edited by Jessica Berman and Jane Goldman

Virginia Woolf Turning the Centuries: Selected Papers from the Ninth Annual Conference on Virginia Woolf, edited by Ann Ardis and Bonnie Kime Scott

Women in the Milieu of Leonard and Virginia Woolf: Peace, Politics and Education Ed. Wayne K. Chapman and Janet M. Manson (1998)

Woolf Across Cultures Ed. Natalya Reinhold (2004)

All volumes of *Woolf Studies Annual* are available, including:

Woolf Studies Annual 6 (2000): The *Three Guineas* Correspondence, edited by Anna Snaith

Woolf Studies Annual 8 (2002): The Fawcett Library Correspondence, edited by Merry Pawlowski

Woolf Studies Annual 9 (2003): *Virginia Woolf and Literary History Part 1*, edited by Jane Lilienfeld, Jeffrey Oxford, and Lisa Low

Woolf Studies Annual 10 (2004): *Virginia Woolf and Literary History Part 2*, edited by Jane Lilienfeld, Jeffrey Oxford, and Lisa Low

Woolf Studies Annual 12 (2006): *"Letters to Readers From Virginia Woolf"* edited by Beth Rigel Daugherty

Woolf Studies Annual 19 (2013): *Special Focus Virginia Woolf and Jews*, edited by Mark Hussey

TULSA STUDIES IN WOMEN'S LITERATURE

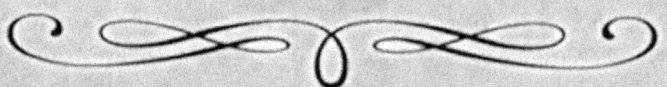

Subscribe now for
Spring 2017, Vol. 36, No. 1

@TSWLjournal
Utulsa.edu/tswl
Like us on Facebook!

Mosaic, an interdisciplinary critical journal

Upcoming Issue

50.3 (September 2017): Letters

This special issue is on the theme of philosophy's, literature's, or any other discipline's, letters. Traditionally, letters have been regarded as "non-serious" or at least as superfluous to the critical enterprise proper (consider Kant's division of Plato the letter-writer from Plato the philosophical father). But can letters themselves be considered critical forays and/or keys to the inheritance of scholarly work? Might letters put the serious/non-serious opposition into question? This issue considers letters in relation to understanding a writer's or artist's body of work; alternate histories; friendship; auto-bio-graphy; archival and digital repository research; email and electronic posting.

Recent Issue

50.1 (March 2017): The *Mosaic* Interviews

Part of *Mosaic*'s year-long 50th-anniversary celebration, this special issue gathers between two covers all of the "Crossings" interviews that *Mosaic* has featured since 2001. In addition to 16 interviews led by Dawne McCance, Editor, with the following leading scholars, artists, and writers, the issue also includes a new interview with Rebecca Comay, Professor of Philosophy and Comparative Literature at the University of Toronto:

- Mary Ann Caws
- Rodolphe Gasché
- Linda Hutcheon and Michael Hutcheon
- Peggy Kamuf
- David Farrell Krell
- John P. Leavey, Jr.
- Alphonso Lingis
- Kristin Linklater
- Erín Moure
- Michael Naas
- Nicholas Royle
- John Sallis
- Álvaro Siza
- William V. Spanos
- Aritha van Herk
- Roundtable discussion with Sander Gilman, Linda Hutcheon, Michael Hutcheon, and Helen Tiffin

Mosaic, an interdisciplinary critical journal
University of Manitoba, 208 Tier Building
Winnipeg, MB R3T 2N2 mosasub@umanitoba.ca

The twenty-third volume of *Woolf Studies Annual*
was published in Spring 2017
by Pace University Press

Cover and Interior Layout by Rachel Diebel
The journal was typeset in Times New Roman and Arial
and printed by Lightning Source in La Vergne, Tennessee

Pace University Press

Director: Sherman Raskin
Associate Director: Manuela Soares
Marketing Manager: Patricia Hinds
Design Consultant: Sara Yager

Graduate Assistants: Rachel Diebel and Taylor Lear
Student Aide: Kelsey O'Brien-Enders